THE SIXTH MAN

♪ "Welcome to my World" ♪

Harry McIntyre

THE SIXTH MAN
A STRING OF PEARLS

HARRY McINTYRE

iUniverse, Inc.
Bloomington

THE SIXTH MAN
A STRING OF PEARLS

Copyright © 2010 by Harry McIntyre

All rights reserved. No part of this book may be used or reproduced by any means, graphic, electronic, or mechanical, including photocopying, recording, taping or by any information storage retrieval system without the written permission of the publisher except in the case of brief quotations embodied in critical articles and reviews.

iUniverse books may be ordered through booksellers or by contacting:

iUniverse
1663 Liberty Drive
Bloomington, IN 47403
www.iuniverse.com
1-800-Authors (1-800-288-4677)

Because of the dynamic nature of the Internet, any Web addresses or links contained in this book may have changed since publication and may no longer be valid. The views expressed in this work are solely those of the author and do not necessarily reflect the views of the publisher, and the publisher hereby disclaims any responsibility for them.

ISBN: 978-1-4502-7717-4 (sc)
ISBN: 978-1-4502-7718-1 (ebk)

Printed in the United States of America

iUniverse rev. date: 11/17/2010

Acknowledgments

My gratitude and heartfelt thanks to the following people: Marie Trotignon for her support and critiquing skills; Eloise Whittlesey for her line edit of the manuscript, and Ethel Winter, Jo Olason, and Bob Ross for their critiquing skills.

My appreciation to <u>The American Legion</u> and specifically to Daniel S. Wheeler (National Adjutant) for permission to use the calendar page entitled "O'er The Ramparts We Watch", *for which they have* a copywrite dated 1985, for the cover page for "The Sixth Man".

PROLOGUE

The title, THE SIXTH MAN, refers to the fact that during World War II; it took six men, or women, to sustain one man on the fighting line, whether on land, sea, or air. Therefore, while the seventh man was on the fighting line, the sixth man was in training to replace him, or join him, whatever the need may be. The others were important, but not scheduled for, or trained for, the fighting line. It was the sixth man who was in that training position, and I was that sixth man.

The second half of the book illustrates how the young man took his military training, plus the energy and drive from his unfulfilled goal of becoming a pilot and used his disappointment and anger, along with the help of the G.I. Bill, to receive the training and achieve the rewards of a long, and fulfilling professional life as an educator.

Table of Contents

Basic Training 4

The Hospital Visit 7

A New Squadron 10

The Ten Hour Layover 12

College Training Detachment 15

Pre Flight 20

New Year's Eve 22

First Date With Louree 25

Thunderbird Field 30

Solo Flight 33

Flying the Stearman PT-17 38

My First Flight After Soloing 45

A New Family 47

Acrobatics 50

Buzzing 54

The Field Meet 56

My First Check Ride 60

The Surprise 63

The High School Dance .69

More Acrobatics 73

The Misadventure	76
The Trial	79
Another Surprise	81
The Test	83
The Frame Up	85
Delay Enroute	89
Lowery Field	91
Mail Call	93
The Dance	96
The Fifty-Caliber Machine Gun	98
The Black Out	100
A Surprise Letter	102
Louree's Phone Call	104
Becoming an Armament Specialist	106
Louree's Arrival	108
Kingman Arizona	110
Christmas Leave	113
Meeting Old Friends	117
Graduation	119
Crew Distribution at Plant Park, Florida	120
Meeting the Crew	125
First Simulated Bombing Mission	129
3-Day Pass	131

High Altitude Problem	134
The Near Tragedy	136
Hurricane	139
Writing to Louree	141
An Open Bomb Bay	144
Havana Escapade	147
Pending Marriage	150
Reuniting with My Father	152
The Wedding	154
Another Furlough	156
A.W.O.L.	159
Biloxi, Mississippi	162
Louree is Pregnant	164
A Furlough Problem	166
Eglin Field and My Discharge	169
Arriving Home	171
Returning to the Northwest	176
Returning to Southern California for College	178
Changing My Major	181
On to a Four Year College	185
Teaching Half-Day on Emergency Credential	188
Changing Majors Again	192
Moving to Central California	194

Returning to Southern California .196

Student Teaching. 199

Graduation and My First Teaching Job 201

Teaching at Newport Beach. 205

A Working Summer's Vacation .210

Return to the Northwest 212

A New Job in Education 215

Commercial Fishing 220

The John Wayne Marina 238

Returning to Graduate School. 247

Frst Principal Position at Almira 250

Return to High School Counseling 253

Principal Position at Sacajawea 255

Retirement, Divorce, and a New Partner. 258

"The Longest Day" 259

A Second Marriage 267

A Trip to the Baja 268

Vocational Rehabilitation Counseling 289

Alone in the San Juan Islands .291

Retirement Again 303

Conclusion 304

Epilogue 305

THE SIXTH MAN

The Call

It was March 1, 1943, I was seventeen years old, and after qualifying through a series of tests, both mental and physical, had been sworn in to the Army Air Corps. WWII was at its height, and we'd been in the war for one and a half years fighting on two fronts: Europe and the South Pacific. At this time our losses were great in the air war over Germany. Some bombing missions cost us up to fifty percent of our planes and personnel. Consequently, recruiting was intense for pilots, navigators, bombardiers, and aerial gunners, but it wasn't until after seeing a Robert Taylor movie, "Waterloo Bridge," in which he starred as a fighter pilot in the early part of World War II, that I enlisted.

I'm going into the war in one branch of the services as soon as I graduate from high school because of the National Draft, so I might as well volunteer and get what I want regarding branch of service and job. After seeing that movie, I want to be a fighter pilot like Robert Taylor.

The Air Corp placed me on inactive duty at first because they wanted me to graduate from high school and turn eighteen before they call me to active duty. By June both requirements had been accomplished. Now I was waiting for my call up for active duty. School was out for the summer and my childhood friend, Clyde Wilson, and I took on the job of putting a new cedar shingle roof on his folks' garage while I waited for my call to active duty from the Army Air Corps.

Removing the old shingles went fairly fast with the help of a couple of shovels, and we had no sooner stripped the garage roof clean of shingles than my Uncle Earl drove up. He stood at the end of the driveway vigorously waving a white envelope over his head and grinning from ear to ear. I lived with my Aunt Hesper and Uncle Earl and I suspected the envelope contained my "call up,"

I hurried down the ladder to the ground, dogtrotted the length of the driveway, and anxiously took the extended envelope. My uncle seemed as excited as I, and sure enough, the Army Air Corps wanted me to report to Camp Kearns, Utah for basic military training in seven days. Wow!

I guess I would owe a favor to Clyde because the roof job was over as far as I was concerned. I immediately made plans to visit all of my relatives and friends within a two-hour drive before I boarded a ferryboat from Bremerton to Seattle, and then a train bound for Salt Lake City, Utah.

Clyde joined me on my travels to a dozen places to see family and friends. This was natural he should do so because, besides being my best friend, he and I owned a car together; our one mode of transportation. My Aunt Hesper put on a delicious "going-away" chicken dinner for a dozen of my boyfriends and me and I felt very special. After all, I was doing what they wanted to do, go off to war and be a hero.

* * *

My mother and my girlfriend accompanied me on the ferryboat ride to Seattle and escorted me to the King Street Train Station. It was the first time I had ever been in a train station or on a train, for that matter. In fact, I was going into a pilot training program and I had never been in an airplane. It was a sign of the times.

My mother and my girlfriend jockeyed for position to see which one would be the last to kiss me goodbye and mother won out, naturally.

The train came and a lot of other young men and I, bound for the same destination, climbed aboard. The whistle blew; we waved our goodbyes, and were on our way to a whole new world.

As the train progressed out of the city and into the night, the enormity of what I was doing hit me. This was an irreversible decision I had made, and as I looked around the dark railroad car, I read the same message in the faces of the other silent young men.

After a fitful night's sleep sitting up in a train's coach seat, I began to make friends with those about me. As conversation brought up schools attended, families and girlfriends, I joined in with the picture sharing by bringing out my high school yearbook. How could it seem so long ago when I'd only been out of high school less than two weeks? Misery likes company and the friends I made in those first few hours on the train were very important to me.

After traveling twenty-four hours, the train covered the one thousand-mile distance and we were in Salt Lake City where Army buses met us and whisked us to our new home, Camp Kearnes. It was about ten miles out of town in an exceptionally arid part of the world. We stopped seeing houses about five miles back and as we approached Camp Kearnes we were told it had started out as a Japanese internment camp. If you can imagine what an internment camp would look like, barbed wire fences, tarpapered single-story barracks, no trees, no shrubbery, and housing several thousand young, disillusioned men.

As we pulled into camp the soldiers not in a formation of some sort, met us with a common refrain: "You'll be sorry!"

Basic Training

After bundling up our civilian clothes and sending them home via the post office we now had army issue. Everything was new except my dress uniform. The short, stocky Italian clerk at the clothing warehouse prized himself at being able to look at you and tell what size you needed in clothing. He was right until he came to my dress blouse. He called out 38 short and I said no, I wear a 40 short. He handed me the 38 short and it was a perfect fit; today I wear some sizes bigger. That's what the years and a good appetite does for you.

We were issued our bedding and assigned to a barracks as a unit called a flight that was predetermined by someone. My new friends and I made our beds according to instruction from our drill instructor that would take a position in our lives just one step below Jesus Christ, he informed us. Soon we were ordered into formation outside the barracks dressed in our new uniform of the day, fatigues. These were olive drab coveralls; not too far from being one size fits all.

Next, we were lined up according to height, which put me at or near the end of the line. This would be my place in a flight formation, which consisted of four columns of ten men. The tallest soldier was at the front of the line and tapered down to the shortest at the end of the line; that was my country. The drill sergeant instructed us how to do a few basic maneuvers and we marched off to the mess hall for our first army meal. I have no idea what the menu was that day; it's probably just as well.

We were free to walk back to the barracks after dinner and those of us who smoked combined this into the walk. We had been taught how to police our butts, which is to say, we were taught not to throw our cigarette butts on the ground. As instructed, we stubbed them out on the sole of our shoe, and then tore a strip from the side of the butt so the remaining tobacco could freely fall to the ground. We then rolled the remaining paper into a tight ball and threw it to the wind. Can you imagine what the grounds would look like if thousands of G Is threw twenty butts a day on the ground. On this issue the army made sense.

The first night was a long one for me. Taps sounded and lights were out, soldiers stopped talking and were left to their own thoughts. It was apparent some had no thoughts and were soon snoring; they were the lucky ones. All good and bad things come to an end and I was awakened by the canned music of a bugler whose job it was to wake us up; he succeeded. The drill sergeant in his best drill instructor voice informed us we were to be dressed in the uniform of the day and be in formation in front of the barracks in five minutes. Is that possible? No, but we tried.

Roll was called and reported to the first sergeant that was responsible for the four flights that made up our squadron. He instructed us what our day would consist of, and so the day began. It started with close order drill, which we needed badly, a lecture on military procedure, an introduction to fire arms in preparation for a trip to the firing range, physical training, and free time. Free time consisted of showering, shaving, etc., putting your spot in the barracks spotless, with bunk bedding made up so tightly a quarter would bounce off it when tested at the daily inspection. I had no idea the army was so particular about how our spot looked or how we dressed.

In the evening, if we didn't have a G.I. party, we had time to write letters in the day room, or take an evening stroll, or just lie around the barracks and complain. Many honed complaining to a fine art, as it did relieve the tendency to want to go AWOL.

In the beginning we were really excited when told we were going to have a G.I. party after dinner. This excitement was soon dispelled when we learned it meant scrubbing the barracks floor, bathroom, and day room from end to end and side to side. Oh, yes, we were learning the army way of doing things. The drill instructor oversaw the party and we performed admirably. Mail call was a thrill, if you received mail. If you didn't, it was like not receiving a present on your birthday. We had sent our new addresses home the very first day and in a week it started to pay off. My girlfriend at the time did an admirable job. There was no higher point in the day than to have a letter from a loved one.

However, you didn't just rip it open and read it, you treated it like manna from heaven. One choice of procedures was to go to one's bunk and carefully lie down on your quarter-tested bed and retrieve a candy bar from you footlocker you were saving for just the right moment. If time permitted you could go to the P.X. and purchase a candy bar or coke, or both. Then you were ready to carefully open the letter and devour every word along with your treat-of-choice. That's if you had any money.

The Hospital Visit

After the first week, routine made life easier, and then it all changed. I was doing pull-ups on an overhead bar as directed when I experienced a stabbing pain in my lower abdomen. I immediately suspected what the problem was because I had been in the Bremerton Hospital overnight two weeks before I received my orders to report for active duty. It had been an appendicitis attack. They iced me down and gave me medication, but with no talk of an operation.

I didn't mention this to the military because I was "gunny" at that point of time and didn't want to miss my call to report for active duty. The Bremerton hospital had learned I was my own financial support system when they checked me in, so they probably put two and two together and figured the military would be providing an operation soon.

As I dropped to the ground from the bar, I was physically helped to the dispensary nearby and immediately ambulanced to the base hospital. Within three hours I was on an operating table and the troubling appendix removed.

Because there had been no room in the ward for patients having operations, I was put in a pneumonia ward prior to the operation. This made me a celebrity, being the only one having an operation. The fact that I probably would get pneumonia didn't seem to be a concern to anyone. A medical orderly was assigned the job of shaving my private parts before the operation. This immediately brought a large audience, which encircled my bed with more than enough comments about the procedure. Obviously the pneumonia patients were starved for entertainment of any kind.

After the operation I was given a private room for three days to deal with my post-operative delirium. On the third evening I had visitors. This was a welcome surprise although I wasn't in my best form yet. Three of my new friends from the flight took the trouble after a full day of training to change into a suntan uniform and walk a mile to see me. They even brought me cigarettes, a magazine to read and a Hershey bar. I was touched by their kindness and concern.

Fifteen minutes into the visit one of them said, "Harry, would you do me a favor?"

"Sure, Chuck, what is it?"

"Would you open you other eye?"

I had lain there talking to them for a long period of time and didn't realize I had only one eye open. That gives you an idea of my physical and mental condition. After another fifteen minutes they excused themselves with the normal goodbyes given by eighteen year-old soldiers. After I promised not to seduce any of the female nurses, they left in good spirits as having done a good deed for a comrade.

I was transferred from my private room back to the ward and instructed to stay prone for another four days. I made new friends and eventually was back on my feet. However, as soon as one becomes vertical he is assigned duties like carrying bed pans, running errands about the ward that the seriously ill cannot do for themselves: carrying food trays, dispensing and dispersing spit cups, and keeping water glasses full.

After a few days I was allowed to go to the hospital day room in another building. As I walked by the desk at the entrance, I admired a large bouquet of flowers on the desk. I bent close to smell and admire them when I noticed a florist's card attached with my name on it in bold writing; I was speechless.

When I found my voice I asked, "How long have these been here?"

The Red Cross attendant offhandedly said, "Three days."

I firmly informed her, "Those are my flowers; why weren't they delivered to me?"

With no sign of chagrin she replied, "They were so pretty, I thought everyone should enjoy them."

I picked up the vase holding the flowers, showed her my identification bracelet and informed her the decision was mine to make, not hers. It's hard to look imposing standing there in your bathrobe and slippers, so I turned around and determinedly shuffled back to my ward where my friends and I could enjoy my first-ever bouquet. In retrospect, my mother and my girlfriend had gone together and sent them as soon as they learned of my operation. Ironically, in the mail that day I received a letter from my girl friend asking if I liked the flowers.

* * *

Because of the type of my operation, I was required to stay in the hospital for three weeks followed by a three weeks convalescent leave. The announcement about the leave got my attention and I could hardly wait until I got my furlough. Traveling a thousand miles by bus is no way to convalesce, but I wasn't going to argue with the Army. I arrived into the waiting arms of the two females who saw me off just a month earlier, but I was ten pounds lighter and a lot wiser about the ways of the world and the Army. I connected with Clyde and the three of us, my Washington girl, Clyde, and I were off on a three-week time of constant activity… so much for convalescing.

A New Squadron

When I returned to Camp Kearnes I was assigned to a new squadron as I had missed nearly two months of training. I once again had to make new friends with a group of cadets being given basic Army training prior to entering the cadet flight-training program. In the Army's infinite wisdom, everyone received the same basic nine-weeks training regardless of whether they were going to be a foot soldier or a pilot.

Several weeks into the new training, I awoke one morning without the bugler's help. I arose on one elbow and noticed the sun was shining; strange, our reveille was 4:45, and the barracks was totally empty. This made no sense! As I lay back on my top bunk totally perplexed, the doors abruptly swung open at the far end of the barracks and my loud-talking new barracks buddies came pouring down the center aisle. Again I arose on one elbow and demanded, "What's going on?"

The first one down the aisle said, "McIntyre, what the hell are doing there? We've been on a forced march all night."

I feebly repeated, "A forced march?"

"Yes, a forced march. The sergeant came in after midnight and rousted us all out in full field packs and we've been on a march all night long. You didn't hear any of this?"

"No, I just awoke."

By now a dozen worn-out, sweaty, grimy barracks buddies formed a sea of faces as I lay there on my side looking down at them. Then someone broke the spell by bursting into laughter. The others saw the humor in the situation and joined in. I had the day off with the rest of them. Being in a top bunk with a noticeable swale to it resembling a hammock, I had been overlooked and innocently slept right through the whole noisy procedure--- honest.

The Ten Hour Layover

All good and bad things come to an end and we graduated. I'm not sure graduate is the right word. Paroled might be closer to the truth. We were excited to be leaving and our entire flight had been assigned to the first step in the aviation cadet program, College Training Detachment located at Arizona State Teacher's College in Tempe Arizona. "C.T.D.," as its called, is a three-month attempt by the army to polish us up from being raw recruits to officers and gentlemen; all army programs aren't one hundred percent successful.

Our method of transportation from Camp Kearns, Utah to Tempe, Arizona was by train. It was a long, hot, boring ride through southern Utah, Nevada, and finally into more friendly California. We were compelled to go south to Los Angeles, and then take another train east to arrive at our destination, Phoenix. This two-train journey gave us a ten-hour layover between trains and to our surprise; we were going to have free time to do what we could devise.

Suddenly the trip became less boring and we started planning how we would spend those precious hours. There were four of us sitting together in a day coach and a friend sitting across the aisle. The five of us hung out together and Dick said, "I've got a great idea. I'll call my folks and they'll come down to the train station and take us out to our house for dinner." We told him, "That isn't exactly what we had in mind."

Being eighteen-years old, we had girls, dancing, and food on our minds. We weren't old enough to go into a bar and our idea of food was hamburgers and milk shakes. The age for cadets being eighteen to twenty-seven years, some of the legal-age cadets had a different itinerary in mind.

Dick refused to let go of his idea, which wasn't like him. Normally he went along with the crowd and was just an easy-going kind of guy. He wasn't the heartthrob type; in fact he reminded me of a cartoon character named "Sad Sack" having a skinny build, and usually looked like an unmade bed in his uniform. What he had going for him was his pleasant disposition; so his determination on how we should spend our free time was surprising.

After much haranguing, we reluctantly told him, "Go ahead and call them." The next time the train made a stop; he was off like a shot and called home. He returned bubbling over with good news. His dad and his uncle would pick us up in two cars accompanied by his sister, and take us out to the house for dinner. We received this news with as much enthusiasm as we could muster, while really feeling like sacrificial lambs giving up a good time on the town for a family reunion for a buddy. So much for our thoughts of amore, dancing and food. Well, mom's pot roast would be a welcome change from mess hall food.

* * *

The train pulled in and there was his reception committee: his dad, uncle, and sister, but with four of her girlfriends. This was a total surprise. Dick had got what he asked for, but had kept what he asked for a secret from us. Incidentally his sister was a looker, which was another surprise, as were her girlfriends and they were about our age. Unbelievable! Things really got interesting when after the usual introductions we were led to two Lincoln limousines. Suddenly, we seemed to be coupled up and on our way to Dick's house and his mom's pot roast.

The house was more than a house, it was a mansion. Dick never mentioned his dad and uncle owned an airplane-parts factory and were wealthy. We met his mother and aunt who led us to a dining room that easily held thirty people and a three-entree banquet. The five of us were being treated like returning heroes when all we had accomplished so far was to survive army basic training. However, we warmed up to our new role in life, and everyone had a good time.

You can imagine the looks we received from the rest of our flight when we returned to the train station in two limousines accompanied by five girls. *It just doesn't get much better than this.*

College Training Detachment

Soon we were back to reality and on our way to the Arizona State Teacher's College in Tempe, Arizona. The college is now the University of Arizona with over twenty thousand students; in 1943 it had six hundred coeds and twelve civilian male students. I was wrong in my assumption about things not getting much better then our ten-hour break. Imagine sending seventy young, red-blooded males into a social situation like this? Three flights of us with a flight graduating each month, and a new flight coming in each month kept our cadet population at 200, while the co-ed population exceeded 600. Consequently, we cadets were in great demand… unbelievable!

A comparison of life at Tempe to our life at Camp Kearns could be likened to the difference between heaven and hell. We lived in dormitories and ate in the college dining facilities. As cadets our food ration doubled and the ladies running the food facility reveled in feeding us the very best. If our officers hadn't worked us so hard, we would have gained weight. They were determined to polish us up to compare favorably with West Point cadets. In addition to physical training and close-order drill, we had daily courses in military etiquette, physics of flying, navigation, speech, and one-day-a-week flight training at Sky Harbor Airport.

We flew in Aironka Cadets, a small two-passenger plane similar to a Piper Cub. We weren't there to solo, but to learn hands-on how to fly a small aircraft. I looked forward to those once-a- week flights and now knew I'd made a good choice to become a pilot. Now, I was the kind of cadet they were looking for: "Gunney."

We marched as a flight everywhere we went during the day, but we were given ninety minutes free time each evening with freedom of the campus. At the perimeter of the campus were two ice cream parlors, which were full-to-overflowing with coeds and cadets each evening from seven to eight-thirty. A jukebox blared the latest hits, but unfortunately no room for dancing.

We would sit four to a booth, make a coke last a little over an hour, smoke our cigarettes with gay abandon, and pretend not to be checking out the coeds and vice-versa. Within a short time couples began to form and a few wives of cadets added to the gaiety. The Mills Brothers were popular singing songs like: "Glow Worm," "Paper Doll," "Dinah," "Daddy," and many more.

One day a friend said, "Harry, my girl and I are having our usual night at the Malt Shop, and she has a girlfriend who wants to meet you."

"Really," I stammered. "Do you know this girl?"

"Yes, she's a looker, and besides, she has her own car."

Well, far be it for me to stand in the way of destiny. "Count me in. I'll meet you there as soon after seven as possible."

I walked in, all confidence with my "Mr. Cool" face on, and there they were looking directly at me. For a moment I hesitated, I hadn't expected a Latin girl. As a northwest boy, my experience was mostly with Scandinavian, Irish, German, or English girls. Her black eyes, hair, and light skin set off her comely features and figure. The seat beside her was empty, and I extended my hand as I sat down. She smiled and extended her hand.

After I acknowledged my friend and his girlfriend, whom I had met before, he said, "Courtney, this is Harry." We nodded and smiled at each other. Conversation came easily, and I automatically reached for and lit a cigarette.

As I sucked in on the cigarette, she said, "Aren't you going to offer me one?"

I'm sure I looked shocked, I'd never gone with a girl who smoked. I tried to slide into a "how-stupid-of-me" look as I pulled out my pack of cigarettes. I'm sure my hand shook as I took a cigarette out of my pack and put it in my mouth, lit it off my cigarette and casually handed it to her. After all I'd seen Clark Gable do that in *It Happened One Night* with Claudette Colbert.

We got on famously and as my friend and I prepared to leave as time had run out, she asked, "Aren't you going to ask me to the dance?"

"What dance?" I stammered.

"The dance next Saturday night put on by the girls in Glenbrook Hall," she replied with laughter in her eyes over my discomfort. "Each month a girl's dormitory puts on a formal dance and that's what this meeting is about today. Didn't John tell you?"

John and his girl had already left the malt shop to give us space for a goodbye. "No, John didn't tell me. However, will you go with me to the dance?"

"Yes, Harry, I'd love to."

"Why don't we meet here tomorrow night and discuss it further?" I suggested.

"It's a date... see you then." We rose and I escorted her to the door and to her waiting girlfriend. John had already gone on, as walking with coeds on campus during the week was against the Army rules for cadets. The college may have had some input on that rule too.

* * *

The first two months of the three-month program at CTD went by quickly and smoothly, as did my relationship with Courtney. We had gone steady from that first meeting which found us at the Malt Shop five nights a week and a date in town on Saturday. There was only one fly in the ointment. The Army had several permanent-party soldiers there to oversee the college program from the Army's point of view: a Major, a Technical Sergeant and a Staff Sergeant. Unfortunately, the Technical Sergeant had eyes for Courtney.

I don't blame him, but he was an old man of twenty-seven. He didn't make life easy, and I received punishment walking 'tours' during my free time for miner infractions of numerous army rules. A tour is one hour of walking one hundred and forty cadence a minute with a rifle marching with a military bearing. I couldn't be with Courtney during our special daily hour and fifteen minutes when I had a tour to walk.

This evolved into a crisis situation when the upper class flight was scheduled to ship out for the next phase of training called Pre-flight at Santa Ana Army Air Base in Santa Ana, California. Being scheduled to leave at ten o'clock on a Saturday night, they were short one man to fill out their roster. Guess who the tech sergeant picked from the lower class to fill that spot?

As I approached the Charge of Quarter's desk to pick up my Saturday pass, the cadet on duty handed it to me and then suddenly blurted, "McIntyre, you're scheduled to ship out with "A" Flight tonight as an alternate."

"What? Is this a joke?"

"No joke, Harry, I got the word from the tech sergeant."

I was momentarily stunned and stood silent, my mind raced. I needed a solution. *Only one thing to do,* "Tell him you didn't see me." I turned and walked quickly out the door with my pass in hand and headed for Courtney's dormitory.

When she came down the spiral stairs she took one look at me and knew something was wrong. I walked her to her car in the parking lot, "We've got to get off campus fast and stay out of sight until ten o'clock tonight."

"What's wrong?"

I quickly told her. "If you don't want to do this, say so and I'll go back to my barracks."

"I don't want you shipped out a month early, that's for sure. Let's go."

She drove and I stayed out of sight until we got off-campus. Later, when she dropped me off at my barracks at eleven o'clock, I was met at the C. Q.'s desk by a visibly angry tech sergeant. "Where the hell have you been, Mister McIntyre?" (Incidentally, cadets were always called mister, but in this case it wasn't a sign of respect.)

"I've been in Phoenix having dinner and going to a movie. What's wrong?" I asked innocently.

"You were supposed to ship out an hour ago with "A Flight" as an alternate. Because we couldn't find you, I had to send someone else."

"I had no idea I was an alternate," I lied.

"I had the MP's looking for you; they obviously looked in the wrong places."

"I guess so… here's my pass, so, if that's all, I'll head for my bunk."

A still angry and suspicious sergeant said, "That's all, MISTER." He quickly turned and walked out the door. The truth is, Courtney and I bought take-out food at a drive inn and parked in a secluded spot out of town, as we thought the MP's might be looking for me.

I especially enjoyed the last month at CTD and then shipped out with my flight as scheduled.

Pre Flight

Our train arrived in Santa Ana, California near midnight in a downpour of rain and cold wind. We stood in flight formation, chilled to the bone because we were now used to the Arizona climate. Buses eventually took us to our squadron area and we were assigned to a barracks. For the first time a barracks felt inviting, as it was a permanent structure with steam heat. After a hot shower we made up our bunks and soon it was lights out. I lay there a long time thinking of my three months at the college, and now I was back in the real army.

It was nearing Christmas and we were busy with classes, testing, close order drill, and physical training. This phase of training was called pre-flight and we would be tested mentally, physically, and psychologically to determine: if we would train to be a pilot, navigator, bombardier, or out of the training program for good. I don't know what the percentages were in each category, but I was elated to be on the list for pilot training. I would receive three months ground school training in my new specialty, and then sent on to flight school.

Because I had new bunkmates, I had a new circle of friends. Ralph Andrews (Andy) and I became close friends and spent each weekend pass together during that three-month period. At Christmas we signed up and were invited to a local home to celebrate the day. The couple had two teen-age sons, so we played touch football with them and their neighborhood friends as we waited for Christmas dinner. This dinner was turkey with all the trimmings, but it wasn't in the same league as Dick's family dinner. However, it was nice to be in a family home celebrating Christmas rather than in a mess hall.

New Year's Eve

The next weekend was New Year's Eve, so we caught a bus to attend a dance at the Balboa Ballroom in Long Beach, California. Nat King Cole and his Trio were the entertainment. He was at the zenith of his career and put on a good show. Because it was New Year's Eve, all of those in attendance were couples, which left us with no one to dance with. Disappointed, we returned to Santa Ana and stayed the night at the Y.M.C.A.

We had spent nearly all our money with just enough left for food and bus fair back to the base. I noticed a cadet dance was being advertised to be held right there at the Y.M.C.A. that very night …exactly what we'd been looking for. Andy and I both liked dancing, and we jitterbugged with each other occasionally in the barracks; I led. I had one of the few radios around as I brought it with me when I returned from my rehabilitation leave after my operation.

We spent the day at the Y.M.C.A. using their athletic facilities and the pool table to pass the day until the dance that evening. Finally it was time for the dance and we were one of the first ones there. In fact we listened to the band warm up. It was a local five piece group with a very limited repertoire; however, beggars can't be choosers. Cadets and single girls started filling the gymnasium, and we eagerly looked over every girl that walked through the door. Guess what? All were taller than Andy and I.

Discouraged, we reclaimed our garrison hats from the hat check girl and walked down the steps to return to the base early. Suddenly two short, attractive girls walked toward the steps. Andy and I exchanged glances and with unspoken understanding did an about face and walked up the steps behind them. We again checked our garrison hats, to the surprise of the hat check girl, and returned to the dance.

When we entered the dance and they were nowhere in sight, we cruised the perimeter of the dance floor in our best cruise style. Much to our chagrin, they were not there. We reconnoitered and determined to take another cruise around the perimeter of the dance floor. Suddenly they came walking out of a hallway that led to the restrooms. Of course, how could we be so stupid? Everyone knows girls don't just walk onto a dance floor, they have to have a mirror check first.

They looked even better than our first impression. It's funny how one minute you can be in the depths of despair and the next minute you're on cloud nine. Andy and I smiled at one another reading each other's mind. I darted across the dance floor first and reached the girl in the lead as the band started to play "Embraceable You." When I asked her to dance in my most suave and subtle manner, to my delight she smiled and nodded a "Yes." Andy followed suit with the same results.

The four of us gathered for introductions after the orchestra had played three numbers. My partner's name was Louree and Andy's was Donna. The girls were best of friends, students at Fullerton Junior College nearby and enjoyed attending cadet dances when the opportunity arose. Because they lived in a neighboring town, they were staying the night with Louree's aunt and uncle in Santa Ana. We asked them for the next dance as the orchestra interrupted our interrogation.

They both held out a hand to us and we were off and running. After three more numbers it was intermission and Andy and I skillfully directed the girls to the refreshment table where we partook of punch and cookies. The four of us seemed to have an instant camaraderie and the evening flew.

When the last dance was announced, Andy and I suddenly realized we would have to act fast or forever live a life of regret. I asked, "May we walk you home?" They accepted our offer. While the girls got their coats and hats from somewhere, Andy and I retrieved our garrison hats for the second time and reviewed the situation. Because we were broke, we couldn't offer them a treat so we decided to tell them our plight. They graciously said that was no problem.

When we arrived at Louree's aunt and uncle's house they invited us in for introductions. A second aunt and uncle were there and soon we felt like family. They offered us hot cocoa and cookies, which we readily accepted as Andy and I had been on a very limited diet all day.

We said our goodbyes with the promise of a date in Fullerton the following week, and briskly walked to catch the last bus to the base. We could be seen hooting, hollering and giving each other high fives as we scurried along celebrating our good fortune.

* * *

During the week we followed a course of films, *Why We Fight* that graphically told the story of what preceded WWII and what was going on now. We were *carefully taught to hate* the enemy so we would pull the trigger when the time came. Some would call this brainwashing. Ground school courses in our new specialty: pilot training, navigation, or bombardier was now added. In addition: physical training, close order drill, and the week topped off with a huge parade on Sunday.

Because of our large number, twenty thousand, it took two hours to pass in review, squadron-by-squadron, and flight-by-flight. After inspection on Saturday we received a twenty-four hour pass from noon Saturday until noon on Sunday, the highlight of the week for us.

First Date With Louree

After the ten-mile bus ride from Santa Ana to Fullerton, Andy and I checked in to the quaint, Spanish style, *California Hotel*. Actually it was the only hotel in a town of twelve thousand people, which, I discovered, meant a ten-block walk to her parent's home. We called to determine an appropriate time for our arrival for our date. Donna was to be there in order to simplify the logistics.

We met Louree's parents, Pat and Vida, and her two younger sisters, Joyce and Patty. It was a typical American family living in a typical American neighborhood, which made us feel right at home. You'd have to be in the Army to appreciate the joy we felt in just being there. It was a giant step back into normalcy; a sharp contrast to the Army, especially in wartime.

We took Louree and Donna to dinner and a movie spending half a month's pay in the process, but Andy and I lived for the moment. However, the girls and Pat and Vida were good at math, so they suggested we stay at their home next time to eliminate the cost of a hotel room and of dining out. In fact Louree's parents offered to lend us the family Ford sedan if we wanted to go to a dance in the next town, Anaheim. With gasoline rationed at four gallons per week, it was quite a generous offer. We gratefully accepted, being in the early stages of falling in love and always short of money. Vida's down-home, Texas cooking was an added bonus.

* * *

The training during the week seldom varied as we followed a three month's course preparing for our next step: for some flight school; others bombardier school, and for the rest, navigation school. Some had been 'washed out' for failure to pass the psychological and physical testing at Santa Ana. Those of us scheduled for flight training would eventually be segregated for either single engine planes or multi-engine planes. I was scheduled for single engine and I have no idea what the selection process was.

* * *

The next weekend Andy and I traveled by bus to Fullerton and walked to Louree's parents home. We were greeted like family, and after an afternoon in Hillcrest Park, dinner at home, and the loan of the family sedan, the four of us arrived at the Anaheim Dance Hall. It was great fun, different from the many public dances where the military, single girls, and women often dominated. This was more family oriented with mostly civilians of all ages. The orchestra members were older having been the house-orchestra for years, however they played most of the modern big-band songs of the decade.

The girls were attractive in colorful dresses showing off their good figures. Louree and Donna were both brunettes, about five-foot two with eyes of brown. Andy and I were in uniform as required. In peacetime the military have a choice, not in wartime. However, I'm sure we both felt handsome in our uniforms. After exchanging dances several times, all too soon the evening ended.

* * *

After Sunday breakfast, we returned to the base being due at twelve o'clock for the parade. Pat and Vida were great hosts and I envied Louree having such wonderful parents. My own family life ended at the age of fourteen when my parents divorced, and scars inflicted would last a lifetime.

The four of us decided to spend the next weekend together celebrating Louree's nineteenth birthday; this made her four months older than I, which she didn't let me forget. I shopped for a present for her at the P.X., my only choice of shopping sites, and settled on a pair of silver earrings in the shape of the fighter plane P-38; a plane I hoped to fly.

Her birthday party consisted of her intimate family, Donna, Andy, and I. Vida prepared a wonderful Baron of Beef roast dinner, with all the trimmings and a lovely birthday cake. Louree seemed appreciative of her gift from me and immediately put the earrings on. After dinner we went to the local theatre and her sisters, Joyce and Patty, joined us. That restricted our togetherness to handholding only; no stolen kisses in the dark… RATS!

* * *

After a casual Sunday morning breakfast, we said our goodbyes and caught the bus back to the base. Andy and I were in the same barracks, flight, and squadron, so our main concern for the rest of the day, Sunday, was the parade. All squadrons were in the parade except the permanent party members. The parade was a test of our skill in close order drill and a way for each of us to know we were a part of something very big and very organized. Also, it was a way for the top brass to entertain visiting dignitaries by showing us off.

The weather was still warm in the fall in California and it took a while to get all of the squadrons with their individual flights of forty men each in place. This meant a lot of standing and waiting. Sometimes I could feel my shoes sinking and adhering to the warm asphalt, so when given the order "forward march," it wasn't that easy to do. If the band wasn't too loud, you could actually hear a sucking sound as you took your first two steps extracting your shoe soles from the hot asphalt.

All the cadets were relieved when the parade was over and we could go back to our barracks and take off our dress uniforms. Sunday night in the barracks was a kind of breather when we could get mentally and physically ready for the next week. Letter writing was always on the agenda and I sat down in the day room that Sunday evening after my third date with Louree and wrote a 'dear Jane' letter to my girlfriend back home. I told her about Louree and suggested she date others also and not spend her high school senior year sitting out the school dances.

She was hurt and angry suggesting we go separate ways, which we did. Writing the letter wasn't an easy thing to do, but it was the right thing to do. After some soul searching, I determined I wasn't ready for a romantic commitment with anyone at age eighteen. In addition to a girlfriend, I also had a correspondence with my mother and my seventeen-year-old cousin, Dolores, who was like a sister to me. Dolores periodically supplied me with homemade tollhouse cookies, which was a real touch and taste of home; my buddies enjoyed seeing that shoe box sized package come in the mail.

The weekdays were always busy from 4:45 a.m. to 6:00 p.m. The day ended with a couple of hours of free time each evening before taps at 8:00 p.m. to take care of our personal lives. I usually called Louree in the middle of the week and we planned the next weekend. She suggested a boy-girl party that would include three of her girlfriends, assuming I could bring three of my boyfriends including Andy. She suggested we go to the Long Beach Pier, which was an amusement park about fifteen miles from Fullerton on the Pacific coast.

Donna and her older sister were two of the girls, plus a tall girl named Janet whom I matched with a tall cadet friend of mine, Dick White. Of course Andy was with Donna and her sister was with a friend of mine who was a non-stop, stand-up comedian. Everyone had a great time and we got together once more as a group.

The three months at Santa Anna Army Airbase came to an end and we said our goodbyes with a promise to write. I shipped out to Thunderbird Field, which is outside of Phoenix, Arizona. Andy, to our dismay, was sent to a different flight school in California, and we never saw each other again until after the war.

Thunderbird Field

Life at Thunderbird Field was magic. We were finally going to learn to fly and to solo, which meant we would do most of our flying alone except for occasional instruction from our instructor and the much-dreaded check flights by check pilots who had the prerogative of either passing or failing one. This would demote the cadet to the regular army as a private and then be sent to a specialist school for additional training.

We lived in attractive bungalows that provided sleeping quarters for eight cadets, and a study room with individual desks. We ate in an attractive mess hall, which held several hundred always-hungry cadets. There were two hundred American cadets and sixty Chinese cadets at Thunderbird Field, so we ate in shifts. The food was good as we were fed on double rations as cadets and we sat at tables set for four. Everything was different from what we had become used to at Santa Anna.

When we walked about the base alone, which wasn't often, we were instructed to stop when we came to a corner, look in all directions, then up and down, then extending your arms, like wings, and fly around the corner. It sounds silly, but it taught us what to do when we were flying alone and about to do a maneuver. Learning to really look in all directions, including up and down, doesn't come easy or automatically; it has to be taught.

A very creative person who drew plans for the field planned it to look like a giant thunderbird when one flew over it at five thousand feet.

In the middle of the buildings portion of the overall design where two identical rectangles were needed in the design, they placed two identical swimming pools. The pools were well attended in the evening's free time as the weather was warm, even in February and March.

We were divided into groups of five and assigned an instructor. My instructor's name was Norbert Lypps, a small, dark-complected man, was a fine gentleman, soft-spoken, and extremely patient. These qualities obviously endeared him to us. Our flight instructors were civilians, while the check-riders were military. I knew none of the other four in my group, but that soon changed as we all had the same goal-- to become pilots.

After introductions, we each took an initial flight with Mr. Lypps. This included a take-off with him at the controls, and with our hands loosely on the dual control to get the feel. This included a trip around the landing pattern and shooting a landing.

Our training plane was a Stearman PT-17; a bi-plane with two open cockpits and dual controls; the instructor sat in the front cockpit. It had a two-wheel landing gear with a tail wheel. The plane's engine, a seven cylinder radial design, boasted of having two hundred horsepower. The Sterman was a very good training plane, maneuverable, and forgiving.

* * *

Our day consisted of a half day devoted to flying and a half-day for ground school plus one hour of physical training. A squadron flew in the morning or the afternoon; mine flew in the afternoon. Our day started at six with a five mile run before showers and breakfast. We enjoyed the cool temperature during the morning run; the day grew progressively warmer as days are prone to do in Arizona; even in February and March.

After breakfast, we marched as a flight to each of our classes, which consisted of navigation, aircraft engines, flight ground school, and military etiquette. After lunch, I marched with my flight to the flight line to meet my instructor, Norbert Lypps, and the four other cadets under his tutorage. Their names were Jack Manthei, Bill Wandtke, Billy Miles, and Bill Graves. It's unusual that three guys with the same first name should end up in a group of five cadets?

Each of us had been assigned an hour flight with our instructor each day in the beginning. We were scheduled to solo after eight to ten hours of instruction. If you couldn't solo in ten hours you were washed out. It was a reasonable length of time and all five of us made it; I soloed on April first, 1944. I had just completed eight hours of dual flying instruction, and when Mr. Lypps directed me to a dirt auxiliary field to shoot touch and go landings; I had a feeling that this was it. After several successful landings, he told me to taxi over to the sidelines of the field, which I did. He then stood up in his front cockpit position and climbed out of the airplane.

Solo Flight

He smiled and said, "It's all yours." I felt ready for the challenge and taxied to the end of the dirt field and turned around into position for takeoff. Several other planes were shooting "touch and go's," so I waited until the quarter-mile-long runway cleared, then pushed the throttle forward. Holding forward pressure on the stick and steering the plane straight down the two hundred-yard wide dirt strip using my foot pedals, the die was cast. As I reached fifty-five miles per hour and when the plane began to feel light, I sucked the stick back toward my belly and I was airborne.

Being free of the earth was an exhilarating feeling and I looked back and down at Mr. Lypps standing on the ground watching. I read the gauges and with my left hand on the throttle and my right hand on the stick, I was flying, solo. Then reality hit me, *I've to get this thing back down.* When I reached 500 feet of altitude, I backed off on the hand throttle, pushed the stick forward to neutral, and prepared for a left turn to stay in the traffic pattern to ultimately return to my starting point.

I kicked the left foot pedal and simultaneously moved the stick from neutral to the left with a little back pressure to keep the nose of the aircraft from dropping as I did a ninety degree turn to the left and still maintaining my 500 feet of altitude. After several hundred yards of flight I repeated the maneuver and was heading back the way I came, only now I was off to one side of the runway.

I flew the length of the field plus several hundred yards beyond and did another left turn maneuver. After another two hundred yards of forward flight and another left turn maneuver, I was approaching the field where I started. I now had to descend five hundred feet to shoot my landing, so I cleared myself visually and started my descent by pushing the stick forward and easing to 'off' position on the hand throttle. As I approached the ground at fifty-five miles per hour, I dare not make any mistakes.

I simultaneously lost altitude and speed, and as the ground approached, the plane wanted to drift because of a side wind. I dropped the wing on the wind side to correct for the drift and I was doing a "dead stick" landing, as I had been taught. Just a second or two before the wheels touched down, I sucked the stick back into my gut and the tail wheel dropped. Rolling about thirty miles per hour, I had to avoid the temptation of hitting the brakes too soon or too hard. With my feet lightly on the brake and rudder pedals I taxied to the side of the field where my instructor stood smoking a cigarette, with a big smile on his face.

He gave me thumbs up, flipped his cigarette away after one last puff, and climbed into the front cockpit. I had done it. I had successfully soloed.

He turned and said over his shoulder, "Take us home."

* * *

On the weekend we were given a 24 hour pass, so I decided to return to Arizona State Teacher's College and look up Courtney Luna, as it was only a twenty mile bus ride from Glendale, where Thunderbird Field was located, to Tempe. I was coming unannounced, as Courtney and I weren't writing, and I was taking my chances we'd connect. As I walked on campus everything was just as I remembered it and being Saturday evening, I stopped at the malt shop for to see if she was there.

She wasn't, but I learned that one of the girls' dorms was sponsoring the monthly formal dance that evening. I went immediately to Courtney's dorm and made contact by house phone. She was happy and surprised to hear from me, but had a date for the dance due to pick her up even as we spoke. She came downstairs to the foyer, and we sat in an alcove where she could watch the front door as we talked, awaiting his arrival.

Our relationship was now one of friends, but with no expectations as I had written her about Louree. After a half hour and when her date hadn't arrived, I told her I would be happy to escort her to the dance. She agreed and lead me outdoors into the flower garden. She bent over, picked a large rose and made herself a corsage deftly avoiding the thorns.

We returned inside, but at that moment her date made a hurried entrance. Breathlessly, he blurted out he'd been given extra duty and not given an opportunity to contact her. He apologized for being late and for being without a corsage, so the homemade one was pressed into service. I was quickly introduced and, just as quickly, they said goodbye.

As I walked back to the malt shop, I mulled over my situation. *It's Saturday night and I'm twenty miles from the base; what to do?* Before I could arrive at a decision, I recognized a girl walking toward me. She recognized me also and said, "Harry, what are you doing here?"

"Hi Ann, I came to say Hello to Courtney, which I did, but she's off to the dance with a date."

"I would have liked to have gone to the dance," Ann admitted, "but I'm flunking a history course and I have to outline a portion of the book to save my grade."

"Do you want some help? I'm available."

"Really? I'm not good at that sort of thing. Maybe with your help I could get the assignment done. You're sure you want to spend your Saturday night doing this?"

"I'm sure, let's get at it."

We went to the small library in her dorm and worked until eleven o'clock with me dictating the outline of the paragraphs from her textbook and with her typing nearly as fast as I could talk. We had been at it for two hours and were exhausted, but the assignment was complete. She walked me to the front door of her dormitory and thanked me profusely.

I told her, "I didn't expect to spend Saturday night this way. However I enjoyed the mental workout and being able to help a friend." I should mention Ann was the girlfriend of a former roommate of mine at Tempe, and they still were an 'item'. We parted with a hug and I walked off campus the three blocks back to the center of town. There was a small hotel on main street where I rented a room for the night.

* * *

The next morning I checked out and went in search of a restaurant for breakfast. The entire small town seemed to be asleep, but in the middle of the block was a little café with a dim light on. However, as I prepared to open the front door, I noticed a CLOSED sign in the window. I strained to look inside, cupping my hands to the window and peered in. I could see a man and a woman standing by a table near the back of the long, narrow dimly lit café.

They saw me and the man turned and walked to the front door. Opening the door, he said, "We're closed." Then he paused, looked me over briefly, then added, "My wife and I are fixing our breakfast, if you like bear steak you can eat with us. We don't open on Sunday."

"I'll be happy to join you for breakfast. I've never eaten bear steak, but I'm game."

We introduced ourselves and they asked about my Army life. We had a comfortable time together over breakfast. They had a son in the service and I could understand their motivation to invite me for breakfast. The bear steak was delicious and did not have a strong game taste. When I offered to pay, they declined. I said my goodbyes and walked to the bus stop to return to my base. It wasn't the weekend I envisioned, but it was a good weekend after all.

Flying the Stearman PT-17

Life at Thunderbird fell into a comfortable routine as long as you were satisfied to only have two hours per day to call your own. The best time of the day was being on the flight line and having the opportunity to fly one hour per day. Once you soloed, the more complicated learning began. The stall came early in the training because if you asked too much of the plane and subsequently went into a stall you'd better know how to get out of it or you become a vital statistic. Not too many fliers walk away from diving head first into the earth.

Mr Lypps, flying in the front cockpit, told me to raise the nose of the plane without adding additional power, which ultimately produces a stall. I followed his instructions and the whole plane started to vibrate and shudder. He said, "Now I'll show you how to get out of this. Let the plane fall off to one side and start its spin downward." That's exactly what happened, and after three complete rotations heading earthward he said, "Because we're spinning to the right, kick the left rudder and dump the nose straight for the ground.

This stopped the spinning, much to my relief, but didn't change our direction, which was now straight down. Looking at the earth from that angle isn't a whole lot of fun. His voice came over the headphones, "Now Mister, gently, but steadily, pull back on the stick and see what happens."

What happened was we didn't become a statistic that day. The nose of the plane began to rise from the vertical and eventually we were flying straight and level. He turned and smiled at me knowing he had given me a thrill. He then had me do it again to be sure I had the sequence correct. There are some things in flying or perhaps in life you had better always get right, and coming out of a stall is one of them. I should mention you should have five thousand feet of altitude when doing this or doing acrobatics, which sometimes brings on a stall, when you don't get the maneuver right. Therefore, most of our flying was at or above five thousand feet giving you time to recover from a mistake in a maneuver.

One the way back to the field we were flying at five hundred feet of altitude over agricultural farmland. Suddenly he pulled the throttle back and shouted, "Shoot an emergency forced landing." After I got through the shock of the command, I realized I was to put into practice what he had told us about emergency forced landings.

He had told us to first determine the wind direction so we could land going into the wind, which would result in having a shorter landing approach. We could determine wind direction by looking for smoke coming out of a chimney or a flag flying, or sometimes the way branches moved in trees. I did this and saw an open field to our left that would require a 180-degree change of flight direction. I made the turn as the plane started to lose altitude and lined up with the fence posts, now approaching into the wind. When we were about thirty feet off the ground he jammed the throttle forward and the emergency landing drill was over. He shouted, "Well done, Mister." I was relieved.

While we flew at this lower level he also talked me through the pylon eight maneuver. He said, "Chose two points of reference about three to five hundred yards apart on the ground." I did this and chose a small building on one end of a field and an object out in the field about four hundred yards apart. He said, "The idea is to do a large figure eight around them to get practice doing wing overs or flying U-turns."

I practiced a couple of these and he was satisfied that my turns were acceptable. The acrobatics we would be taught, because we were to be fighter pilots were: chandelles, slow rolls, snap rolls, loops, vertical spit 's' turns, Cuban eights, English bunts, and pylon eights. All this would come in good time starting with the easiest to the more difficult.

* * *

After a full day comprised of ground school, physical training, and flight training, we looked forward to two hours of free time. During the warm weather, and it was warm even in March, the two swimming pools were popular. I had some expertise in diving and was selected to represent my squadron in a month-end athletic competition including swimming and diving. I needed to expand my repertoire and did so with the help of a fellow cadet. I saw him do a front kip with a back half gainer, and a one-and-a-half layout I wanted to learn.

I approached him even though we would be competitors in the future contest. He told me to meet him the next evening at the pool, but suggested I dress in my long underwear as I could count on bad landings at first. The long underwear would take the sting out of the mistakes. I did this and learned the dives after many attempts. I received all kinds of smart remarks from my friends, but I now had what I needed, a total of five dives for the competition.

These included: a swan dive, a jackknife, a forward one and a half tuck, a forward one and a half layout, and a front kip with a back half-gainer.

My new friend, Arne, and I decided to go to town on Saturday and demonstrate our diving skill at the municipal swimming pool in Phoenix. The swimming pool was crowded, but they did have a good one-meter board, which is what we needed. We went through our dives and attracted some attention.

After a dive, as I came up the ladder at the edge of the pool, a girl standing nearby appeared to be straining to read the name carved on the silver bracelet I wore. Being the ever suave and subtle eighteen-year-old, I said, "Don't break your neck." I then held my arm in such a way she could read my name.

She deliberately and slowly read it as I stood there with one foot on the pool ladder and the other on the pool apron with my arm extended. She then stepped back, smiling a smile of invitation. Quick to respond, I said, "Now that you know my name, what is yours?"

We stepped off to one side to avoid people climbing in and out of the pool. "I'm Rae Staniford." She turned around with a nod of her head, continued, "This is my friend Peggy." I then became aware of a girl standing nearby waiting, watching the drama of our meeting. I acknowledged Peggy as Arne joined us. I introduced him to Rae and Peggy and we walked from the pool as a foursome. We spent the next hour that way and then it was time for the girls to leave. They were taking a bus to downtown Phoenix, and then would transfer to another bus taking them to Peggy's house.

The girls were high school friends and looked to be seventeen or eighteen years old. Both were brunettes, attractive, and the right height for Arne and me. They were easy to talk to and the four of us hit it off right from the start. Rae, who lived in a suburb of Phoenix, was spending the weekend with Peggy and her folks.

While we waited with them for the transfer bus we sat as two couples, but apart, due to available seating. I approached Rae for a date for the following weekend, and she accepted. She told me she lived in Glendale, an area not too far from Thunderbird Field, so it was agreed we would meet at the bus station in Glendale, as I would be riding a bus to get there.

As far as I was concerned, Arne was on his own with Peggy and they didn't pursue their relationship.

* * *

Their transfer bus arrived and the girls went on their way. Arne and I caught a bus back to the base. I spent Saturday night just hanging out with my bungalow friends, and caught up on my letter writing and studies Sunday morning. There was to be a U.S.O. show that afternoon comprised of a group from Mexico; I planned to attend.

As I finished my studies I was the only one in the bungalow when I heard a rapping on the door. When it suddenly swung open, there stood Lt. Lipinski, the Military Arts Instructor. His eyes swept the room as he determined I was the only one there. Obviously irritated he said, "Mister, do you speak Spanish?"

"No, Sir. *What's this about*? Well, I did take it in high school, but it wasn't one of my better subjects."

"You'll have to do, come with me. I need a chaperone for the female singer with the Mexican band performing today. She speaks no English and I want you to stick with her like glue until she leaves. I don't want any of these horny cadets getting smart with her… do you understand?"

Dumbfounded, I could just nod my head. Lt. Lipinski was a little taller than I, ramrod straight, and all Army. He hurriedly took me to the all-purpose room where twenty or so entertainers in Mexican costumes, awaited show time. I was quickly introduced to this attractive young woman who stood smiling at me, extending her hand. I accepted my job for the day, wondering if I would wake up and discover this was but a dream.

I was instructed she needed to be taken to the Ladies room to freshen up before the performance. Of course I had to be told its location, also I was told where to have her, and at what time for her act. We did a lot of smiling at each other, and with the aid of hand gestures and my few words of Spanish, we managed.

She was charming and we got along well; I only wished I was a couple of years older. Uncomfortably, I waited outside the ladies room while she freshened up. Several of my friends walked by on their way to the performance when she walked out of the Ladies room and joined me. Their mouths dropped open as she laughingly took my extended arm and we walked off together like old friends.

We arrived at the right time and I stood in the wings while she performed. She had a wonderful singing voice, and was well received by the cadets. With her looks, she really didn't have to open her mouth. All too soon, I escorted her to the group's bus, where we said our goodbyes, and surprisingly she gave me a quick hug and a kiss on the cheek. Therefore, I was well rewarded for my duties, and a lot of cadets, and probably a few officers, were envious.

I told my cottage roommates, "See what happens when you stay in and study."

They had some snide remarks about Lt. Lipinski's choice for a chaperone, which I have chosen to forget.

* * *

Each day Mr. Lypps and his group, of which I was one, would come together at the flight line in a sort of huddle, and he would give us our flying assignment for the afternoon. It consisted of one of three things: flight instruction with him, solo flying, or a ride with an Army check rider. The check riders were all military pilots whose job was to be sure only suitable pilots succeeded. Their checklist not only included all the skills necessary to fly the Army way, but personality and attitude were on their checklist. These last two items weren't talked about, but they were there. One other factor entered the picture as the tide of the war changed, and we weren't losing 50% of our planes, as was the case at the beginning when I joined the Army.

This meant the check riders didn't need to pass as many cadet pilots because the law of *supply and demand* became a big factor. The Army Air Corp had taken in thousands of young men, who qualified mentally and physically, to train to fly the huge armada of airplanes coming off the assembly lines. As the war progressed, not only did we have more of our planes in the air against the enemy, but the Axis powers, Germany, Italy, and Japan, weren't keeping up with our assembly lines. Even though we were also supplying England and Russia planes and supplies under a program called Lend-Lease.

Consequently, as the need for new pilots lessened, being told one had a check ride brought on immediate anxiety. If a cadet failed a check ride, he was given a second chance a few days later. If he didn't pass the second check ride, he was immediately out of the program, reduced in rank to a private, and returned to the war effort as a crewmember on a bomber. To become a bomber crewmember required specific training as an aerial mechanic/gunner, an armor/gunner, or a radio operator/gunner. Everyone on a bomber crew except the pilot and co-pilot had a gun position in addition to his specific job.

As we cadets broke from the huddle each day, one would go with Mr. Lypps immediately. The rest of us waited our turn to fly with him. Because there were only so many planes available of the four to five hours on the flight line, one might spend several hours waiting to fly. This was not wasted time, however, as we talked to each other about all we were learning. Hand gestures of placing one hand on the other and simulating flying the different maneuvers often accompanied this. If one stood back and looked around the waiting area at the small groups of cadets, it was a humorous sight to see.

My First Flight After Soloing

The following day I was assigned an airplane for my first flight alone, wonderful! It takes two people to start a Stearman Pt-17, so I commandeered Jack Manthei, who wasn't busy, to be my crank man. We walked out to the plane together. I should say he walked, and I hobbled as I was wearing a seat-pack type parachute. Once there, I climbed into the back cockpit, settled in, checked the gauges, and prepared to start the plane. This is where Jack came in. He had to crank the starter engine with the aid of a huge crank, which was thrust into the side of the engine. This cranking method was better and safer than pulling the prop through, as engines had required in that era.

Once the engine caught and the airplane became alive, it was now my time to be a real pilot. I slowly taxied out of the parking area and onto a taxi runway that led to the end of the main runway. Several planes were ahead of me, and I was satisfied to play follow-the-leader. When my turn came to do a ninety-degree turn onto the field, reeve my engine to clear carburetion, and another ninety-degree turn to face the line of takeoff, I did so quickly, as other planes waited behind me.

I again cleared myself visually and started to move slowly at first down the field, but by pushing the hand throttle forward I gained speed. My goal was to have enough speed by the time I reached the middle of the runway to ease back on the stick and become airborne, which I did. What a glorious feeling to once again be free of the earth in an airplane! Everything looks different from that perspective, and I felt exhilarating power.

I had been told to fly out to an auxiliary field and do a few "touch and goes" to get used to landing and taking off solo. I cleared myself visually and entered the traffic pattern of the field along with other planes. Some had an instructor or check rider and a cadet; others were solo, it was as if I'd joined a new brotherhood.

* * *

The workweek came to a close with the routine of flying, ground school, and physical training strictly adhered to. This was the end of week number two of a ten-week training program. I felt very fortunate to have Thunderbird Field as my primary flight school as everything was top drawer. Living in a bungalow for eight cadets instead of a barracks was a big plus. Having two swimming pools, another. The grounds were well manicured and the hangers, operations, tower, and runways were all conveniently laid out as compared to a typical Army flying field, which was much more austere.

I learned the base had become operational in 1942 and was owned by Southwest Airways, Incorporated. Five thousand students had preceded me, and seven hundred of these students were Chinese officers training to fly combat in the Far Eastern war theatre. There were four squadrons of American cadets and one squadron of Chinese cadets.

The Chinese did not wear their insignias of rank, consequently they were treated like the rest of us. Their age ranged from twenty-one to twenty seven. Ours ranged from eighteen to twenty seven.

Civilian instructors gave both flying and ground school instruction. Flight Officers of the Army Air Force made progress check flights and final check flights on each cadet. A total of 65 hours of flight was given and 109 hours of ground school. The five-mile run each day plus calisthenics assured one of being in good physical condition; a necessity when flying open, twin- cockpit planes, especially if you are doing acrobatics.

A New Family

Saturday noon was a high point in the week, as we received a twenty-four hour pass. I caught the bus that stopped outside our gate and soon arrived at the bus station in Glendale, the closest town to the field. As I stepped off the bus, I saw Rae waving her hand from the window of a Chevrolet coupe parked across the street. I returned her wave and she motioned me to get in. We exchanged words of greeting, although a little awkward at first, soon our conversation became normal, and we headed for her folks home just three miles down the road.

It being a typically pleasantly warm spring day in Arizona would be thought of as a hot summer day for a young man from Washington State. As we drove along through the rural countryside, talk came easily until suddenly the car's engine stopped. Rae braked the car to a stop and tried to start it, unsuccessfully. I got out, opened the hood, and started looking for a problem. I checked the spark plug wires, the gas line, and then took a rock and tapped the fuel pump housing. I told Rae to try starting it again. She did, and it started.

After magnanimously accepting words of praise from Rae, we arrived at her home without further incident. The house sat back on five acres of land, as did the neighbor's houses. It was apparently an area of gentlemen farmers who made their living working elsewhere. The house was gable roofed and probably had a couple of small bedrooms upstairs. Her mother and sister came out of the front door as if expecting us as we stopped in the middle of the circular driveway. I was introduced to Marie, her mother, and her younger sister, Connie.

Rae had invited me to stay the weekend, so I had my shaving kit with a change of socks and underwear inside. I was shown a single bed in a room that obviously was Rae's bedroom. We then met in the kitchen and shared a welcome glass of cool lemonade. A young couple joined us who were living upstairs. The conversation got around to the car stopping on the way to the house.

The young man started to laugh at our explanation of what happened. It seems the car was his that Rae borrowed to pick me up. It stopped because Rae evidently had driven faster than fifty miles per hour, as he had installed a governor to limit the speed of the car, for whatever reason. We all had a big laugh at Rae's expense and I immediately lost my automobile mechanical problem solver status.

Rae's father, Don, came home shortly before dinner, as he worked in an automotive parts house in Phoenix. I soon learned the family included the young couple in all of their activities as she was a relative of Marie's who was expecting her first child. I also learned Marie was a nurse and an excellent cook… soon proven as we sat down to dinner. It seems, I had lucked out again and became a part of another great family. For a guy who left home at age 16, this was wonderful.

After dinner, Don told us the family car was at our disposal if we wanted to take in a movie in town. We jumped at the offer, as we wanted some time alone to get to know each other; the movie was secondary. Driving a car almost made me feel like a civilian again, and the movie was not one remembered, but the rest of the evening was. On the way home we stopped for an ice cream Sundae in Glendale and our first kiss as we got into the car to drive homeward.

After a late breakfast on Sunday, Don, Rae and Connie drove me to the main gate at Thunderbird Field five miles away. My pass expired at noon so we said a quick goodbye with an invitation to spend the next weekend with them, with one exception; Rae would pick me up at the main gate. I walked the short distance to my bungalow and seven guys, who were waiting for a rundown, as I was the only one in the bungalow that had spent the night away from the base. It's hard to be humble at a time like that.

* * *

The five-mile run in the morning before breakfast became easier as we were getting in great shape physically. We looked different as a group now as we were introduced to one of the traditions of Thunderbird Field. During the first few days we marched as a flight to the barbershop, and each given a severe butch haircut, no exceptions. When I say severe, I'm saying hair a half-inch long at the front, the highest point, with an immediate reduction in length in all directions south. I had a butch haircut when they first became fashionable in high school, but that haircut was long compared to this haircut.

It made an immediate difference in our appearance; for some, drastic. I remember one Italian cadet with dark, long, wavy hair, became almost unrecognizable, and he came close to weeping. We soon got used to it, and when in town we were immediately recognized as being from Thunderbird Field. We looked better when our suntans took over the skin exposed at the first cutting. This haircut wasn't something you let grow out, however; that happened only after you left Thunderbird.

Speaking of suntans, I might add, many of us had peeling facial skin due to the sun and wind exposure when flying open cockpit airplanes in Arizona. I had a constantly peeling nose being a fair-skinned Anglo-Saxon and only hoped someday I'd stop peeling and heal.

Acrobatics

The third week of training included an introduction to acrobatics, which was fundamental in being a fighter pilot. Mr. Lypps and I were flying at 5000 feet on our way to a remote part of our flying area when he patted himself on the top of the head indicating he had the controls. He immediately dropped the nose of the plane below the horizon to picked up speed. Then suddenly he pulled back on the stick and we started into a loop. As the plane headed upward we soon went over backwards at the top of the loop.

At this point my vision blurred, everything looked gray, and the engine seemed non-existent. I could feel us start down the backside of the loop and the engine kicked in as my vision cleared. At the bottom of the completed loop we were once again flying straight and level. It was thrilling, and now it was my turn.

I did everything he did and completed a successful loop, including 'graying out' at the top. Later he explained this was normal for the body to react this way when a pilot puts on three or four 'G's on his body suddenly. He assured me I would always come out of the 'gray-out' or red-out, or black–out, whichever happened, when I started down the backside of the loop, as the blood now returns to one's head due to gravity working for him and the release of the 'G' force on your body. I began to see why we needed to be in top physical condition for this training.

* * *

The next Saturday afternoon, Rae waited in the borrowed car at the main gate as per our arrangement. We drove to her home, this time being careful not to exceed fifty miles per hour. We spent the day just enjoying being together and playing a few table games with her sister, Connie. That evening after dinner we would return to the base, as there was to be a dance outside near the swimming pools.

We borrowed the family car and I drove us to the base. The band was a local group comprised of eight members who played the latest "big band" type music. Rae was a good dancer and I loved to dance, so we really enjoyed ourselves. Dancing outdoors on a balmy evening was a new experience for me being from the Northwest.

Actually, there were more observers than dancers because of a lack of women. About a dozen girls from a local USO had been bused in and were kept constantly dancing. Only a few cadets had dates like I, due to the short amount of time we had been there. A few officers with their wives or girlfriends also attended.

Of course, my bungalow buddies were anxious to see and meet Rae. I begrudgingly sat out a couple of dances as several of them asked Rae to dance. Some of the Chinese cadets attended the dance, but never asked a girl to dance. They seemed to enjoy the music and watching others dance. After a couple of hours the dance came to an end and Rae and I returned to her parent's home, where I had been invited to stay the weekend.

After a leisurely late Sunday breakfast, her father, accompanied by Rae and Connie, again drove me to the base. Rae gave me a quick hug as did Connie, and I returned to another week of military life. When I arrived at my bungalow, I was surprised to learn a group of Chinese cadets had been there asking about me. This was a puzzle and my roommates had no explanation.

Several hours later, I was busy catching up on my letter writing when they returned. I knew one of them slightly from a casual meeting at the pool the preceding week, a Captain Chinn. He was about twenty-five years old, slender build and about my height. He was the spokesman for the group of five. They had seen me at the dance and wanted me to teach them how to dance. This was a bolt right out of the blue. I was flabbergasted, but agreed.

I learned it was high on their list of things to do while in the United States, to dance with an American girl. They determined I was a good dancer and would be a likely candidate to be their teacher. Suddenly, our bungalow became a dance studio. I lined them up on one side of the room and turned my back to them as I stood before them. I showed them a basic two-step and then had them follow me as I repeated the maneuver.

We did this a few times and I added music from a record player belonging to one of my bunkmates. Once they got the feel of the steps to the music, it was time to couple up. This brought about a lot of laughter and good-natured teasing. After an hour we called it a day and I promised to give them another lesson the following Sunday.

Captain Chinn and I became friends and being the son of a Chinese general, he offered to get me a job flying as a soldier-of-fortune for China in their anticipated war against the Communists. He and his father were on Chiang Kai Shek's inner council. I told him I would consider it, but first I had to learn how to fly.

* * *

The next time Mr. Lypps and I were up he taught me a snap roll. The maneuver happened so quickly and effortlessly I was amazed. As he moved the stick quickly and sharply to the left, he kicked the right rudder hard and we were going over, upside down, and out of it in less than 30 seconds. I guess that's why they call it a snap roll.

He indicated it was my turn. I duplicated what he did and it happened. I now had two things to practice when I had a solo hour coming up tomorrow. Mr. Lypps had me shoot the landing at the end of our hour and said, "You'll have a check ride coming up after you log fifteen hours. I'll see you get the hours, so plan on Friday."

This was good news and bad news. Good news because he thought I was ready for a successful check flight. This was bad news only because I was nervous about my first check flight. I put aside my anxiety, determined to practice, practice, and practice. I had two more solo hours before my check ride, which should give me the polish I needed.

Buzzing

As I took off solo the next day I decided to see if I could find Rae's house from the air. I gained 500 feet of altitude and then maintained it as I recognized the road she lived on. It was a simple matter to follow it until I recognized the house. It was later in the afternoon and she was probably home from school by now, so I decided to do a fly over and see what happened. Nothing! I decided to do an emergency practice landing which involved determining the direction of the wind, choosing a field where you could set down if you had to, and go down to within fifty feet of the ground then abort the landing as this was only a practice, emergency landing.

I chose the field next to her house and came down within fifty feet of the ground. I watched, hoping she would come out and recognize me. As I came to the end of the field, I continued looking back, and sure enough, there she was. She came out of the house and was looking at my plane from a distance of several hundred yards.

I did an immediate U-turn, or wingover and reversed my path of flight. Being an open cockpit plane and being only fifty feet off the ground, I came within several hundred feet of her and she recognized me with my goggles up and waving as I flew by. I could see her clearly as she stood waving and smiling; I was delighted. I then immediately pulled back on the stick to avoid the trees that lined the road that ran in front of her house.

Then I thought this would be a great time to climb to 5000 feet and do my acrobatics. I made climbing turns as steep as I dare without stalling and soon reached my needed altitude. First I did a loop; that had to impress her. Than I did a snap roll; then I repeated these two maneuvers. That was my full repertoire up to this point in my training. Drats! I looked at my watch and my flight time was nearly up. I had to head for the main field and get in the traffic pattern for my return landing.

I would have liked to have said goodbye to Rae the way I said hello, but time didn't allow it. I just rocked the plane from side to side signaling goodbye. I returned to the base, shot my landing, and walked on air as I left the parked plane. I didn't tell any of my flight group, as I'm sure the Army wouldn't approve. However, I called Rae on the phone that evening and she was excited to see me actually flying. It doesn't get much better than that.

The Field Meet

The day of the field meet and diving competion arrived and there was excitement in the air. All five squadrons competed against each other and it was strictly a fun affair. The field events were first, which included: 75-yard dash, 220-yard relay, 880 yard run, broad jump, high jump, shot put, and discus.

Then came the diving contest; there were no swimming events due to the short length of the pools. Each squadron had one diver representing them and I was 'it' for squadron three. I had practiced my five dives daily for several weeks and felt I had a chance to win or come close. Of course, I would be competing against my teacher, Arne.

Diving is like a lot of things in life, if you were 'on' that day, you were good. If you weren't, you were less than good. With five dives you had a chance to be both good and bad. My first dive was a swan dive and it was O.K., but not enough height for my liking. The other divers took their turns and each chose their own dive. Each diver's repertoire didn't have to be the same as their competitors, so you weren't matching dives, but everyone had a swan dive.

Several of the divers shouldn't have been in the competition, so it was basically a three way race. I followed the swan dive with a jack-knife; this time I had enough height. I followed this with a one and a half tuck, and then a one and a half layout. So far my weakest dive had been my swan dive. Arne was matching me dive for dive, which surprised me as he had a larger repertoire of dives. Maybe he was making it easier for the judges.

It now became a two-way race between Arne and me. My last dive was my most complicated dive and was 'showy' off a one-meter board; the front kip with a back half gainer. My approach on the board gave me good height and I brought my legs up like a front jack knife, and then opened up, throwing my head back to the board into the back half gainer. It was the best I had ever done it, and in my mind all my dives were good except my first dive. I just didn't get enough bounce out of the board on that one.

I wish I could say I caused an upset that day, but not so. I came in a respectable second, as I had a good teacher. My squadron, especially my bungalow mates, was happy with my performance and that meant a lot to me. It was time and effort well spent and an additional plus was that I had met Rae because of my diving.

* * *

The next Saturday she was waiting, parked in the borrowed car outside the main gate. I always looked forward to these meetings, as she always greeted me with a kiss. We arrived at her home and I was surprised and pleased to meet her maternal grandmother. She was tall and stately, with graying jet-black hair, a kind, but knowing face that always seemed to know what you were thinking. It was apparent she was a full-blooded American Indian.

Rae introduced her as Sta Ha Re Sa, a Pawnee name meaning "Indian Princess." Her father had been a high-ranking warrior in the Pawnee Nation. The long beaded dress she wore was made of an exquisite material and later I was told valued at one thousand dollars. She extended her hand graciously and looked deep into my eyes saying in a well-modulated voice, "I've heard a lot about you, Harry. It's a pleasure to meet you."

Rae's mother being one-half Pawnee, made Rae one-fourth; this accounted for her dark coloring, attractive features, and athletic build. Rae's father, of Scottish heritage, thus the name Staniford. Rae looked like both her mother and father, as did Connie.

I immediately liked Sta Ha Re Sa, who asked many questions about my cadet life in the Army. I could tell her opinion of me was important to the family, being truly the matriarch. I sensed I had passed a test of some kind and felt very comfortable with her.

Rae and I went to the movies again in the borrowed family automobile and got to know each other better. Being young, falling in love, life was in the fast lane during the war years. 'Immediacy' was the name of the game, as one didn't dare look too far into the future because it could be a blank page.

We arrived home at the appointed time and shared hot cocoa in the kitchen with the family. I asked if I could sleep on the couch, as Sta Ha Re Sa would need a bedroom. This solved their unspoken problem; they didn't have to ask me to sleep on the couch.

The next morning, after the eight of us had breakfast, Rae drove me back to the base. Each weekend was the same, yet each different.

* * *

That afternoon the five Chinese cadets came to the bungalow at the appointed time and I started out with them where I left off the preceding Sunday. I could tell they had been practicing and I'm sure they took a ribbing from their fellow cadets. However, they were determined to learn, so they could dance with an American girl. It helped they all spoke English and were well coordinated. I'm sure each of them had his own story to tell, but there was no time for that.

I lined them up and stood before them facing the same direction as they, so they could follow my moves exactly. First, without music to be sure they had the two-step routine down pat. Then I showed them out to use this two-step to make turns, then full circles. They remembered well from last week, and I had them couple up with the better dancers taking the girl's part. I became Captain Chinn's partner. We put on a Glen Miller record *Tuxedo Junction* and danced through to the end, in spite of some missed cues, but with the instructions, "keep going."

They did well and I decided to teach them the box step so they could dance to waltzes and slow numbers. We started out the same as the two-step with them mimicking me slowly step for step. The box step was easy to visualize and by the time the hour ended they had all they needed to ask an American girl to dance.

In appreciation they invited me out to dinner the next Saturday evening and then to a public dance in Phoenix. If Rae hadn't been in my life I would have accepted, but time was running out, and I preferred to be with her. They went and had a grand time, they later informed me. I felt satisfied I could be a part of their happiness, and they thanked me profusely.

My First Check Ride

Each afternoon started the same: in a huddle with Mr Lypps, and our individual assignment for the day. Today, being my check ride day, made me the first of the group to do this. If Mr. Lypps thought I was ready, then *he should know*, I reasoned. The check rider, Lt. Butzow, sat in a nearby plane waiting for me, and he looked all business. I climbed into the back cockpit, which is not that easy to do with a seat-type parachute strapped to you, and he motioned me to taxi to the point of take-off on the main runway.

He signaled me to proceed with the take off and I pushed the throttle forward, both feet lightly on the rudder controls. The tail lifted as we reached fifty-five miles per hour, the plane began to feel light, and I sucked slowly back on the stick becoming airborne. He directed me to a remote flying area and to climb to 5000 feet. This I did and he asked me to do a snap roll, loop, and a chandelle. This I did successfully, and he then directed me back to the field.

I realized I was doing everything mechanically and had put a damper on my emotions. He was a very stern-faced man, but probably handsome, if he had chosen to smile. When at 500 feet of altitude, but not in the traffic pattern, he suddenly pulled back on the throttle cutting off the engine. He then shouted, "Forced Landing" and I immediately looked to determine wind direction. A flag flying in a schoolyard off to one side gave me the answer.

I could see I had to change my direction of flight 90 degrees, and an open field lay ahead that would accommodate us. We were losing altitude rapidly without power, but it was do-able. I started my turn and hit my approach point to the field right on the button. At thirty feet of altitude Lt. Butzow pushed on the throttle, the engine caught, and he signaled me to take us up to 500 feet and to enter the traffic pattern.

So far so good, I thought and started my ninety-degree turns to get us to the approach we needed for the landing. I made my last turn, lined up with the runway, and cut the throttle coming in 'dead stick'. Being a warm day, I could see heat thermals rising from the tarmac before us. Thermals were to be reckoned with as they had the ability to lift your plane, then when you passed through them… drop you. That's exactly what happened and it resulted in a rough landing, but safe. Fortunately, we both knew I had no control over that without the use of the throttle.

I taxied back to our starting point and when we stopped rolling, he shut the engine off. He got out of the front cockpit, turned, and gave me thumbs up. I sat there for a long moment as anxiety drained out of my body; *I had passed.*

As I entered the waiting room, I was surprised to see Lt Butzow talking to Mr. Lypps. *Was I to be worried? He'd given me thumbs up, hadn't he?*

Mr. Lypps signaled me over as Lt. Butzow walked away. Mr. Lypps said, "You passed Mister McIntyre, but he had one negative comment. He said you let the nose rise too quickly on the take off. That could lead to a low altitude stall with no time to recover. Remember, we talked about that."

"Yes, I remember. I guess I was thinking ahead to my first turn out of the pattern. I won't let it happen again."

"Good! Let me tell you what happened to one of my former students with that problem. Even being warned, he kept letting the nose of the plane rise on take off. Frustrated, I dumped the stick forward to emphasis what I wanted. Unknown to me, he hadn't fastened his seat belt and he came straight up out of the cockpit and slid down the fuselage to the vertical stabilizer."

"Good grief," I gasped. "What did you do?"

"I flew a low pattern and shot a landing with him riding the tail of the plane; he didn't do that again." Mr.Lypps was smiling as he walked off.

THE SURPRISE

Rae, waiting for me as usual, was always a high point in the week. She had informed me earlier her folks were giving her a birthday dinner this Saturday night. With this advanced warning I had a present for her when I climbed in the passenger side of the older coupe. She asked, "Is that for me?"

"Yes, it's for you."

"Are you going to give it to me now?"

"No, I plan to give it to you at your birthday dinner."

"Bummer! I can hardly wait."

"Don't get too excited; I'd hate to disappoint you."

"Whatever you've chosen to give me, I'll just love, and it'll be special."

"Which birthday is this, Rae? And don't tell me you're older than me."

"You don't ask a girl her age."

We drove into the circle driveway in front of her house, she stopped the car and planted a kiss on me right there in front of God and everybody. Going inside, we joined Connie and her mother in the kitchen for a tall, cool glass of home-squeezed lemonade; always a welcome treat on a hot spring day.

I really enjoyed the weather, now acclimatized from the cool winter weather in Santa Ana, even though Santa Ana was warm compared to

Utah in the fall of the year. I still sported a sunburned nose and brow because of the hot wind from open-cockpit flying.

Rae and I could accept each other's skin infirmities because Rae had an acne problem. Still a pretty girl, but it was a cross for her bear. I had gone through an acne problem at an earlier age, and her problem made my constant peeling nose and brow easier for me to accept.

It's funny how unimportant things can sometimes seem important; especially when you're eighteen-years old.

We spent the afternoon playing board games with Connie, dancing to records like *In The Mood, Chattanooga Choo Choo, It Might As Well Be Spring, and Moonlight Serenade*. I gave Connie a dancing lesson, as she was twelve-years old and wanted to be a part of the fun. Now being an experienced dance teacher, I felt comfortable in the job. Besides I didn't have to have a building fall on me to know Connie had a crush on her big sister's boyfriend.

That evening after Don arrived home from work we sat down for the family dinner including the young upstairs couple, Rex and Lyrene. Grandmother Sta Ha Re Sa had returned home to Prescott, Arizona a few days earlier. Marie prepared a lovely chicken dinner with all the trimmings and we ate leisurely as their custom. Conversation was always easy and constant, as all joined in.

Finally the time arrived for the coup de resistance, the birthday cake, and Marie brought in a beautiful three-layer, frosted cake with all candles blazing… all fifteen of them. Everyone, but me, said "Happy Birthday." I sat in shock! *She's only fifteen.* Suddenly everyone was looking at me, including Rae. Recovering my composure as best I could, I smiled and said "Happy Birthday."

It seemed everyone there knew I thought Rae was my age; she looked it. Now some things began to make more sense and some things didn't. *Fourteen-year-olds don't drive cars. Of course she didn't drive the family car, only Rex and Lyene's car with the governor on it and only on the country roads to and from the base and the bus stop.*

More mature girls, don't usually act as brazen as Rae at our first meeting at the swimming pool; a fourteen-year old might. She seldom talked about school, or her friends, and perhaps I didn't ask.

All of this ran through my mind as I quietly sat eating her birthday cake. I noticed she occasionally looked at me, but said nothing. Eventually dinner was over and she opened her gifts, including the leather-framed picture of me taken at Santa Ana dressed in my cadet dress uniform. I'd had several copies made at the time, and she was pleased with the gift.

We excused ourselves to take a walk. "Her first words were, "Does it make any difference with you that I'm fifteen? I'm still me."

"No… it takes a little getting used to… but you're right, you're still you, and I'm still me."

* * *

Ground school was always the less interesting part of the training experience, but I put up with it. The next week of flying for me started off with a solo hour and Mr. Lypps had instructed me to do some Pylon Eights, Forced Landings, and Touch and Goes. It was early in the afternoon and Rae wouldn't be home from school, so I put aside any thoughts of buzzing her house. Anytime I did that I would be pushing the edge of the envelope.

The Touch and Goes went well and I felt like I was getting pretty good at landing 'dead stick.' This was always done at an auxiliary dirt field to keep the main, paved runway as free as possible. Even so, it was always busy because of the many planes in the air at the same time. Thunderbird Field was a mile square, but had a flying area of about thirty miles square. There were three auxiliary fields several miles out in the rural areas surrounding the field.

They were usually busy with solo cadets doing Touch and Go's like me. I had been warned about the Chinese cadet's landing idiosyncrasy.

At first I thought it was an exaggeration, but this day I found it to be true. It seems that once they entered the traffic pattern to shoot a landing, they were-going-to-shoot-a-landing.

There were many times when we had to go around the traffic pattern more than once, because there were too many planes in the process of landing. The safest thing to do was to abort one's landing and go around. It seems once the Chinese pilots decided to land, there was no turning back. This led to some close calls on the landing strip and an occasional ground loop by a plane trying to avoid another plane on the ground.

On my third Touch and Go, I was coming in on the final approach and had just shut off my engine when I became aware of a plane coming in over the top of me. It was a solo plane and at first I thought it was going around… not so. He was going to shoot a landing ahead of me, and if both planes are 'dead stick', it's courting disaster. I dropped down a bit and watched him. Sure enough, he cut his engine when he should have gone around. I had the right of way, being first, but who wants to be *dead right*?

I eased my throttle forward turning on the engine to turn aside, and then rose above him. Sure enough, he was Chinese. I went around in the pattern watching him and thinking, *is it possible a nationality can have a universal trait of 'single mindedness' or whatever you might want to call it?* When I saw him shoot his landing and then take off immediately leaving the field, I breathed a sigh of relief and shot my landing without incident. I can only hope he realized he came close to causing a collision.

Mentally returning to the assignment at hand, I found a long, plowed field over which to perform my Pylon Eights. To be true to its name, it needs two reference points on the ground around which to fly, forming a figure eight that's lying on its back. I saw a large tree at one end I could use as one pylon and an object far off in the field as the other. I now had 100 feet of altitude and made a left turn around the vertical line suggested by the tree. I then rolled on to my right side to go around the other vertical line suggested by the object on the ground. After doing a right bank, being careful to keep the nose of the plane from rising, I completed the turn and headed back to the tree. I reversed the roll on my side and did a left bank around the tree. Everything was going well and I started back making my roll in the same spot and started my bank at the same place, when I realized I had misjudged and the object was farther than I had planned. I lengthened my run and banked around the vertical of the object and suddenly burst into laughter. *No wonder I misjudged the distance; my ground object was a moving tractor.*

This obviously wasn't my day, so I called it quits and headed back to the field. I shot a successful landing and carefully taxied up to the hardstand where the plane belonged. Climbing out of the cockpit, I took off my parachute, and walked across the tarmac to the operations waiting room. Suddenly I felt exhausted and now realized, my near miss at the auxiliary field had taken its toll.

* * *

Later in the week I had a late afternoon solo flight and found myself heading for Rae's house. *I needed to practice my emergency landings, didn't I?* I rationalized. *After all I had aborted that part of my last solo flight. Mr Lypps would want me to do this.* I followed the road to her house and flew over thinking she might wonder if it was I. Sure enough, she came out the back door of her house and stood with eyes shielded by her hand, looking my direction.

I did a chandelle turn and came back over the field next to her house, with about 30 feet of altitude. I pulled back my goggles and waved. She waved back and we could easily see each other. I then pulled back on the stick to hop over the trees and power lines coming at me. To my surprise, after I had cleared the obstacles mentioned, the plane started to settle… not maintaining normal flight. *Good grief, I've asked too much of the engine.* I dropped the nose as much as I dared at that low altitude, to give the engine a chance to catch up. *It's doing it, thank goodness I'm maintaining altitude, and I won't do that again.*

I then started my climbing turns and reached five thousand feet. I started acrobatics with a snap roll followed by a loop. I then brought the nose up without increasing the power and forced a stall causing the plane to shudder and fall off to the left into a spin. After three complete turns downward, I pushed the stick forward and kicked the right rudder. The spinning stopped and I had lost fifteen hundred feet of altitude. Pulling back on the stick, I leveled out.

I waggled my wings in farewell and headed for an auxiliary field for Touch and Go's. After three of these, I had used up my time and headed home; happy to have seen Rae and had the opportunity to show her she was going with a real pilot.

The High School Dance

The next Saturday Rae was waiting for me in her usual parking place; a place where she could watch the main gate. As soon as I walked out, she drove up to intercept me, and we were off on our fantasy twenty-four hours together. We never did anything unusual; just being together was enough.

Now that the cat was out of the bag concerning her age, she invited me to a high school dance. I had been to a lot of high school dances back home, but this would be different. I would be in uniform, as there was no option during wartime. Her folks would provide us with the family car, and we would have Saturday dinner at home, as usual.

Rae was excited about the dance and came to the dinner table dressed in a skirt, blouse, and sweater. She was attractive with her dark-brown hair stylishly fixed in a pompadour and soft waves framing her face. It wasn't a formal dance, but I would be formal. The dress code at the base hadn't changed to summer wear, so I would be in my olive-drab dress uniform with suntan shirt and tie, brown oxfords, garrison cap, and cadet brass.

I had asked about buying her a corsage, but she said it wouldn't be appropriate. I would have asked her out to dinner, but her folks seemed to enjoy having a big dinner with all of us there. I think it took the place of their regular Sunday dinner, which I couldn't attend.

The big moment came when we were ready to leave and Don took our picture as we stood in our finery. We arrived at the dance when it was in full swing in the high school gymnasium. An attempt at decorating with crepe paper ribbon tried to make it more festive, but decorating a gymnasium is next to impossible.

The band was the North High School's jazz band and they were pretty good. I checked my garrison hat and Rae led me onto the floor in the middle of a dance number. I looked about for other service men and there were a few. However, the rest of the dancers were the usual high school students and for the boys, dirty cords were in vogue. The girls were dressed like Rae for the most part, and soon we relaxed and got into the music. We danced well together.

There was a short break between each set of three numbers and Rae introduced me to her friends. I could tell she was showing me off, as it isn't every sophomore girl that had a military man for a partner. I use the term, man, loosely as many of the senior boys and girls were nearly my age, some looked older. Rae's friend, Peggy, was there and after the three of us briefly talked about our first meeting at the swimming pool, I asked her to dance; it seemed the thing to do. While dancing with Peggy, I noticed Rae had been asked to dance by a boy probably her age and height. I didn't get a chance to meet him, but I asked Rae about him. She said, "He's a boy I started elementary school with and we've been friends a long time."

"You and he dance well together."

"Thanks, but I much prefer you and me dancing together, so let's, as this is a ladies choice and I don't want any of these hell-cats getting a shot at you."

"Your wish is my command," I joked.

We stayed to the end of the dance and totally enjoyed ourselves. I secretly liked my roll as being older and uniformed. We stopped for ice cream in Glendale, not the hangout close to the high school. The Glendale ice cream parlor was a place we both liked and we didn't have to put up with the high jinks of the loud crowd back in Phoenix. Maybe we were both growing up.

* * *

Rae drove me back to the base on Sunday and a U.S.O. show was scheduled after the Parade. It was to be a comedian and I thought how different it would be for me from the last U.S.O. show with the Mexican musicians and the lovely senorita. I smiled to myself as I sat on my bunk and thought about that while waiting for the parade.

The parades at Thunderbird Field were short and sweet compared to Santa Ana's parades. It didn't take long to march two hundred cadets in review, but they were colorful with the American, Chinese, and Thunderbird Field flags proudly carried; it was a spectacle.

I guess the Army Air Corp thought it important to remind us how to march to band music and look like a military outfit, not just a bunch of flyers lounging around the flight line, waiting for their turn to take off.

The show was a disappointment. I sometimes thought the U.S.O. program was an opportunity for new and borderline talent to get experience, and a refuge for 'has-been's that didn't want to be forgotten. Of course there are exceptions like Bing Crosby and Bob Hope, but that wasn't the norm. They traveled to the big military audiences, like Santa Ana, where I had seen both of them.

After the show we went to the mess hall for dinner and then to our bungalows for letter writing, studying, or just shooting the breeze. We did have the option of taking a swim, which many did because of the 80-degree weather. I was still writing Louree and I chose not to mention Rae, as I didn't want to lose that relationship as I had with my letter to my former girlfriend, Francie Lou.

Louree and her folks and sisters were important to me, but I was young and deprivation was not one of my long suits. You've heard of sailors who had a girl in every port? This seemed to fit me as well at eighteen, as I just wasn't ready to put all my eggs in one basket. I was sincere in my feelings and intentions, but marriage, or a relationship like marriage, just wasn't one of my intentions.

When I finished my letter writing to Mom, Louree, and my cousin, Dolores, the cookie baker, it was time for lights out. I lay in bed and listened to taps being played over the loudspeaker system, concluding it had more going for it than reveille.

More Acrobatics

The next afternoon on the flight line, I drew a training session with my instructor. We climbed into the two cockpits of the Stearman PT-17, and Billy Miles was the crank man. After he had wound us up, so to speak, I gave him the signal for contact and the Stearman sprung into life. I then taxied to the end of the main runway facing the direction of the wind.

In taxiing it is necessary to make constant turns in order to see ahead; especially when you're sitting in the back cockpit. This meant you had a zigzag, not a straight-line course. When we reached the point of entrance to the main runway, I turned the plane with the aid of the rudder 180-degrees to face down the runway. After clearing us visually, I steadily pushed the throttle forward to reach our target speed of 55 miles per hour; then with slight backpressure on the stick we were airborne. Mr. Lypps gave me thumbs up and pointed upward, indicating I was to take it to 5000 feet of altitude. Once there, he signaled he was taking over the controls by jiggling the stick and tapping himself on the top of the head.

He dropped the nose of the plane to pick up speed; then brought the nose up above the horizon and moved the stick steadily to the left while giving foot pressure to the right rudder. The plane rolled over, upside down, and I felt myself slam into the side of the cockpit with my right shoulder. I felt that I was hanging on my lap-type seat belt. He immediately reversed the controls and the airplane continued to roll over to level flight. He looked back at me and shouted, "That's a slow roll, now you do it."

I had heard a slow roll was similar to a snap roll, but more controlled and you lose the advantage of centrifugal force with the slower maneuver, resulting in a shoulder slam into the side of the cockpit and hanging on the seat belt, if only momentarily. I followed through precisely as he had, and with the same results, including the shoulder slam.

He then asked me to do a chandelle turn, which is one way to gain altitude when you have limited space. I dropped the nose (put it on the step) to gain speed. Then I gave right rudder and right stick in a controlled fashion to not over correct and let the nose rise, then gave it more rudder to come around 180 degrees, and at the same time gaining altitude. A series of chandelles will give you a lot of altitude in a limited space.

He was satisfied and told me to return to the base. I purposely lost altitude and returned to the main runway. After getting into the landing pattern, I followed the traffic and shot a good landing. When I had taxied and parked the Stearman, Mr. Lypps congratulated me on my progress. This was a boost to my ego, although I wasn't having an ego problem at the time.

I wish I enjoyed ground school as much as I did flying. However, I rationalized it was necessary to know about the workings of all parts of an airplane including the engine in order to be a good pilot. We had a test each week in this course and always passed. I enjoyed the navigation course because it was mathematical, which came easy for me. Morse code, sending and receiving, was a challenge, but I passed their required receiving level of 15 words per minute.

* * *

The week flew by, and it was Saturday with Rae waiting at the gate. During a phone conversation in the middle of the week, we decided on a return to the swimming pool outside of Phoenix where we met.

We traveled by bus, as no car was available beyond picking me up at the gate. It turned out to be a good way to spend a warm 80-degree Saturday afternoon.

We swam and sunbathed and I gave Rae a diving lesson, but her heart wasn't in it. However, I must say: in a bathing suit Rae didn't look like a fifteen year old. No wonder I thought she was my age. Once I adjusted my mind to the situation, it was a good relationship; satisfying both of us. We returned home in time for Saturday night family dinner, as was expected.

That night we drove down to the ice cream parlor and Connie joined us. Rae's family didn't attend church, so Sunday was a leisurely morning with a big breakfast and a walk afterwards to aid digestion. I had to be on base at twelve o'clock to accommodate the parade and any recreational activities scheduled, so Rae drove me in Rex's car. I felt fortunate to have this totally different life experience once a week and each week Rae and my relationship grew stronger.

The Misadventure

As we eight cadets sat around in the bungalow waiting for parade time, the conversation centered on our flying experiences beyond the scope of instruction. This led me to share my buzz job on Rae's house and her response by standing in the yard, waving. In so doing I violated my pledge to myself I wouldn't share this information with anyone. Well, the cat was out of the bag.

* * *

The next afternoon Mr. Lypps gave us our assignments for the day and Bill Graves and I were both to fly solo later in the afternoon. *I could buzz Rae's house and show her my new slow roll*, I reasoned. *I would be killing two birds with one stone: practicing my new maneuver and showing off as well.*

I took off in my assigned PT-17 and headed for Rae's house flying at 500 feet of altitude. Following the road to her house, I was shocked to see another PT-17 about 400 yards ahead of me doing the very thing I planned to do. It made a turn where I planned to make my turn and then buzzed the house. Right on schedule, Rae came out and started waving to the plane and the person in that plane. I was fighting for an answer. *Surely Rae didn't have two boyfriends that were cadets.* I made my turn and saw the surprised look on her face as I flew by at a lower altitude with my goggles pushed up on top of my helmet.

Then a light bulb went on for me...that was Bill Graves ahead of me. He, alone, knew my buzz story and had a solo plane the same time as I. *Well, I'll fix him.* At the end of his run over Rae's house, he started climbing turns to leave the area. For him it was a big joke; for me it was a challenge in front of my girl that needed to be met.

I followed him up turn for turn, and eventually he reached the altitude necessary for acrobatic practice. We played follow-the-leader through several maneuvers and then I decided to pull up along side him for close visual contact. He looked back to watch my approach when suddenly he started pointing for me to look behind. I turned my head and saw the problem coming at us, a Stearman PT-17 with both cockpits occupied. This meant trouble if it was an instructor and a cadet; it meant double trouble were it a check rider and a cadet.

Well, the fat was in the fire; in either case we were in trouble. Close flying was forbidden and considered 'dog fighting', which was an event to be saved for actual combat. To escape, Bill turned away and went 45 degrees to his left and downward. I did the opposite and headed for a remote part of the practice area at this altitude. I felt a sudden rush of relief when I looked back and saw no one pursuing me.

I practiced my 'slow rolls', but my feeling of relief was short lived. I could see a dual occupied plane coming directly at me from a distance. I decided to find out if I was his quarry by putting my plane in a stall, which led to a wing over and a spiral downward. After three complete turns I took it out of the dive and the other plane hovered directly above me. The person in the front cockpit pointed for me to return to the field, with him following every foot of the way.

When I taxied up to a parking area, Bill Graves was sitting in his plane with a hangdog look on his face. The other plane stopped directly behind me and directed us, in no uncertain terms, to report to operations. The arresting officer was a check rider, Lt. Wolpers. He was angry because he had to abort his check ride to deal with us, and he was determined to see us punished. Bill and I had no excuse, and had been taught as cadets not to give excuses.

The operations officer instructed us to turn in our parachutes and restricted us to our bungalow for the rest of the afternoon. We were also told we would have a hearing before a review board tomorrow morning and they would decide what discipline would be meted out for our flying violation.

We silently returned to our bungalow, went to our bunks, and lay there buried in our own private misery. *This could be the end of my flying career.*

* * *

That evening after dinner in the mess hall I used the public telephone and brought Rae up to date. I told her I would call the next night and tell her the results of our hearing scheduled for the next day. It's strange, Bill Graves and I still had nothing to say to each other.

We were both to blame for what happened; he started it, but I finished it. However, what the check rider saw was only what happened at 5000 feet of altitude; me in pursuit of Bill. I wondered how that would play out at the hearing. I came to realize my flying style had become an extension of my personality, a show-off. I definitely needed to clean up my act.

I saw the parallel between my flying and my automobile driving. The preceding year in high school I totaled my pretty Plymouth convertible showing off by racing another car on the way to a school picnic. *Maybe I wasn't the kind of pilot the Army needed… or maybe I was exactly the kind of pilot they needed… time would tell.*

The Trial

The hearing was held at ten o'clock in the administration building with Captain Caldwell presiding and flanked by two other officers sitting at a long oak table. Lt. Wolpers sat off to one side and Bill and I sat side-by-side facing the three officers at the table. It was a grim-faced panel we faced. Captain Caldwell asked Lt. Wolpers to give his testimony.

He was very explicit about what he saw and his effort to apprehend us. We were asked if we had anything to add or detract from his testimony. Because we didn't, he was dismissed so he could get to his job as a check rider.

I determined, if they didn't pursue the 'why' of what happened, I would not use it as a defense because the buzzing of Rae's house might be more of a violation than our present charge of Dog Fighting. The panel excused us temporarily while they came to their decision.

After a short period of time we were called back in. Captain Caldwell, a mild speaking, middle-aged man, looked sternly when he scolded us for our indiscretion and said our punishment would be fifty hours on the ramp. Bill and I gave an inward sigh of relief, saluted, did a military about face, and walked briskly out of the room. Once outside the building we congratulated ourselves for not being washed out. What a relief.

Fifty hours on the ramp meant we would give up free time, probably for the remainder of our stay at Thunderbird. When others were swimming or relaxing we would be walking for fifty minutes out of each hour, in a military manner, at 140 cadents per minute. On weekends we would walk Saturday afternoon until dinnertime, then walk Sunday morning from nine o'clock until lunchtime. At this rate it would take three weeks to satisfy the penalty and take us to the end of our stay at Thunderbird Field. Obviously, someone on the panel was good at math.

Bill and I returned to our morning classes and then to the flight line that afternoon. Our instructor was not pleased with us, and neither of us flew that afternoon. I called Rae that evening and she was relieved to hear I hadn't been washed out. I also filled her in on the punishment and how it would affect our relationship.

She asked if I'd still get a pass for Saturday night. I told her I thought so, but I would be walking until six o'clock and again back at it by Sunday morning at nine o'clock. She said she'd be there to pick me up and have me back on time Sunday morning. She wanted to see me as much as I wanted to see her.

Another Surprise

The next day I received instructions to report to Captain Caldwell in the Administration Building. I reported immediately and had no idea what this could be about. *The decision had been reached. What more is there to say? Well, I'll soon find out.*

Captain Caldwell sat at his desk looking at me in a fatherly way as I stood at attention before him. "Mister McIntyre, I'm going to give you some advice that is to be just between you and me. Is that agreed?"

I'm sure I looked shocked, but I stammered, "Yes Sir,"

"Lt. Wolpers is angry with our decision to give you a second chance. He sees you as the instigator of the violation and has said he will 'get you'. I don't know what he has in mind, but I feel compelled to warn you, as I don't agree with him."

I stood silently taking in what Captain Caldwell said and replied, "Thank you, sir. I'm sorry he feels that way, but I'll watch out for him."

Captain Caldwell said, "That's all, Mister McIntyre."

I left, puzzled by all that had been said, and determined to deal with whatever might be ahead. I returned to my classroom, Aircraft Engines, and noticed the instructor watched me closely as I sat down deep in thought.

* * *

Mr. Lypps had both Bill Graves and me assigned instructional flights the following day. He seemed to have set aside the violation and everything appeared to be back to normal. He had me go through all of the maneuvers he'd taught me and seemed satisfied. After the landing he said, "If the plane, for whatever reason goes into a ground loop, hit the rudder hard on the side the plane is turning and it will straighten out."

It was a maneuver I never hoped to use, but it's nice to know what to do in case it happens. Ground loops usually occur on landings and can be caused by over correction on the part of the pilot, a strong cross wind, or a rough landing surface.

The Test

The next day in engines class we got our weekly test back… and I failed it. I was surprised, but I knew I would have a chance to take a comparable test again. Fortunately, it was two strikes before you're out in the Air Corp. I studied the test pages and realized I had been so distracted by my flying violation and hearing, I hadn't studied enough for the test as I always had previously. *Well, that's easily resolved. I'll study for the test, and give it my highest priority.*

I talked to the teacher the next day after class and asked when I could take the retest. He seemed very negative about the whole situation and I knew he wasn't my friend. He said he'd have it for me in two days and I would take it during class. I theorized he resented having to be bothered with the retest at all. I shrugged it off and set up a time to prepare, which wasn't that easy as my free time was devoted to walking tours.

What was left was ten minute snatches here and there, and I'd do some memorizing as I walked tours. At the same time I had to keep up with the new information from the engines class for the weekly test. I began to feel pressured, but I was determined to get through this. I was being punished, but given a second chance in the flying portion of my training; does trouble come in threes?

The next two days was a blur. I took the test and felt good about it. The next day the instructor informed me during class …I had failed the test. I was shocked! I sat through the class hearing nothing, lost in my own thoughts. *How could that be? How could that be?*

I stopped to talk to him after class. He said, "I have a meeting Mister McIntyre; there's really nothing to discuss."

"I would like to see the test," I stated.

He snapped, "It's home." Turning abruptly he walked out of the classroom.

The Frame Up

I walked to my bungalow and sat on my bunk feeling totally defeated. My bunkmates came in and were strangely silent. One person in the class had overheard the conversation between the instructor and myself and the word spread like wildfire. Their quietness was understandable, what could anyone say? The thing that was happening to me was the very thing every cadet feared.

I left the bungalow to report to operations to walk my tours in hopes there would be someway out of this. Bill was already there and had begun a tour. We had been in this mess together, but now I had an even greater problem. It looked like I was going to be washed out after all, for an invalid reason. I started my tour and spent the next fifty minutes lost in thought, going over and over how I could have failed that test. I just didn't believe I failed it.

It was a long night and I'm not sure I got any sleep. I went through the motions of being a cadet in training until I reported to the board at ten o'clock. Captain Adams headed the washout board and two officers sat on each side of him at the same long oak table.

As I entered the room I thought, *I don't like the looks of this. I've never seen these officers before and they don't look happy to be here.* I stood at attention while the charge was read, "Failure to pass the course in aircraft engines." Captain Adams asked, "Do you have anything to say?" I knew the answer that had been drummed into me in cadets, No

Excuse, Sir, and that's what I mechanically replied, "No excuse, Sir." My mind screamed *I want to see the test!* But my voice said nothing. No one there seemed interested in delving into the case, in asking why? It was cut and dried…I had failed the test and that was that.

Captain Adams announced coldly I was relieved of my appointment as a cadet and would be transferred to the regular Army in three days. He asked matter-of-factly, "Which of three positions do you wish to train for now: radio/gunner, aerial mechanic/gunner, or armament/gunner?"

I asked, "Which has the shortest training period?"

He replied, "Armament."

I replied, "So be it."

"You are dismissed private McIntyre."

It was over! *Where was the show off, devil-may-care cadet when I needed him?*

Captain Caldwell was right; Lt. Wolpers had his revenge. I was beaten; he had won.

* * *

I called Rae as promised and to my surprise her grandmother answered the phone. She evidently had been filled in regarding my dilemma, "How did your hearing going?" she asked.

"They washed me out!" I blurted. There it was, it was the first time I had verbalized it… and it hurt.

There was a long silence on the other end of the line. Finally, "I'm sorry," she replied softly.

I felt like crying… but big boys don't cry. I thanked her and asked if Rae was there.

"She's still at school, Harry, but she'll want to hear from you."

"Tell her I'll call later in the afternoon."

"I will, but I'll let you tell her about washing out."

"Thanks. It would be best coming from me."

I returned to the bungalow where my roommates had just returned from ground school. I'm sure they saw by the look on my face what happened at the hearing, so I took the initiative and told them I'd been washed out.. They were somber; they knew this was no joking matter.

I filled them in on all the sordid details and they were angry that I had been treated like I had by Lt. Wolpers and Frank Nelson, the engines instructor. "Those two guys are as thick as thieves," interjected one of my roommates.

"What do you mean?" I asked.

"They drive to the base together every day."

"Really? How do you know that?"

"I've seen them. They could even live together for all I know."

"Well, now I know what I've suspected, when the Nelson left my test home, it wasn't by accident. I think I'll talk to Captain Caldwell. He was the one who warned me about Lt. Wolpers in the first place. He may have a solution."

"Good luck," several replied in unison.

* * *

I went to Captain Caldwell's office and, thank goodness, he was there. His secretary called him on the intercom and motioned for me to go in. He was sitting at his desk, looking very serious. I stood at attention with my hat in my hand. He said, "I'm sorry to hear you washed out, Mister."

"Not as sorry as I am, sir. If I might ask, why did you warn me about Lt. Wolper?"

"I didn't like his arrogance and his attitude about taking matters in his own hands."

"Did you and he talk about it?"

"No."

"Did he say what he was going to do to see I got washed out?"

"No."

"Is there any way I can get another hearing?"

"No."

"Did anyone see or ask to see my failed test?"

"No."

"Why not?"

"Because there was no reason to. When one of our instructors tell us a student has failed a test, we believe them."

"Don't you think it was strange it wasn't available to me?"

"Yes, but that isn't the first time that has happened."

"Really?"

"Yes, really."

"Well, I guess I finally see the handwriting on the wall."

"Yes, Mister, and I'm sorry, but I can't fight this battle for you, as I can't win it either, and I'd put myself in jeopardy. I've already done something I've never done before… by warning you."

"I appreciate that sir." I rose from my chair, saluted him, did an about face and knew I had done all I could do as… ' This is the Army Mr. Jones.'

Delay Enroute

Later that afternoon I called Rae and told her the bad news. "Oh no!" she cried. "What happens now?"

I told her, "In three days I will be given a ten day delay-en-route to report to my new base at Lowry Field in Denver, Colorado."

"It doesn't take ten days to get to Denver, Colorado; what are you going to do?"

"I can fly home or stay here with you, that is if you want me to."

"What do you want to do?" she asked.

"My first choice would be to stay here."

"Then do it, as I'm sure the folks would love to have you here. You know, they look upon you as the son they never had."

"You talk to them, and if it's O.K. with them, I'll stay here for the first eight days and give myself two days to travel to Lowry field and report for my new life in the Army."

* * *

The next three days were the longest of my life. Everybody was busy, and I had nothing to do, but wait. I didn't go down to the flight line, as I didn't want to face my instructor, Mr. Lypps. I was ashamed. The few places available to spend my time was the day room to play phonograph records or read, my bungalow to write letters or read, the mess hall three times a day, or the pool.

I did some of each and finally the third day arrived. I had my new orders plus a travel voucher in hand. It came time to say goodbye to my friends and that was the hardest part of the whole ordeal. When the final moment came and I had my two barracks bags packed, I shook hands all around with my bungalow buddies with brief goodbyes. The last one in line was Campana who handed me an envelope filled with dollar bills. He chokingly said, "This is from all of us. It won't make up for what you've lost, Harry, but it should take you on a good drunk."

Totally surprised, I thanked them and made a quick exit; all of us knowing, I wouldn't spend it that way. I chalked his words and the money up to their way of saying "We care."

* * *

I had called Rae and she was waiting at the gate. We tried to make light talk, but weren't very good at it. When we arrived at her house, I unpacked for my eight-day stay, hung my dress uniform up, and never had a uniform on for a week. I became a civilian again, if just for a little while. Rae and I were like a couple of high school kids on spring break; in fact it was spring break for them.

Don suggested, "If you drive me to work and pick me up at the end of the day, you and Rae can have the use of the family car."

I agreed and Rae and I played for eight days. However, all good and bad things come to an end and it was time for me to catch a bus to Denver, Colorado. After the goodbyes at home, Rae saw me off at the bus station with a tearful goodbye and a promise from me to write and call once a week. I was apprehensive, but there were no choices. I was a private in the Army headed for more training, but now as an armament/gunner on a B-17 or a B-24, once again, alone.

Lowery Field

The bus ride was uneventful and the weather and the scenery pleasant; I arrived with time to spare. Checking in to headquarters, I was assigned to a flight and squadron. The barracks were similar to those in Santa Ana, but it soon became apparent everything wasn't spit and polish as in cadets. In fact everyone in the barracks was a washed out cadet and each one had their story to tell. They were no longer 'gunny.' To the contrary, they were turned off with the Army, but they were there and would be for the duration of the war plus six months…assuming we won.

I thought I had a negative attitude because of my wash out, but I didn't hold a candle to some of these guys. It would be a week before the next class in Armament started so we were assigned to K.P. for that time. This was rubbing salt into the wound. We got up at 5:45 and were bused from Lowry Field # 2 to Lowry Field #1 for their mess hall. A flight line and an airstrip separated the two fields. Lowry #2 was training only and Lowry#1 was a typical Army airfield.

I had never had K.P. before, which was remarkable due to the fact I'd been in the Army over a year. I made up for it having it seven days in a row. The days were long, starting at 6:00 a.m. and ending at 8:00 p.m. It didn't leave time for anything else and made us look forward to the start of school, which would bring an end to the K.P. duty.

One evening we missed the last shuttle bus to Lowry #2, meaning a long walk around the airstrip of about one and one half miles. We were tired after fourteen hours of K.P. so when some one suggested, "Let's cut across the airstrip," it sounded like a good idea at the time. After all, it was dark and the light from the control tower that swept over the landing strip once a minute provided a challenge to authority for a bunch of washed-out cadets.

About six of us chose to do this; the rest of the work party walked the U shaped route to our barracks. When we came to the edge of the light path, we timed it and started our sprint across. It was farther than we thought and we obviously were seen because soon a jeep with three MP's in it showed up behind us. They couldn't break their own rules by driving across the airstrip after us, so they chose to drive around and catch us on the other side.

On each side of the airstrip was a drainage ditch about as deep as we were tall. We decided to use it as a way out of our dilemma. It provided a place to be out of sight, but it also provided a foot of water, slippery rocks, large clumps of grass, and cattails. You never know all the facts when you make a decision? We traversed the ditch for about the length of two football fields and then saw an open field ahead to our left that separated us from the rows of barracks… our goal.

We dashed across the open grassy field using nearly all of our fading energy, and we could see the lights of the jeep coming up the road toward us, but we made it to the row of barracks. We quickly worked our way past several barracks and entered one to collapse from exhaustion in their dayroom. Choosing to sit on the floor because we were such a muddy, wet mess, we then looked at each other and collapsed into gales of laughter.

It took some time for us to explain to the occupants of the barracks why we were there. Fighting fatigue, hysteria, and hiccupping, we finally blurted out our adventure. After resting, we made our way to our barracks and arrived shortly before those who chose the long way home. We decided it was one of those things you only need to do once.

Mail Call

After a week, I received my first mail and was shocked at the number of letters I received from Louree. For some reason I had stopped getting letters from her about a week before I washed out. Then with the delay-en-route and the week here, it had been nearly a month since I heard from her. Now I had a stack of her letters before me to read. I put them in the order they were written and realized soon after I started reading she had been looking for a letter from me on a daily basis and had received none.

Eventually she had come to the conclusion that our relationship was over, and I wasn't going to write anymore. When I didn't hear from her, I didn't write as I was dealing with the washout. It saddened me to read each letter as her hope of hearing from me dwindled until finally she said this would be her last letter.

Even though I cared for Rae, I cared for Louree too. I immediately wrote her a letter bringing her up to date about the washout and what I was now doing. I didn't mention the delay-en-route as that would be hurtful. I walked a mile that night to post it so I could start to make things right again with us and ease her apparent pain.

* * *

Class started and it was like a breath of spring after the week on K.P. I made friends easily as everyone was in the same boat of being shipped alone into a bunch of strangers. The one common denominator was that we had all been cadets with the same dream; a dream that was shattered, and misery likes company. We marched as a flight to class and spent a session in the morning and afternoon with physical training at the end of the day. Soon we had a routine that made life easier and I was writing and receiving mail from Rae and Louree.

The first course subject was the fifty-caliber machine gun. Standing at the front of the classroom the instructor began, "This is best recognized as the gun barrel sticking out of the turrets and side openings of American bombers like the B-17 and the B-24. It is all one man can carry, and then only a few feet. Therefore, it is designed to be stationary and is 'the gun' on bombers and some fighter planes.

Of course the bombers payload is in the bomb bay in the form of a variety of bombs. The turrets located on top (upper local), and bottom (lower ball), of the plane are for protection only and have twin mounted 50 caliber machine guns. The single mounted 50 caliber machine guns are: one in the nose, two at the waist of the fuselage, and one at the tail of the fuselage."

The instructor has convinced us the importance of the fifty-caliber machinegun. He now surprises us by saying, "Your job as the Armament Specialist aboard your bomber, besides being in charge of the bomb bay and everything that goes in it and out of it, is to keep all of the fifty caliber machine guns and turrets operating. This means, if one of the single guns or turrets malfunction, it is your job to fix it." That got our attention.

"That may not sound difficult to you," he continued, "because you know we're going to teach you how to do that. The hard part is the conditions in which you will be working to accomplish your job during the flight. Remember you're at 30,000 feet and it's cold because every thousand feet of altitude means a drop of two degrees of temperature. That equates to, if the ground temperature is seventy degrees, it's ten degrees up there." He paused talking for effect.

Convincing himself we were all paying attention, he continued. "That means you can't take off your leather insulated gloves… or your hands will freeze. So we'll teach you to disassemble the guns completely in order to correct malfunctions and the turrets to some degree for the same purpose. And because most missions are ten to twelve hours long you won't always have daylight, so we'll teach you to do it blindfolded.

There it is, gentlemen… your test on the fifty-caliber machine gun and each of the turrets will be to accomplish your task with your gloves on and blindfolded. Are there any questions?"

I wanted to ask, "Has anyone ever done this?" But I just sat there, waiting to begin learning my new job.

The Dance

After being there three weeks, we were paid and three of us went to town together to have a steak dinner, then attended a public dance. We spent most of our time just watching the dancers and enjoying the band. As usual, there were far more military men than single girls; I noticed a couple of girls who were together between dances, but one stood alone during the dancing. As soon as the music started, the prettier one of the two always was asked to dance leaving the other to stand-alone. She was occasionally asked to dance, but refused.

This puzzled me, so on a whim I asked her to dance. She shyly smiled and said, "No thank you. I don't dance."

"You don't dance? I blurted. Why are you here?"

"I'm with my sister; she can't come here unless I chaperone her."

"Would you like to learn how to dance, right now? I can teach you."

"Oh, no! I'd be too embarrassed."

"All we'll do is walk to the beat of the music." She hesitated, and that's all I needed. I took her hand and walked her into the crowd of dancers. I faced her and said, "Follow me." I walked backwards and she followed. Soon I could tell she was feeling the music and matching her walking steps with it. The music stopped and I escorted her off the floor; she was smiling. I took her back to her sister who was surprised to see her walk off the dance floor with me.

I introduced myself to Sirella and Maria. I soon learned Maria was married with a two-year old boy who their folks were taking care of that night so the girls could have a night out. Maria's husband was in the Army overseas and being older, was Sirella's chaperone for the night.

Soon the music started and one of my friends asked Sirella to dance. I turned to Maria and asked, "Would you like lesson number two?" She smiled and I led her onto the dance floor.

We picked up where we left off for a minute, and then I stood beside her and introduced the two-step. She caught on quickly and I added a turn doing the two-step. We had all we needed to enjoy a dance number.

When we returned to Sirella at the side of the dance floor, she was ecstatic over Maria being able to dance. Maria and I danced several more numbers and one of my buddies asked Maria to dance. She hesitated at first, but I encouraged her to accept, and she did. Now I asked Sirella to dance and she accepted.

She was a good dancer and I felt I had returned to some normalcy in my life. Expressing myself through dance was an important part of my life I had determined back in high school.

I wasn't looking for a girlfriend, I had two at the time; I was in need of a dance partner. After the dance my buddies and I walked the sisters to their bus; then we caught ours back to our life in the Army.

The Fifty-Caliber Machine Gun

In the morning class we concentrated on the fifty-caliber machine gun and turrets that used them. In the afternoon class we concentrated on bombs, their releasing mechanisms, and the layout and intricacies of the bomb bay itself.

Our instructor, standing at the front of the classroom behind a long table loaded with bomb related paraphernalia, started his lecture. "The bomb, whether it's a hundred pounder, a five hundred pounder, or a thousand pounder has to have a carrying and releasing device. This is called a bomb shackle and like all mechanical things, they don't always work. Therefore, you, being the Armament Specialist aboard the bomber, have to know how to either fix it or how to make it work manually." He held a bomb shackle up for all of us to see.

"Releasing it manually can be challenging," he continued. "If you're on a bombing run and one or more or all of the bombs doesn't release, it's your job to release them. Bombing runs usually are at thirty thousand feet of altitude, therefore you're bundled up in heavy fur-lined clothing, boots, helmet, gloves, and if you're in the bomb bay, you're on an oxygen walk-around bottle with a three minute supply of oxygen." He looked around the room to determine if we were following him closely. We were, as this would be our role in a matter of a few months and we all knew it.

Satisfied he had our undivided attention, he continued. "The bomb bay layout is such that a foot wide 'cat-walk' runs down the center of the bomb bay dividing it into two bomb bays. There are racks of bombs: on the inside of the fuselage wall, on each side of the catwalk, and on the opposite fuselage inner wall. Therefore, there are four racks of bombs and each rack holds up to forty bombs depending on the weight of the bomb; most bombs are 'hundred pounders.'

"Are there any questions so far?" There were none, so he continued. "If a bomb release fails to work, it's your job to take a screwdriver, like this, and manually release it by turning this screw on the side of the shackle." He held up the shackle and demonstrated.

It looked like a pretty simple operation, to me and I thought he was making a big deal out of it unnecessarily.

Being satisfied we were all with him, he continued. "If it's next to the catwalk, it's easy to release. If it's on an outer fuselage wall, it requires one to straddle the open bomb bay with one foot on the cat-walk and the other foot on the aluminum rib of the fuselage, which is about an inch wide; just wide enough to hold the edge of your foot if it's turned sideways."

If some of us were only half-listening before, this got our attention.

Warming up to his subject the instructor continued, "Remember, you are heavily dressed and on a walk-around oxygen bottle with a limited supply of oxygen." As an aside he added, "It pays not to look down, as you're over an open bomb bay and the first step is thirty thousand feet down." He paused for effect, which he got. "Now reach out with the screwdriver and turn the screw in the shackle ninety degree; that will release the hung up bomb."

We sat quietly, taking in the mental picture that had just been painted for us. He could see he had captured his audience. Smiling, he continued. "Don't allow yourself to run out of oxygen, or you'll pass out in two minutes or less, and be dead in five. If you have more work to do in the bomb bay, get another bottle. Oh yes, I forgot to mention, often when working over the open bomb bay, it is so tight space-wise you probably won't have room to wear a parachute. Are there any questions?"

The Black Out

The class discussion that followed was brief, and we filed out for a cigarette break before marching back to our barracks area. It was now three o'clock and we were due to be at the physical training site at three thirty. This meant a change of clothing into our sweats or just the top with shorts and tennis shoes as we had been told we'd be doing a distance run today.

We arrived as a flight and had calisthenics before the run. This would limber us up and help prevent injury. I had won a physical fitness award at Thunderbird Field, so I was in pretty good shape. We ran against the clock and a mile usually was easy for me to do. However, today was different. I usually paced myself so I had a kick at the end for a competitive sprint to win.

I ran this race according to my plan, but when I turned up the speed at the end I ran out of breathe to the point I had to stop, drop to my knees, and gulp in air deeply and rapidly. A PT instructor saw my plight and stopped to help me. "Are you O.K?" he asked.

When I felt capable of standing, I did. "I don't understand, I've never done this before."

He asked, "How long have you been here in Denver?"

I replied, "Three weeks."

"You're not acclimated yet, we're a mile high here. Don't run any sprints for a couple of weeks, you'll be O.K."

I followed his advice and learned a lesson about the body shutting down when it doesn't get enough oxygen for the task at hand.

A Surprise Letter

At mail call, which occurs daily immediately after lunch, the orderly stands on the top step of the barracks entrance and calls out the name on the envelope in his outstretched hand. That person responds with a "yoh" and takes the extended letter. Everyone there obviously wants a letter, but everyone won't get a letter. The trick is not to show your disappointment too much, if you don't receive a letter, or your joy too much if you do receive a letter. This game is to protect the non-receivers feelings.

This day I hit the jackpot and received letters from Louree, Rae, and my mother. Going to my bunk, I stretched out to read them as I had twenty minutes before flight formation would be called to march us off to our afternoon class. I read mother's letter last and immediately sat up on the edge of my bunk. *She wants to come here and wants me to send her money for bus fare.* Shocked, I reread the letter.

In all fairness I should say mother never had enough money since the divorce because she boarded my two sisters out, which cost twice as much as the support money my father was required to pay each month. Therefore, I had taken out an allotment for her from my Army pay in order to make this arrangement work.

Mother was a waitress and during the war years could get a job anywhere. She said she wanted to see me and would get a job in Denver for a month to pay her expenses. Mother was a hard worker, and I knew she would make her plan work. I wrote her back and sent the money.

*　*　*

I met her Trailways bus; then we took a city bus to the base, as I had arranged for a three-day stay for her in quarters the Army had for visiting relatives of servicemen. This would give her time to find a room in town and a job to support her trip. All I could afford was to pay her bus fare.

We ate dinner each night in the P.X. and spent the evenings in the lounge. I had talked to my squadron commander and received permission to do this. Mother started work on the third day in a restaurant near the state capitol in Denver, and acquired a room close by that was usually rented to legislators; fortunately the legislature wasn't in session.

In our long talks when we were together, I learned mother was running away from a broken relationship with a boyfriend and just felt she needed to get out of town for a few weeks. It worked for both of us, as we could be supportive of each other with our individual problems. It wasn't long before mother told me she'd met an officer from the base who had asked her for a date and she had accepted. Evidently, her broken heart was healing.

Louree's Phone Call

My focus now returned to my schooling and the routine of school became comfortable. I was lying on my bunk after a full day when an orderly came in the barracks shouting out my name. I responded and he informed me I had a long distance call on the phone at squadron headquarters. This kind of thing just didn't happen. I jumped up and ran the half block to headquarters. The C.Q. handed me the phone and I was surprised to her Louree's voice. "What's wrong?" I asked.

Her voice was weak and shaky. "Donna's been killed in an auto accident I and four other girls were in three days ago."

"Are you hurt?"

"No, I was one of the two lucky ones. Five of us were pushing a car from the back when a car came from behind and hit us. Donna is dead and two others are seriously hurt."

"Oh, my god!"

"Daddy wanted me to call you, as I'm at my wits end."

"Oh, how I wish I was there to console you."

"I wish you were here, too. Mother wants to take me out of town to visit relatives in Texas and says we can go by way of Denver to see you, if it's okay with you."

"Of course it's okay with me."

"I feel better already; I'll write to give you the details."

"I can arrange for you and your Mom to stay in guest housing on the base for three days, so let me know when, and I'll make arrangements."

"I'd better hang up now as this is long distance."

"Just remember, I'm here for you."

"Thank you, and I love you."

"I love you too, Louree. I'll wait for your letter… and thank your folks for making this call possible. Goodbye."

I stood there in shock over what I'd just heard. I thanked the C.Q. for his part in getting me to the phone, and walked back to my barracks, my mind in a swirl.

*　*　*

I returned to my barracks and filled my bunkmates in on why I had received a personal phone call handled by headquarters. They were sympathetic to the situation and told me so, then returned to their own personal worlds. I lay down on my bunk and thought *I'll wait for Louree's letter giving me the date and time of their arrival before I asked headquarters to provide them with housing. It's crazy… usually I'm alone; now I have my mother in town expecting most of my free time. Now, Louree and her mother are coming who will be expecting that same free time. I'm glad mother has a new boyfriend; maybe she can cut me some slack.* I rolled over and called it a day.

I phoned mother and told her my dilemma and she said no problem, between her new friend and her job she was wondering how she was going to work me in satisfactorily. That took the pressure off, and I decided to call Louree long distance in two days to be supportive and perhaps get information on their planned trip.

Becoming an Armament Specialist

My training continued and I was learning more about machine guns, turrets, bombs and their fuses than I wanted to know, but I reasoned *if your required to do something you might as well do it to the best of your ability, doing so may save your or your crew's life. After all, getting out alive is the name of the game.*

As I attended classes day after day I began to feel like an Armament Specialist and looked forward to graduation, then on to gunnery school. Upon completion of training we would all be promoted to the rank of corporal, which gave us a measure of prestige and a higher salary. I could easily stand some of both.

I made new friends as time went on and two of these new friends were twin brothers, Ron and Don. They were identical twins and this had indirectly caused their washout from pilot training. It seemed one was a better pilot than the other and when Ron's check ride came due; he became anxious and shared this with his brother. Don, the better pilot, offered to take the check ride for him, and like a lot of things, it seemed like a good idea at the time, but it wasn't.

They got caught and both immediately washed out. It was the Army's way of saying, "Don't prank with us." They accepted their fate, like we all did, and tried to make the best of it, though they too, lost their dream. It was a lot easier to take… being washed out if you were out because you couldn't pass the flying tests. At least one of them could have, but like me, were washed out even after passing the flying tests.

Louree's Arrival

I called Louree two days after her phone call to me to be supportive and to find out if and when they were coming to Denver. It was evening and she was at home to receive my call. Making a long distance call from an Army base sixty years ago took some doing. You had to walk to the Post Exchange building, wait in line to get a public phone, and have the right change to pay for the call for the first three minutes and then additional coins if you talked over three minutes.

"Hello, Louree, this is Harry."

"Hi, what a surprise."

"How are you?"

"I'm in a lot of pain mentally, but I'm surviving."

"I wish I could help you."

"Seeing you will help me, and mother and I are leaving in three days and will arrive in Denver by Southern Pacific on Friday at 8:15 p.m."

"I'll be there to meet you and we'll take a taxi to the base, where I'll have on-base housing for you for three days. Will that work for you?"

"That will be perfect. Mother can set up the rest of the trip's schedule now to get us to Texas and back home."

"I hate to sign off now, but the operator just gave me a fifteen second warning."

"I look forward to seeing you, Harry, and I love you."

"I love you too, Louree; until Friday… goodbye."

* * *

The next day I received permission from my sergeant to go to headquarters to make arrangements on housing for Louree and her mother. I had no problem doing this as it was standard procedure and one of the nice things the Army did for their soldiers.

I was able to get a weekend pass and met Louree and her mother, Vida, as scheduled. We spent an hour together before it was time to call it a day, as I could see the strain in both their faces from the recent tragedy and the train trip. It was good to be together again.

The next morning I was there to take them to breakfast and spend some quality time with them. That afternoon I'd set up a meeting with mother at a park close to mother's room. They were meeting each other for the first time and it went all right in spite of the fact mother was surprised that any mother would bring her daughter over a thousand miles to see a soldier she had known only a short time. Mothers are like that, I'm told.

The next day I was there early to take them to breakfast and to church. We spent the day touring the Colorado Capitol grounds and Vida excused herself to return to their room on the base giving Louree and I some alone time.

The next morning they caught a taxi and returned to the train station to continue their journey to Texas. I could not see them off as my weekend pass was over and I was once again a soldier.

Louree's tragedy brought her back into my life and I could see how important I was to her. So, the long and the short of it was, I was in love with two girls. I've learned I didn't have a corner on that market, especially in wartime.

Kingman Arizona

Our three months of training was coming to an end at Lowry Field and mother had returned home to be near her two daughters. It was good to see her and spend some time with her, which I did as often as the Army and her job allowed. Louree and Vida had returned to their home in California and I continued to write to both girls, each of them oblivious of the other's existance.

Finally the day came when we sewed Corporal strips on our uniforms and shipped out to air-to-air and air-to-ground gunnery training in Kingman, Arizona. It was October and the weather in the high country of Arizona was turning cold.

The Army Air Base was bleak in appearance and in a bleak looking part of the state; we weren't too far from the southern rim of the Grand Canyon. Our barracks were of the one-story temporary type with tarpaper on the outside and a potbelly coal stove in the middle of the barracks as a source of heat. As winter came on, trying to stay warm was the name of the game. We were issued long underwear and a short coat in addition to our overcoats for warmth.

Class began and soon we would be flying practice missions with fighters coming from nearby bases to run attacks on us. Our machine guns used cameras not bullets to show our success in making hits on the passing fighter planes. The fighter planes would be learning the different patterns to fly to attack bombers and we would be learning to defend ourselves. We will learn to drop bombs on targets at our next school. We will arrive there as a complete crew, wherever it is.

One afternoon after class I happened to walk into a graduation ceremony of a class ahead of us. I arrived at the point where they were handing out five silver bracelets to those five gunners who had been the best in one of the five phases of our training: air-to-air gunner, air-to-ground gunnery, ground-to-air gunnery, simulated flight gunnery, and physical fitness.

I sat in a back seat in the auditorium and watched the drama on stage intently. Each airman came up as his name was called and received his silver bracelet presented by one of the five officers on stage. The audience applauded loudly as their fellow airmen received this coveted prize. When the last one came up to receive the award for physical fitness, the officer shook hands with the airman then sank to his knees in feigned pain from the pressure of the handshake. The audience laughed at the gesture and the graduation came to an end.

That night the new airmen would be sewing on sergeant strips and pinning silver wings on their uniforms. In addition, five of them would be wearing a silver bracelet with flight wings engraved on it and U.S. Army Air Corp engraved above the wings. I walked out of that auditorium determined to be the recipient of a silver bracelet for physical fitness. I didn't know how good a gunner I would be, but I knew how to train my body to be ready for the fitness test everyone took to determine who got the top spot and the bracelet.

I set up a training schedule I would follow after our workday was over. I needed a challenge like this to help heal the sore spot in my gut for washing out of pilot training. I made it a point to learn what the final physical test consisted of. The different physical maneuvers to be tested each had a number of times of execution, which was deemed one hundred percent. For example: a dead lift from a parallel bar with the back of your hands facing you, called an overhand lift, and if you did twenty five of them in sequence, it earned you a one hundred percent rating.

There was only one test that wasn't rated on a percentage basis. This was the two hundred forty yard shuttle. The point was to run against a stopwatch picking up a small block of wood putting it down forty yards away, then turning and go back and pick up another block and do the same. When you had three blocks of wood at the far end of the course, you sprinted for home or the finish line and the clock stopped. This was my greatest challenge because I knew some of the contestants had been college runners.

Each evening I worked on the different categories until I reached one hundred percent. I knew I could run fast, but I didn't have access to a stopwatch, so I would just practice the skills this race required and hope for the best.

Christmas Leave

Christmas season arrived and we were given a three-day pass, if we wanted one. Most guys didn't because we were in a very isolated area with no cities of any size nearby and they chose to just hang out on the base. The mess hall did serve a good turkey dinner. I was one hundred and seventy miles from Glendale and Rae. It was possible, if I hitchhike there and took a bus back to insure I arrived back at the base on time. I had enough money to ride one way on the bus, and I was an experienced hitchhiker.

I left as soon as I could after a full day of training; the weather had turned cold. I had on my long underwear, my wool uniform and my overcoat to combat the cold. It was dark by the time I got on highway 40 and obtained a ride east to the junction of highway 93 that led south to Glendale. It seemed few cars were going south and I spent three long, cold, lonely hours until a trucker finally took pity on me.

It was an eighteen-wheeler, and I was so stiff from the cold I had trouble climbing up to the cab. His first words were, "I'm not supposed to do this, but you looked pretty forlorn standing there in this God-forsaken place.

I thanked him and said, "It's pretty cold out there, and I've been there a long time. In fact, I was just about to give up."

"Where are you going?"

"Glendale."

"We'll be there in three hours."

"Really? That should put us in about 6:00 a.m."

"Correct. What's in Glendale?"

"My girlfriend."

"She must be something to have you doing what you're doing."

"She is."

I took off my overcoat as I warmed up in the toasty warm cab of the truck. "How cold do you think it is out there?"

"It's below freezing, and the wind makes it even colder."

"I'm pretty tired, do you mind if I doze off?"

"Be my guest."

* * *

I awakened sometime later, refreshed. Looking out the windshield, I noticed the road seemed steeper and curvier. Glancing at the speedometer I asked, "Are we really going eighty miles an hour?"

"Yep. It doesn't feel like it because we're sitting high off the road."

I stared at the off-road vegetation fly by the side window as we wound our way down from the high plateau of northern Arizona and wondered *is this where I should be? I set myself up for my washout with dangerous flying, but this is more dangerous than that. If this guy misses a curve or an animal walks out on the road, we're dead.*

To get my mind going in another direction I asked, "Where are we?"

"We'll be coming to Wickenburg shortly, and Glendale in an hour."

"Wow, I must have slept a couple of hours."

"You did, but you obviously needed it. Nap some more if you want; I don't mind, as I'm used to traveling alone."

As the road straightened out when we reached a lower altitude, I settled back, relaxed, and replied, "No, I'm okay now." He talked about his family and asked about my army career, just small talk, and soon he was saying, "Here's Glendale, where do you want off?"

"At the bus stop, if it's not out of your way. I know how to get to my girlfriend's house from there."

"That's it right up ahead."

I thanked him profusely, and we said goodbye. It was just beginning to get light and there was no traffic as it was not quite six a.m. I recognized the road to Rae's house and walked the three miles arriving before anyone was up. Fortunately, I knew how to get in with a hidden key. I quietly walked to Rae's bedroom and bent over her sleeping form to awaken her with a kiss.

My kiss did the job intended and arms wrapped around my neck as I bent over and prolonged it. Finally I stepped back and discovered to my amazement I was kissing Connie, her twelve-year-old sister. At first I was speechless. Eventually I mumbled a disjointed apology, and she just smiled impishly, saying nothing. I excused myself and went into the living room to lie on the davenport and wait for the family to awaken.

* * *

I told Rae about my mistake concerning Connie and she just laughed. It was good to be with a family at Christmas time to really enjoy the season. Lyrene had delivered her child some months before and there would be a child to share Christmas. The tree, the house decorations, the extra food treats, plus the sumptuous Christmas Day dinner and just being among loved ones were all the things you didn't have when you were on an Army base at Christmas time.

Because I hadn't done any Christmas shopping, Rae and I went to Phoenix to take care of the problem. Eventually I had gifts for everyone except Rae. As we strolled the boulevard sidewalk, we passed a woman's dress shop that brought me to a halt. There in the window was a mannequin that had a dress on I thought would look good on

Rae. "Would you be interested in a dress like that? I think it would look great on you."

"It is a lovely dress but I'm sure it's far too expensive. Someday you can buy me a dress like that, and I'll love it."

"Let's go in find out if it's in my league."

"Well, I guess we can do that if you really want to, but this is kind of an exclusive woman's dress shop."

We went in and I asked a middle age saleswoman about the dress. She looked at the two of us standing together and for some reason hesitated for a long moment before she answered. When she stated the price it was affordable. "If they have the right size, we're in business." They did, and Rae looked like I thought she would, great! And I said, "We'll take it."

The sales lady wrapped it beautifully and with a maternal smile, handed me the box. We walked out the door, and I noticed she was still watching us as we turned and walked arm-in-arm to our car parked up the street.

That evening the family gathered around the large tree in the living room and the gifts were distributed. When Rae opened her gift from me everyone was surprised by the nature of the gift, and Rae couldn't wait to put on a style show. She did, and I sat back like diamond Jim Brady enjoying the show.

All too soon my three-day vacation was over, and I was driven to the bus station to return to Kingman Army Air Base one hundred and seventy miles north. I would get there late at night, but before my deadline.

Meeting Old Friends

One day while walking from my barracks to the mess hall, a voice called out, "Hey, McIntyre." I turned and there were two of my friends that had visited me in the hospital nearly a year and a half earlier when we were in basic training.

"My gosh, Chuck and Dick, I can't believe it. I see you're still in cadets, what are you doing here?"

"We're in our last phase of pilot training and flying co-pilot on the B-17's used here for gunnery practice. What happened to you?"

I felt happy and deflated at the same time, if that's possible. Happy to see them, but ashamed I'd washed out of pilot training. "I got too big for my britches and was washed out for dangerous flying in primary flight school." It was easier to explain my washout that way, than say I'd been blackballed out of cadets by a check rider.

"Gee, that's tough. Where are you going now?"

"I'm on my way to the mess hall."

"We are too, only we eat at the officer's mess," replied Chuck. "I've got a great idea. Why don't we put cadet brass on you; then you can join us."

"I don't think I want to do that. I'd like to spend some time with you, but I don't need trouble, like impersonating a cadet."

"I think that's a great idea," joined in Dick. "I have extra brass in my foot locker and it's on the way to the officer's mess."

"I don't know; I'd hate to screw up again."

"You won't get caught. They're so laid back here, nobody would care if you did get caught," cajoled Chuck.

"Well, all right, let's do it."

After putting cadet brass on my collar and cap, we headed for the officer's mess hall. We had a steak luncheon, and I didn't enjoy one bite of it, all the time thinking *if I hadn't washed out, I'd belong here and be just weeks away from getting my commission and pilot wings.* After lunch they walked me back to my barracks, I returned the brass, shook hands all around and we went our separate ways.

* * *

The last two weeks of training required the squadron to relocate to a military outpost called Yucca. It was so isolated only a train track and a landing field were available as a means to get there. We flew every day in B-17 bombers and the training was intense. One day we flew into the Grand Canyon and took some unusual pictures of the canyon walls with our gun cameras. The pilot confiscated all the film that day, as he wasn't suppose to fly inside the Grand Canyon and he didn't want the evidence lying around in the form of film.

I kept up my daily schedule of physically training after evening chow, but it took a lot of discipline as my body was tired at the end of a long flying day. It was exciting to see the fighter planes coming at us from all directions and fighting them off with our fifty caliber machine guns shooting film, not bullets. When the film was developed and viewed, we learned how successful we'd been, or if we'd become a casualty.

Graduation

Graduation day finally arrived and I knew ahead of time I had won the top spot in the physical training department. It had been a close contest and as I predicted, a half dozen guys had attained one hundred percent in all the categories, which meant the two hundred yard shuttle was the deciding event. They raced us three at a time, and I had the shortest time by a second. The runner-up wanted to have a re-run with just the two of us competing.

I have to admit I didn't like this guy because of his superior attitude, as he appeared to see himself as the big-time college athlete, and I the little guy that got lucky. I refused his request and said, "What have I to gain by a re-run? I've already won the contest." He was furious, but the physical training officers and sergeants got a big kick out his dilemma; I don't think they liked him any better than I.

As I analyzed the race later, I think my short stature helped me because of the nature of the race with the four starts and stops. I had trained hard and had the strength and the wind for the race, but we'll never know the results of the 'race not run.' I received the silver bracelet and the officer who gave the award to me did exactly what he had three months earlier when I accidentally stumbled in on that graduation exercise; he sank to his knees in feigned pain when we shook hands. The audience laughed and applauded, and now we were airmen with the rank of sergeant.

Crew Distribution at Plant Park, Florida

We shipped out as a squadron to Plant Park Base in Tampa, Florida for crew redistribution. We would be there only a week or two at the most. Just long enough for them to assemble us into ten-man crews to fly B-17 bombers. Our squadron boarded a troop train at Kingman, Arizona for the 2500-mile trip, which would take us four long uncomfortable days.

On the fourth day we were in northern Florida on our way south to Tampa, and I had written letters to Louree and Rae and wanted to mail them as soon as possible. It was frustrating to write letters and not be able to send them for the lack of a postal box. When our train stopped at Tallahassee, I looked beyond three sets of railroad tracks and a short city block to see a mailbox. Throwing caution to the wind, I jumped down from the train and dashed the distance to the box, deposited my two letters and immediately turned and sprinted back toward the train. To my horror, when I came within a hundred yards of the train, it started to pull out of the station. I had to catch that train; otherwise I was AWOL.

Picking up speed as I approached the middle set of the three sets of train tracks, I misstepped and my toe caught the first rail, sending me sprawling. My knees hit the second rail, but I immediately jumped up and was able to climb onto the train just as it began to gain speed. Breathlessly I found my seat and sat down, exhausted. *Thank goodness,*

I mailed my letters and caught the train. Suddenly my knees started hurting as the leg muscles began tightening above each knee.

Standing up, I discovered my legs were stiff to the point that I was not able to walk. I had one of my friends find the Officer in charge of the squadron to tell him of my dilemma. The officer came to my seat and determined it was true, I couldn't walk. With the aide of the conductor, he contacted our new base and asked them to have an ambulance meet us at the train station. I was embarrassed about the dilemma I had caused, but there was nothing I could do; I simply couldn't walk.

The ambulance met us with a medic aboard, and because they had no hospital, I was taken to a one-room dispensary at my new base. Plant Park, a county fair grounds in Tampa, had been converted to a bomber-crew assembling and assignment center. Our living accommodations were rows of double bunks under the enclosed grand stand. There were probably only three hundred men there for crew distribution, so everything was on a small scale. I spent the night in the dispensary occupying the one bed there, and the next day given a bunk with the rest of my squadron. With the aide of walking crutches, I could get around. They had given me pain pills in an effort to relax the leg muscles and control the pain.

As a crew redistribution center, everyone had nothing to do, as we waited for the crew lists to be made up. Several days went by and I was able to get around better, but I still relied on my crutches, as the muscles above my knees were still in spasm. Each day I felt more mobile and when offered a twelve-hour pass, I took it. A new friend, Frenchie Martineau, accompanied me on the bus to a county park and USO advertised on the bulletin board located in nearby St.Petersburg across Tampa bay.

It was pleasant to be out in the sunshine and away from the confines of our makeshift base. The entire flora about us appeared tropical, and the park had an attractive sandy beach. We moved about the park at my pace, and eventually worked our way to the USO building. After lunch we were told they were going to have a dance there that afternoon.

When the orchestra tuned up, they sounded promising, so we decided to stay and just listen to the music, as Frenchie didn't dance and I couldn't dance.

As the day progressed, I walked more easily as my leg muscles began to slowly return to normal. A mixed crowd had gathered and the band began its first number. I noticed a young woman, probably a year or two my senior, standing at the edge of the dance floor. We exchanged glances, and I got the message she would accept an offer to dance. To her, I was probably an injured war hero with my crutches, my wings, and my sergeant's strips.

Without giving it a second thought, I handed my crutches to Frenchie and slowly walked to face her. "I'm game if you are."

"I'm game." We slowly moved away to the beat of the music. I introduced myself and she replied, "I'm Marilyn, happy to meet you, Harry. Is this your first time here?"

"Yes, we're here to pick up a crew and continue our training."

"You aren't returning from overseas then. Why did I see you with crutches?"

"It's a long story, but I'm getting better with each step we take."

"Really?"

"Really."

We danced to the end of the number, and the next, and the next. By that time, my leg muscles had completely relaxed and Marilyn and I danced every other dance until the end of the afternoon dance. Frenchie and I escorted her home, and I asked her for a date the next afternoon to see a movie. It's marvelous, the rebound power of the young male body.

* * *

When I rang the doorbell at Marilyn's house, I was met by her mother. She invited me in and said Marilyn would be down in a few minutes. She abruptly turned and faced me, "I want you to know Marilyn has to be very careful about her reputation as this is her first year as a high school English teacher."

I'm sure my mouth fell open. I assured her we would do nothing to tarnish her reputation. We were going to take in a movie and would return immediately home. This seemed to satisfy the mother just as Marilyn entered the room. Although she said nothing Marilyn's face revealed she suspected what the conversation had been. We excused ourselves and left for the movie.

As we walked toward the theatre I said, "I had no idea you were a teacher."

"Mother gave you the third degree, did she?"

"She is concerned about your reputation."

"She is too concerned about my reputation. She doesn't think I should be going to the USO or to be seen with a service man, but that's her old-school way of thinking. I hope this doesn't ruin the day for you."

"No, I'm fine."

* * *

After the movie we walked home, which was only a half-mile away. It was a pretty part of older, but well-established Tampa, near the water. Marilyn and I talked easily and occasionally I was taken aback mentally with the realization I was dating a high school English teacher. I'd had a high school English teacher who was young and pretty, Mercedes Miller, but dating her was not in my world. Of course I was seventeen then and now I'm nineteen with a year and a half of Army life under my belt.

As we walked over a bridge on the way to Marilyn's home, we stopped to admire the river flowing beneath on its way to Tampa Bay. As we turned back to resume our walk, a small group of teenagers ahead and across the street stood watching us and giggling. I looked from them to Marilyn and seeing the expression on her face, knew these had to be some of her students. We continued walking and talking as if we weren't concerned, but she was concerned.

"Those are your students, aren't they?"

"Yes, and I'm surprised how much it bothers me. I guess I don't have a right to a private life after all."

"Yes, you do! Would it help for you to talk to them?"

"No, I'll just wave as we go by; I can't pretend I don't see them."

This is what she did and they smiled in return, but a couple of girls couldn't stifle a giggle. The rest of the walk home was uncomfortable for both of us. I walked her to the front door, extended my hand and said, "I'll be shipping out in a couple of days to who knows where so its been a pleasure knowing you, Marilyn. I hope I haven't caused you a problem."

"You haven't, Harry, nothing I can't handle. Take care of yourself."

"You too." I turned and walked away, never to see her again.

Meeting the Crew

Two days later the lists were posted on the large, long bulletin board in the dining area of our cavernous temporary home under the bleachers. I found my name among the names of eight other men on my new crew; none of which I knew. We were being shipped to Avon Park, Florida to begin the final phase of training prior to being sent overseas. The list read:

Lt. Mitchell (pilot), F/O Fletcher, (co-pilot), F/O Swisher, (bombardier), F/O Noonan, (Navigator), Sgt. McIntyre, (armament/gunner), Sgt. Harrison, (radio/gunner), Sgt. Hughes, mechanic/gunner), Cpl. Smith, (tail gunner), Cpl. Gerber, (lower ball gunner).

We met for the first time in a corner of our large open area and introduced ourselves. It was a little awkward at first, but soon we began to relax. As we sat in a circle, each told something about their personal lives and military background. I was the only one who had any flying experience in addition to the pilot and co-pilot. We sat together as a crew as a train transported us to our new base at Avon Park, Florida, eighty miles southeast of Tampa. Here we would learn how to hone our new skills as a bomber crew on a B-17 prior to overseas deployment in three months.

The officers went to their BOQ quarters and we five enlisted men, were assigned to a barracks where we would bunk together as one crew among many crews.

The mess hall and the airstrip were nearly a half-mile away causing us to take an open-air shuttle bus to get there. We could walk to the other facilities, like the PX, medical facilities, post office, and theatre.

When we walked from our barracks to the above facilities, it was through a tropical forest where we were apt to see wild pigs, large snakes, birds of all hues, and small and large flying insects of all types. We soon learned Avon Park Army Air Base was on the perimeter of the everglades, and the airstrip was a minus twelve feet in elevation. We actually lived in a jungle. This certainly was a change of environment from our last base in arid Kingman, Arizona.

When we were issued leather flight suits, boots, and helmets that were sheep wool lined, it seemed strange gear for the tropical climate we were experiencing, even in January. However, we were reminded most of our flying would be at thirty thousand feet of altitude and the temperature would drop two degrees per thousand feet, meaning a hundred degrees on the ground equated to forty degrees at thirty thousand feet. We carried our flight gear in a large canvas bag and put it on only in-flight as we gained altitude.

One of the first lessons taught was how to ditch a B-17 when it goes down in water. In the past, a B17 evidently overshot the runway and ended up in Lake Avon about one hundred feet off shore. As a crew, we rowed out in two rubber boats to the partially submerged plane. The lakes are very shallow in Florida and most of the plane was actually out of the water. Two instructors met us each with a whistle dangling around his neck; this looked like a fun exercise.

We were told to go to our crash position in the radio room, which is located forward of the bomb bay and directly behind the pilot and co-pilot's cockpit. In preparation for a crash landing, the crew, with the exception of the pilot and co pilot, sit in two rows on the radio room floor. The first person in the row sits with his back to the bulkhead separating the radio room from the pilot's cockpit. The next person sits between his legs, and so on.

This sounded simple enough, but to get there we had to go through the bomb bay. When we opened the door, to our surprise, we were looking into the jaws of a six-foot alligator. The bomb bay doors had been open on landing causing it to be flooded nearly up to the catwalk, which ran in the center and the length of the bomb bay, which incidentally was our only means to get to the radio room except for a hatch in the ceiling. The instructor nearly fell down laughing at our plight and blew on his whistle. The alligator, on command, swam out of the partially submerged bomb bay to the freedom of the lake.

Once we were sitting in position on the radio room floor, we were instructed to help each other climb out of the hatch and proceed to the wing where we had tied our two rubber rafts. This was our means of escape and we had two minutes to do it. After four attempts we succeeded as a crew, and now knew what to do in a crash landing. However, it's not a happening you choose to spend a lot of time thinking about.

We were now scheduled for our first flight; an easy indoctrination flight of two-hour duration. All went well and Lt Mitchell shot a good landing with me standing immediately behind him and Hughes, the aerial mechanic, standing directly behind the co-pilot. It was nice to know we were in good hands regarding our pilot and co-pilot. Also it had been agreed that I would take an injured pilots place if the situation arose in combat.

We were coming together as a crew and everyone seemed congenial, which is important in a close-knit flying group such as a bomber crew. We would be spending about eleven hours every other day learning to fly and drop bombs in a large wing formation of up to a hundred planes. Most of our missions would be high altitude runs over designated areas dropping sand bombs at ground targets. This would give the navigator, the bombardier, and me a workout.

It was my responsibility to supervise that the bombs were loaded properly in their bomb racks with the releases working. The navigator had to get us to the target and the bombardier had to actually fly the plane remotely by using the Norden bombsight once we were approaching the target. It also vectored in the speed of the plane, altitude, and wind velocity, to enable our bombs to hit the target.

First Simulated Bombing Mission

Our next flight was run as a typical bombing mission from start to finish. We got up at 4:30 A.M., dressed, caught the shuttle with our B4 bag in hand containing our flight gear, and stopped at the mess hall, which was located next to flight operations. After breakfast we reported to an assembly room for briefing.

An officer stood on a raised stage in front of a large map, and pointed out our destination, then told us the number of planes in the mission, our takeoff procedure, our wing forming procedure, our estimated time of departure as a wing, our route to the target area, the location where we would pick up fighter protection, and our estimated time of arrival over the target area. He showed several close-up slides of the target area and his expectations for the mission.

As a crew, we were excused to go to a waiting jeep that would transport us to our planes that sat on a hardstand (an asphalt circle large enough to accommodate a bomber) with a paved approach leading to a taxi strip. It was an impressive sight to see plane after plane leaving their hardstand and taxiing to the end of the runway to take off in one-minute intervals. The mathematics show that planes taking off like this will take nearly two hours just to get in the air and in a formation to fly to the target.

En route we picked up our fighters escorting us partway there and partway back. The lead bomber took us directly to the target where it salvoes its bombs. We salvo our bombs and the wing formation starts its wide 180 degree turn to return home. In actual combat we would expect to fight our way to the target and on our return home. Also we would expect to pick up a flack barrage from the ground guns when we are over the target.

On our return to our base area we are stacked in four quadrants (planes flying in a circle at different altitudes) and given landing instructions from the field control tower. Landing is more difficult than take off due to air turbulence from so many prop-driven planes. Once on the ground we head for our appointed hard stand, shut down the engines and we're home. The next stop is the mess hall, which is ready to serve us, as we had breakfast eleven hours ago. We learned to take a snack with us

3-Day Pass

Our first opportunity to get a three-day pass was coming up at the end of the fourth week of training, and we decided as a crew to go to West Palm Beach, Florida, which is one hundred and twenty miles south of Avon Park. Fortunately, there is a fast train called the *Silver Meteor* that stops in Avon Park if there are passengers with reservations. We made the necessary arrangements and looked forward to two days in a resort setting on the Atlantic Ocean.

At the end of four weeks we were coming together as a group of nine friends with a common mission, have fun. The train was impressive, looking like a silver bullet, carrying vacation seekers from as far away as New York. It was impossible to find nine seats together, so we spread out and met different types of people with the same goal; to have a winter vacation in Florida.

Swisher, our bombardier, and I had seats across from two young, attractive women from New York City. They were putting on a show with their long cigarette holders, but soon loosened up when they learned Swisher was from New York and had a connection with the stock market. Actually he was a player, not a worker. He played the market nearly daily and had more than his share of money, so he must have known what he was doing . As far as the girls were concerned, I just sat back and watched him operate.

After we exchanged names and destinations, he confronted them as they sat smoking their cigarettes, "You are two secretaries from the big Apple looking for a sugar daddy in Palm Beach."

Instead of being angry at his affront, they burst out laughing, "Is it that obvious?"

"Yes, the cigarette holders are a dead give-away," Swisher replied. "Put those away as you've got everything else going for you."

"Thanks for the advice, I don't even like to smoke," replied one of them.

Swisher continued, "We're obviously not what you're looking for, but if you don't find what you're looking for, we'll be at the Holiday Inn for two nights. In actuality, Swisher was exactly what they were looking for, but they didn't suspect that, and he wasn't buying what they were selling.

They acknowledged his offer and then the conversation moved to everyday things. The train made few stops and in two and a half hours we were in West Palm Beach. Swisher had arranged for a rental car and the nine of us filled it to overflowing. At the hotel we had a double room only, so some would end up on a cot or on the floor; it was first come, first serve.

In the afternoon some of us headed for a famous bar down the street called *Wertz*. It advertises *the Atlantic Ocean is across the street from Wertz*. Smithy, Gerber and Harrison had chosen not to join us, and it was just as well as they were underage and non-drinkers. Mitchell and Noonan were of age, but non-drinkers so they went their merry way. That left four of us and I was the only one underage, but it was wartime and most places went by the motto *if you were old enough to wear a uniform and go to war, you were old enough for a drink in a bar or restaurant.*

Wertz was classy and expensive, but not much going on so we had one drink and left to take a walk along the ocean front. It was a beautiful day, but most of the people were older. As the day and the weekend wore on, we discovered this to always be the case. As a group of nine, we ate breakfast and dinner together and broke up into different groups during the day. Soon, it was time to catch our train back to Avon Park, and the time spent in West Palm Beach was okay, but nothing special.

The two secretaries never called us, so their trip must have been successful.

High Altitude Problem

After our return to duty, I developed a toothache while on a high altitude mission. The pain started at fifteen thousand feet, which is the altitude where we would go on oxygen. I asked Harrison for an aspirin, and then another as we approached thirty thousand feet. I wasn't used to taking aspirin, but it seemed to take care of the problem. As we returned to normal altitude flying the pain went away.

Two days later on the next mission the same thing happened. Again I asked Harrison for two aspirin to control the pain, but they didn't eliminate it. As soon as we returned to low level flying the pain went away. I decided to see the dentist, and went on sick call the next day for an appointment. In the meantime I had another mission to fly with the same symptoms. This time, I had my own aspirin.

The dentist was a young officer who appeared to be more interested in the nurses than my teeth. I thought it was poor form when he would shoot them in the rear with a dental water hose spray as they walked by. They thought so, too. He took X-Rays and decided I needed extractions because it was evident I had an abscess running the length of one side of my jaw.

As he was preparing me for the extractions, his boss, the Colonel, walked by and took a look at the X Rays. He asked, "What are you planning to do, Lieutenant?"

"Extract the four teeth below the abscess, sir." This was news to me.

"Bring this man into my office, I'll take over from here."

"Yes, sir."

He led me into the Colonel's office, where to my surprise, was a dental chair. I sat down and waited. The Colonel soon appeared wearing a white smock, now looking like a dentist. He had a pleasant face and disposition and spoke more like a dentist, not like other Colonels I had observed. "Sergeant, I do need to extract one tooth to drain the abscess, but I think I can save the other three teeth."

Good news! With four teeth in a row extracted, I would have to have a partial plate. I told him, "I appreciate the effort, sir."

"What you have been putting up with is what we call a high altitude abscess triggered by the change in air pressure. Where did they put in the plastic fillings?"

"In Lowry Field, sir."

"Someone didn't do a very good job, but this should take care of the problem."

"I was surprised when they took out all my fillings and put in plastic ones."

"That's standard procedure for someone preparing for a lot of high altitude flying."

He gave me Novocain and extracted one tooth near the middle of the abscess. "I'll take you off flight status for three days, and we'll see if this does the job. Make an appointment to come back."

"Yes, sir. Thanks again."

"You're welcome."

Fortunately, the extraction of a single tooth allowed the entire abscess to drain and I had no further problem with my teeth.

The Near Tragedy

One of our training missions extended after dark, and because we were a small squadron of twenty planes practicing air-to-ground gunnery on a strafing mission, we returned one by one to our home field. The mission had been exciting because we flew about fifty feet off the ground and shot at targets in a simulated town in northern Florida. All turrets and side guns were involved except the lower ball, upper local, and tail guns. The mission involved flying down the middle of the street and picking out targets on the ground like vehicles, gun emplacements, and military troops. We were to exclude simulated civilians and real cows.

You might wonder why would there be cows in a simulated town built to be a strafing target? Florida had an open range law and cows would wander in, some said they were driven in, and made dandy moving targets for some trigger-happy gunners. Some cows would get killed; the rancher would bill the government, get paid, and also get the dead cow.

When the officer in charge of the mission stood before us at the briefing, he made it very clear that the government was tired of the game and anyone killing a cow would face a court-martial. I can only say for sure no one on our crew killed any cows. However, the cows were there and when they stampeded, they made an enticing target. I tracked one with my gun sight, but didn't pull the trigger.

THE SIXTH MAN

On our return, it was dark by the time we got within fifty miles of our home base. We had to fly over the Everglades to approach our landing field in our letdown pattern, and I was standing behind the pilot watching the procedure. As field-landing lights appeared a mile ahead of us, we dropped down to one hundred feet of altitude. As the lights grew closer I noticed they seemed different in arrangement.

I pointed this out to Mitch, our pilot, who strained forward in his seat to see what I was talking about. Then Fetcher, the co-pilot, looking out his side window yelled, "Those tree tops shouldn't be there."

A statement like that got everyone's attention. Then the light bulb went on; those weren't the landing lights of the field. Because parts of the Everglades burn every summer, it was a row of tundra and bushes on fire nearly in a straight line looking like the ground landing lights we were looking for. Mitch pulled up to five hundred feet of altitude where we saw the real landing lights several miles ahead. We shot our landing, all gave a sigh of relief, and learned one can get disoriented flying over a jungle in the dark of night.

* * *

The USO sponsored a Saturday night dance at the base and brought in a busload of girls from the small neighboring communities. Some of the WACs stationed at our field also attended. For lack of something better to do, several of us on the crew decided to attend. That part of Florida is very rural and there were no large towns or cities nearby. The dance was held in our gymnasium with several hundred in attendance. As usual, the ratio of women to men was dismal and you had to be fast afoot to get a dance.

A young WAC walked in to the dance late, so I made a beeline for her. She smiled, nodded yes, and we were dancing. She wasn't much of a dancer, but we managed. We danced our three dances just before intermission, so I invited her to the punch bowl where we sat and made small talk. She'd been in the WACs only six months and this was her first assignment after basic training and tech school. She was the base photographer, and in love with her job.

When the orchestra started to play I asked, "Would you like to dance?"

"Yes, but not this set as the fellow walking toward us works in our office, and I promised him a dance. Perhaps the next set?"

Light-heartedly I replied, "That would be great, Private Brown."

She laughed and followed with, "I'll see you then, Sergeant McIntyre."

I had never talked to a girl with rank before, so I tried out the term. We danced the following set and I called it a night.

Hurricane

The next day we were sitting in the barracks playing cards when the call came for all crews to report to operations with flight gear immediately. We were in the path of a hurricane, and we needed to move our planes, "NOW."

Soon the shuttle buses were transporting us to the flight line area and half an hour later we were sitting in the briefing room with our squadron commander standing before us in his flight fatigues.

Raising his hand for quiet he said, "We're in the path of a hurricane that is estimated to pass through here in an hour. We're to fly directly to McDill Field in Tampa, Florida and stay there until further orders. The hurricane path can switch at any time and we might have to move on from there. I'll fly the lead plane, and we won't take time to get in a formation, as time is of the essence. It's only a hundred air miles to McDill, so we should be there in a half hour."

We were dismissed and scrambled to our planes with the help of a small fleet of jeeps driven by permanent personnel. This was standard procedure whenever we flew a mission, as they didn't want people walking where planes were preparing for takeoff. Soon we were aboard our assigned plane in line for take-off at one-minute intervals.

Once in the air, we made a beeline for McDill and a half hour later Operations stacked us in the air when necessary and brought us in for a landing at one-minute intervals. They had us park on a little-used taxi strip close to the barracks. We were told we would be there for several hours at least, so most of the crews spread out their heavy leather, sheep-lined flight gear for substitute mattresses and tried to get some sleep.

I had a "nature call" and told Mitch I'd be back in a few minutes, as I was headed for the nearest barracks to use their latrine. I walked in and there on the first bunk sat Waco Ross, a man from my hometown, Bremerton. Waco was as surprised to see me as I to see him. "McIntyre," he said, "what the hell are you doing here?"

"First, I've got to use your latrine and then we'll talk…don't go away."

A few minutes later I joined him, and we brought each other up-to-date on our lives. Waco was a Native American and taller than most. He had been a star basketball player in high school when I was in junior high school, but I attended high school games and rooted for him and the team. Also, we saw each other at the public swimming beach nearly every day in the summer time when I was in my early teens. He was one of the older boys we younger boys admired.

Regretfully, I needed to cut our visit short to be with the crew if we had to scramble again. I could tell he enjoyed seeing someone from home as much as I. We said our goodbyes and I ran back to the plane.

Nothing had changed; we were waiting out the hurricane and it had held its predicted path. Three hours later we were on our return flight to Avon Park, just as darkness approached.

Writing to Louree

I wrote Louree more often since the tragic accident when Donna, her best friend, died, and Janet lost both legs below the knees. In answering my letters, Louree didn't dwell on the accident any more than was comfortable for her. I let her take the lead, as I was trying to be supportive for her. She became more and more open with me and kept me apprised of the mental recovery process she went through.

It became apparent to both of us this tragedy brought us to a different level in our relationship. Consequently, my relationship with Rae diminished proportionally. Louree, far more mature than Rae, had a special need for someone to share her pain. I felt Rae just needed to become more active once again with her school crowd.

* * *

On one of our regular missions, we were in formation, but still at a lower altitude, when we unexpectedly ran into a flock of large birds. We were at our gun stations when Mitch's voice came over our headsets, "We're dropping out of formation and will be returning to the field. A bird has gone through our Plexiglas nosecone and injured Swisher." There was a pause, and then Mitch continued, "The bird's bill struck him in the forehead, and he needs to see a doctor. Fletcher and Noonan are working on plugging the hole in the nosecone and Hughes and Harrison are in the radio room with Swisher."

Who would have thought you could be knocked out of formation by a bird? I left my right-waist gun position and went through the bomb bay to the radio room. Swisher sat on the floor with his back resting against the forward bulkhead and a silly smile on his face. A three-inch bandage covered the wound and initial bleeding, left a trail of now-dried blood down the right side of his face.

"McIntyre, do you suppose I'll get a Purple Heart for this?"

"Knowing you, Swisher, I'm sure you will."

We all laughed, which broke the tension. With nothing to do, Swisher suggested a game of poker. Swisher loved poker, and we often played it on our return home from missions once we were off oxygen. Smith and Gerber came forward on invitation and the six of us sat in a circle on the floor enjoying the return trip home. Swisher seemed to be feeling little pain and the bleeding stopped. The base doctor applied six stitches to close the wound.

* * *

Hughes and I decided to obtain a twenty-four hour pass and see the sights of Lake Wales, which lay twenty miles north. Hughes, the aerial mechanic on the crew, was the drinker by reputation. I guess he was alcoholic because a bottle opened had to be emptied, or a six-pack of beer finished off. He was a pleasant nineteen-year-old from a wealthy family near Chicago, and we got along well together.

Traveling by bus, when it pulled in to town we were immediately impressed with the beauty of this small city situated on a lakeside. After obtaining a room in a modest hotel, we bought a pint of bourbon, for later, and set out to see the town, which didn't take that long. After some inquiring, we soon determined it wasn't a town for a couple of young military men, as nothing was going on, like a dance. However, we paid for our room, so that locked us in to staying.

We had dinner at a nice restaurant filled with middle age and elderly people, and I'm sure we stuck out like a sore thumb. After dinner we returned to our room and retrieved the bottle for a bourbon and water. Fortified, we took a stroll by the lake with its manicured lawns, wide meandering sidewalk, ornamental trees and shrubs, and ornate, white, metal park benches. Sitting and looking out across the lake, we soon determined it was void of any activity, so we passed the bottle back and forth, taking a pull on each pass.

Drinking straight bourbon out of a bottle isn't my style, but Hughes was in his element. My sips were just that; his were man-sized. However, it wasn't too long before I felt a warm glow in my stomach and a light-headedness, indicating I was on my way to becoming drunk. I'd only been drunk once back in high school, and I didn't like the experience. I told Hughes the rest was his.

We continued to sit on the bench looking out across the lake, when we spotted a pair of eyes skimming on top of the water headed toward us. The large eyes protruded from behind a long ragged jaw, and we realized we were looking at an alligator also looking at us. Not only was the 'gator looking at us, but swimming directly toward us. We sat transfixed as we watched it swim slowly to the lake's edge, twenty feet away.

The alligator stopped momentarily and stared at us; we returned that stare. Then it did what we dreaded it might do. It came out of the water and slowly walked towards its intended evening meal, us. We responded by doing the only logical thing. We each picked up one end of the metal park bench and with one mighty swing and a heave, bounced it off its head. The Alligator was stunned and looked at us curiously for a moment, then backed into the water, and slowly swam away. We did thumbs up, and called it a day. After all, Hughes had emptied the bottle, and we'd had all the entertainment we were going to get in Lake Wales this night.

An Open Bomb Bay

On a mission as we approached the target on a bombing run, Swisher and the Norden Bomb Sight took over control of the plane. At the precise moment the bombs were salvoed, one of the eight banks of bombs didn't release. I immediately put on an oxygen "walk-around bottle" and headed for the bomb bay. I snapped on my chest parachute, as I would be working over an open bomb bay and the first step was thirty thousand feet straight down.

With screwdriver in hand I started releasing the bombs one at a time by standing with one foot on the catwalk and the other on the rib of the airplane. You don't want to shoot a landing with a bunch of bombs hanging from their hardware in the bomb bay. I learned not to look down when I performed this task, and all went well.

Once the bombs were on their way, Swisher closed the bomb bay doors and we were safe to return home. This has to be done relatively fast to be sure you are still in the safe bombing range. Otherwise the pilot would have to break out of the flying formation to return to the bombing area.

In actual combat it wouldn't be a consideration for two reasons: one is that you aren't that concerned about the enemy, and two is to be out of the flying formation makes you an easy target for the enemy fighters. In a formation of bombers gives one some protection from enemy attack, as it's dangerous for the fighters to get too close to six gun stations each bomber maintains. There are nine, fifty-caliber machine guns pointed at the fighter plane; they have speed on their side.

* * *

Training progressed smoothly, and not only our crew grew close as a small group of men with a common purpose, but we were a part of a larger group in our barracks, who became our buddies. Therefore, it came as a surprise when the crew of five men living next to us in the barracks received orders to report to McDill field near Tampa, Florida. This meant they were being switched from flying B-17's to B-29's.

It happened so quickly we hardly had time to tell them goodbye. We shook hands or embraced, and they were out the door. We'd been together in the barracks three months, which is relatively long during wartime. The B-29's were a new bomber for the Army Air Corp and had several advantages. Being considerably bigger than the two work horses, the B-17 and the B-24, it carried more bombs and had a longer flight range. This being important to winning in the Pacific as the war zone covered a much larger portion of the earth's surface.

We knew some crews were being switched from other airfields like ours around the country to learn to fly the new plane, but this was the first crew to leave Avon Park. The B-29 still had some mechanical bugs to be worked out. The airplane jet engine replaced the propeller driven engine and wasn't reliable… yet. In fact there was a saying going around, "A Plane a Day In Tampa Bay." Disconcerting, to say the least. If a B-29 left the airfield for a training mission and returned with three of its four engines operating, it was considered a successful flight.

B-17s or B-24s can sustain flight with two engines, but not the B-29. Therefore, the Army Air Corp was losing as many planes in training as they were in combat. It was shocking, but not totally surprising, when a week later the crew that left, our barracks buddies, was killed because their B-29 did a cartwheel in Tampa Bay. At this point in time, America was definitely winning the war in the European theatre and tooling up for the war in the Pacific… but at what cost.

Havana Escapade

Our crew was getting excited about an overnight flight to Havana, Cuba. This was standard procedure bringing back duty-free booze. Each crew member can bring back one gallon of liquor without tax, but the crew member never sees it, because it is destined for the officer's club. However, the crew would have a night on the town, and Havana was wide-open for anything and everything.

Unfortunately, at this time I experienced a digestive problem, as I had irritated my stomach lining by chewing aspirin when I dealt with the high altitude abscess tooth problem. This put me in the base hospital at the time of the Havana 'night on the town' flight. The crew had a great time telling me of their spree with several having brought an end to their virginity that night. It's probably just as well I didn't go.

* * *

I continued my correspondence with Louree and Rae, but I wrote more frequently to Louree and now felt I was letting go of Rae. From a distance of time and space, it was apparent to me Louree was the type of person I would want to come home to… if given the opportunity after the war. I guess I was growing up and my thoughts of the future became more dominant in my thinking. That's probably a natural phenomena for a man going off to the uncertainties of combat.

My letters to Louree became more personal and suggestive of a future together. She responded in kind, as she was fighting her own war in the recovery from the horrible accident and the loss of her best friend. I did everything I could in my letter writing to help her in this process.

We were both looking for something or someone to hang on to.

* * *

It was May 1945, and I had just celebrated my twentieth birthday when the war in Europe came to an end with the surrender of Germany and Italy on May 8th. This changed everything for our crew, as we had just completed our training and were scheduled to ship overseas with the Eighth Air Force in England in one week. With no war, there was no need, but this left Japan to be dealt with. The timeline was estimated at two years, with the allies and enemy combined loss of life at approximately one million. Yes, war is costly… beyond money.

We were given the opportunity to apply for furloughs, as it would take the military a little while to shift gears and direct all of its fighting force to the war in the Pacific. We, as a crew, were in limbo. We knew we would be going to a war zone the B-17 wasn't really suited for, as the distances between base and target were too far. It was anyone's guess as to what we'd be asked to do.

Louree and I had been talking marriage when I came back from Europe; suddenly I was back, because I never left. I called her on the phone and asked her to marry me while I was on the furlough I had applied for. She accepted.

The furlough came through without a hitch and knowing Fletcher, my co-pilot, would be on furlough too, and in the neighborhood, I asked him to be my best man, as he lived thirty miles from Louree's hometown. All of a sudden life became very exciting, with the wedding plans and the plans for the trip from Florida back to California. I decided to hitchhike using military planes and automobiles to get there to conserve money for the wedding and honeymoon. This meant no fixed date could be set for the wedding until I got there. I'm sure this complicated planning for Louree and her parents, but money was always an issue, as the Army wasn't noted for paying high wages, and I had an allotment for my mother requiring part of my pay check.

Pending Marriage

The day arrived for me to leave, so I obtained a flight from Avon Park to McDill Field in Tampa, then on to Dallas, Texas. After a few hours wait, I caught another flight to March Field, California, only sixty miles from Louree's home. From there, I went to the highway, and two rides later brought me to Louree's doorstep; I had made it in two days. There was a joyous reunion and that evening I asked Pat and Vida for their daughter's hand in marriage.

As they hesitated, Louree said, "I'm going to marry him regardless of what you say."

This was a shock to me: for their hesitating, and for Louree's declaration.

They gave their consent, and the next day we went to the marriage license bureau in Santa Ana, California. Plans were made for us to marry that evening, but we were in for a surprise. The license bureau clerk told us Louree was old enough to get a license, but I wasn't. A woman needed to be eighteen, but a man had to be twenty-one. We walked out of the office stunned, as they said I needed one of my parent's signed consent.

I felt very chagrined at the thought Louree could marry and I couldn't, even though we were both twenty years old. Sitting down on a park bench outside the courthouse, a thought came to me. I hadn't seen dad since I left his home four years earlier, but recently, my aunt had written and mentioned he had moved to Huntington Beach, California and was working as a federal employee at the Seal Beach Naval Ammunition Depot.

I asked Louree, "Where is Seal Beach from here?"

"It's about twenty miles, why?"

I brightened, "Because that's where my dad works and he would be working right now."

Louree turned to face me, "What do you have in mind?"

"I'm thinking we could drive there and see if he'd sign a consent form so we can get married today as planned."

Louree smiled, "It's worth a try. It's still early in the morning, so if we could find him, and he would agree, he'd have his lunch hour to go to a notary for the consent form."

"Let's give it our best shot," I replied offering her my hand. "Everything is set for the wedding tonight; I think this is supposed to happen."

Reuniting with My Father

After a brief search, we found the Naval instillation where my dad worked and stopped the car at the main gate. The marine on duty came over to the driver's side of the car and asked to see my pass. I told him of my mission to find my father and he said, "I'll call Administration. If he works here, they will be able to tell us his location."

After a brief phone call, he gave us a temporary pass for the car and instructed us to drive to a nearby building, as the installation wasn't very big. We stopped outside the building and went inside… and there sat my dad. It had been four years, but he looked the same to me: middle aged, short, stocky, black neatly trimmed hair, parted in the middle, with a very surprised look on his face.

"Harry, what are you doing here?"

I introduced him to Louree and then told him our story and our need for his consent to marry. I could see this amused him.

With his easy smile he said, "If you two want to get married, I have no objection. I can take my lunch hour a little early and we can go to a notary public. You say that's what the court house wants in order to issue you a license?'

"Yes, that would be great, Dad. You and Irene will be invited to the wedding tonight, if we get the license and there is a wedding."

We drove the short distance to town and found a notary public. In a matter of five minutes it was done. As we drove back to his work place he suggested we stop by his house on our way to the courthouse to see Irene, my step-mom. He gave us the address and called to bring her up-to-date.

We arrived and I introduced Louree to Irene. We talked about the whirl-wind we were in, but made sure she felt welcome to attend our wedding, if we got the license, and if the minister was still available, and if the guests are notified, and if the wedding cake has been baked, etc. We made an early exit and drove directly to the courthouse in Santa Ana. It was late in the afternoon and we never thought to call Louree's Mom who was making all the arrangements.

We arrived home and found her in a state of despair over our early departure to the courthouse, and then no word from us.

She blurted out, "Are you two getting married today?"

We told Vida our story, she laughed and she then, skillfully put it all together. Guests were called including my best man, the minister, the baker, and Dad and Irene. The wedding was to take place in Louree's home in a matter of hours and everyone was very busy.

The Wedding

The wedding started on schedule at seven o'clock with a house full of people, including a half dozen of Louree's girlfriends, three sets of aunts and uncles, and my Dad and Step-Mom, plus the minister. The wedding party consisted of Fletcher, my best man, and Louree's sister, Joyce, her maid of honor, Louree, a stunning bride dressed in a fitted white suit and summer hat, with a lovely corsage, and I wore my dress uniform.

The wedding party stood in front of the living room fireplace, backed by a large ornate mirror, facing a living and dining room packed with wedding guests. The wedding soloist, Louree's cousin Onie, stood to one side, and the minister stood with his back to the audience facing the wedding party. Everything went like clockwork, and many said it was one of the nicest weddings they had ever attended. It was an informal, home wedding to be proud of.

We drove the family sedan away from the wedding celebration under a hail of rice, and good wishes. Arrangements had been made for us to honeymoon at Lake Arrowhead, about eighty miles away, where we had rented a one-bedroom mountain cottage for a week. It was a lovely setting and we had a great honeymoon. But all things must come to an end and it was time for me to return to my base in Florida.

* * *

I took the train back to Florida, as I needed to return on a specific date. Louree and her dad put me on the train at Riverside, California for a long four-day trip back. When the train stopped briefly in Phoenix, I made a phone call to Rae to tell her of my marriage, as I felt we should stop corresponding. Unfortunately, she wasn't home. I talked to her dad and asked him to tell her, as she wasn't aware of my plans to marry Louree. There was no further correspondence, and that ended the relationship…understandably so.

Another Furlough

I had no sooner returned to my base in Avon Park, Florida when the crews were told there would be a period of transition, as the Air Corps needed time to change direction from the European theatre of war to the Pacific theatre of war. Therefore, anyone eligible to apply for another furlough could do so.

I qualified, as we accumulate thirty days furlough per year and I had been in the military two years. I was the only one of the crew who applied, as furloughs are expensive and travel is tiring. Of course, I was the only one with a new bride; a few days later I was on my way back to California.

Again, I hitchhiked to McDill field in Tampa with my parachute and B-4 bag in hand, and caught a transport going to Dallas, Texas. From there, I caught another military plane to Phoenix, Arizona. I waited there for twelve hours with no flight available so I decided to hit the highway. The first car that came by was a nearly new Chevrolet sedan driven by an Army officer.

He asked, "Do you have a driver's license?"

I was taken aback for a moment and then replied, "Yes."

"Good," he sighed. "I'm exhausted from driving and I have to be in Los Angeles by eight a.m. It's three hundred and fifty miles and I've got to get some sleep. You drive, and wake me if you need to."

He lay down on the back seat and was asleep before I pulled away from the side of the road; it was two A. M. The car handled well and the road was not heavily traveled at that time of night. I found I could travel comfortably at eighty miles per hour.

In addition to slowing down for towns occasionally, I ran into a roadblock situation out in the middle of nowhere. I barely brought the car to a stop in time to avoid a collision with the two police cars blocking the highway. I thought *this is going to be trouble.*

The officer shined his flashlight in my face and asked me for identification. I showed him my travel orders and driver's license. Then he noticed the officer asleep on the back seat. I told him the story and he obviously believed me because he flagged me on. They were looking for an escaped convict.

Eventually it became daylight and driving was easier. I pulled in to Fullerton at 7:15 a.m., still on the road to Los Angeles, but only three blocks from Pat and Vida's house. I awakened the officer and brought him up to date. I got out of the car with my parachute and B-4 bag in hand and said, "Los Angeles is thirty miles straight ahead; thanks for the ride."

"That must have been quite a ride; you averaged seventy miles per hour."

"It was." I turned, smiling, and walked the three blocks to where my new bride was. I had been gone only two weeks.

* * *

Furlough always goes at warp speed and soon it was time to return to my job in the Army Air Corps. I allowed three days to return, using military hops as my source of transportation. Pat and Louree drove me to March Field, the nearest Army Air Field for my return. After a tender goodbye, I hoisted my gear with travel orders in hand and walked up to the guard on duty. He directed me to the flight line and by eight a.m. I was inquiring about flights headed toward Florida.

The answer I received was not encouraging. "We have no scheduled flights going east today." I needed air transportation to get back to my base in three days, so I waited it out for the rest of the day. They had no place for me to sleep there at operations, as this was a much smaller base than any of the others I used in this manner. The others had sleeping cots and food available.

I decided to hitch hike back to Fullerton and try again the next day. I arrived just as the family was sitting down to dinner and Vida quipt, "You've got a good nose, Harry." However, they were happy to see me and understood the problem.

The next day we did a repeat of the preceding day, but again there was no travel going East out of March Field. Now I was beginning to feel a little panicky, because I didn't have money to fly commercially, nor time to travel any other way and get back before I was A.W.O.L. I hitchhiked back to Fullerton and arrived once again in time for dinner. It was beginning to get comical, except for the fact I might end up in the guardhouse.

A.W.O.L.

The next day began just like the preceding two days, except this time, there was a plane headed for New York City. A long way out of my way, but it was east, and the closer I could get to my base the better... if I ended up A.W.O.L. It turned out to be a hospital plane, so I lay down on an empty bunk and slept to Chicago, and then on to New York City. We landed at a military airfield and they put me up for the night. At the stroke of midnight I was officially A.W.O.L.; not a good feeling.

I couldn't leave the base without detection at the guarded gates, so I went to the flight line and hoped for a miracle. A DC-4 was leaving shortly for Orlando, Florida carrying a group of officers to a meeting. I bypassed operations and walked up to the pilot of the plane and asked him for a ride. He looked me over briefly and said, "Let me see your travel orders."

I thought *if he reads them, I'm a dead duck.* I handed him my travel orders as directed, and he glanced down at them just as his scheduled party arrived. He looked up, saluted the one star general and his staff as they walked by, handed me back my travel orders, without really looking at them and said, "Climb aboard."

I could feel my heart pounding as I climbed the stairs and took a seat in the back of the plane. Placing my gear on the seat beside me, I looked forward surveying more officers than I had ever seen at one place at one time. In addition to the one star general and his staff were several high ranking Naval officers. I smiled to my self, *I'm sitting here with all this brass and I'm AWOL. Oh, Louree, if you could only see me now.*

The flight was uneventful and several hours later we were shooting our landing at the Army Air Base in Orlando, Florida. I knew I would soon be found out when I tried to get off the base, but at least I was within eighty miles of my home field. As I sat looking down at the general layout of the field in order to find the gate, I saw a tree overhanging the fence that surrounded the field some distance from the gate. *Desperate means require desperate measures. If I can use that tree as a means of getting over the fence, I can hitchhike to my base, and the A.W.O.L. status and penalty would be less severe.*

The fence was only six feet high, so I threw my gear over it, scrambled up the tree, and dropped down the other side. I hastily looked about, and to my relief, saw no one. An alley nearby became my path away from the field and to the highway out of town. It wasn't long before a car picked me up heading toward Avon Park. Several rides later I was at the bus stop to my field; I could hardly believe my good luck… so far. I had traveled from New York City, New York, to Avon Park, Florida all in less than a day and I was right outside the main gate to freedom from this nightmare. Of course I'd still have to deal with my commanding officer, if I could just get to him without being caught.

The bus to the base came, and the MP started up the aisle checking passes. I sat at the very back of the bus and stashed my gear under the seat ahead of me. Pulling out an out-of-date Class 'A' pass from my billfold, I nonchalantly showed it to him. He only glanced at it…and I was home free.

I got off the bus near the squadron headquarters, and with my parachute in one hand and B-4 bag in the other, fairly skipped up the steps to my commanding officer's office. *Now my punishment shouldn't be so bad.*

I was on an adrenalin high as I approached the CQ's desk. He looked up and asked, "McIntyre, where the hell have you been?"

Ignoring the question I said, "I need to see Captain Thompson; I hope he's in."

"Oh, he's in, all right, and he'll want to see you, too."

The CQ announced me over the intercom and pointed to the door. I opened it and stood before my commanding officer feeling as if I had completed an unbelievable journey. He looked at me and repeated what the CQ had asked, "Where the hell have you been?"

I told him the story from beginning to end. He sat there chewing on his unlit cigar and drawled, "Sergeant, that's the damnedest story I ever heard. If you could pull that off, I'm sure as hell not going to turn you in as A.W.O.L. Dismissed!"

As I saluted, I breathed a long sigh of relief; did I detected a slight smile as he looked down at my travel orders showing I had arrived one day late.

Biloxi, Mississippi

Shortly after I returned to Avon Park, my crew was given shipping orders to report to the Army Air Base in Biloxi, Mississippi. We were pleased to still be a crew, and our new assignment was to train to be an air-to-sea rescue plane for the Pacific Theatre. This meant, instead of dropping bombs, we would be dropping an especially equipped thirty-foot boat attached to the bottom of the hull of our B-17. This was to rescue B-29 bomber crews who ended up in the ocean either going to or coming from a bombing run to mainland Japan.

Our purpose had definitely changed as a crew; now we would be back in training for several months learning new skills. As the Armament Specialist, I would be in charge and responsible for attaching and detaching the boat to our hull. We were not given a starting date for training, so we bided our time waiting to begin. In the meantime, I sent for Louree to join me in Biloxi. I found a room, with kitchen privileges, about two miles from the base; a handicapped woman in a wheel chair was renting out her bedroom. It was a poor beginning, but housing was at a premium.

I met Louree's train a few days later and it was a joyous reunion. I had to report to the base each day and spend it there even though we hadn't started training. However, I had a pass allowing me to live off base, giving me nights and weekends with Louree.

We spent our free time seeing the sights of Biloxi by bus and bicycle. We could rent bikes for a leisurely ride along the boulevard following the local gulf coastline. One hundred-year-old mansions were in abundance along this boulevard looking out on the Gulf of Mexico.

* * *

With the dropping of two atomic bombs, SUDDENLY, THE WAR WAS OVER IN THE PACIFIC. Not only was it a shock to the enemy, Japan, but also to the United States and the rest of the world, since it had been a secret weapon developed under the authority of President Truman. Because it was so devastating to human life, Japan surrendered immediately and unconditionally.

This was wonderful news, but now our crew was in a permanent hold pattern. After a few weeks the crews were disbanded and some of us given jobs on base that needed to be filled as men with high quota numbers were being discharged. Being an Armament Specialist, I was given charge of an armament shop. I was responsible for ammunition and hundreds of small arms, which included any weapon a soldier could carry. I had three men working under me, and because they had been there when I arrived, everything ran smoothly.

At home it didn't. The landlady had a terrible disposition; probably due to her handicap, since she was wheelchair bound. After one month we moved out. Because finding a rental was the next thing to impossible, Louree answered an advertisement for a part-time housekeeper in exchange for a one-bedroom house, rent-free. The landlord owned a dress shop downtown and needed someone to do some housekeeping and to cook the noon meal; their big meal of the day.

Louree is Pregnant

This worked well for a few weeks until Louree started having morning sickness. It was devastating enough to make us realize she couldn't fulfill her job responsibilities. I went to the Red Cross with the problem, as advised, and they secured an emergency furlough for me, and a train ticket home for the two of us. I later paid for the tickets out of my pay on a monthly basis.

With Louree comfortably settled and under her mother's care, I returned to Biloxi. The Army had six months to discharge those of us in the service for the duration of the war plus six months. Because I hadn't gone overseas, I had a lower quota number and destined to stay in longer than I wanted to. Time dragged and my job didn't keep me busy as guns were now passé, so when I was offered another furlough, I took it.

I had little money to spend, so I relied on my thumb as a means of transportation. I caught a hop to Dallas on a C-47 and then my luck ran out. No flights were going my direction, so once again I turned to the highway. Another soldier joined me and eventually we were offered a ride late at night in an older Cadillac sedan. The lone driver, a large man, pulled out a revolver and warned us not to pull any "funny stuff." We were dumbfounded.

Because we had been a long time getting this ride on a cold night, we both fell asleep from fatigue. We told him we were headed for California by way of El Paso, so when he pulled to a stop and said, "This is as far as I go", we thanked him for the ride. The sun was coming up and we looked about for a restaurant. Spotting a small café down the block, we soon found ourselves inside, sitting at a counter each with a hot cup of coffee in front of us.

Several patrons at the counter were carrying on a lively conversation and they kept mentioning Austin. My friend looked at me questioningly, and I did the same. I asked the man behind the counter, "Where are we?"

He looked at me in disbelief saying, "Your in Austin, Texas, of course." For whatever reason, our benevolent host in the big Cadillac had taken us several hundred miles out of our way. He had turned south during the night when we wanted to go west.

After a hearty breakfast, we hit the road again and several hours later ended up in El Paso. Going to the airbase there, we hopped a ride in a C 47 to March Field, California. We parted ways and I hitchhiked to Fullerton and surprised Louree and her family. Although I will admit... it was getting harder to surprise them.

* * *

Louree's morning sickness had run its course and she was feeling much better. Her pregnancy was showing now and we spent many days doing passive things like visiting relatives and friends. I was establishing a new relationship with my father and stepmother, who now lived just twenty miles away. I'd literally run away from home four years previously, and it was good to have them back in my life; they said they felt the same way.

Louree's sisters, Patty and Joyce, became like sisters to me, and Pat and Vida always accepted me graciously and whole-heartedly. I really felt like I had a family and looked forward to making Fullerton my home after I received my discharge from the Army Air Corp. However, I still had a soft spot in my heart for my hometown, Bremerton, Washington, even though I saw my future in Southern California.

A Furlough Problem

Soon it was time for me to return to my base in Biloxi, Mississippi. I allowed three days to hitchhike rides, either in the air or on the ground, so Pat and Louree drove me to March Field as they had on my last furlough. I hoped a flight would be easier this time.

I checked into Operations and was disappointed with what I heard. Since the war had ended, a lot of military air travel had come to a halt. I pondered hitting the highway to hitchhike, but I really needed a flight, at least part of the way, to get back to my base in three days. I decided to stay there in case a military plane came in and would be going my direction. The pilots were good about giving a serviceman a ride, if it didn't inconvenience them.

At the end of the day nothing had changed, so I talked operations into putting me up for the night. The next day was more of the same, and now it was too late to hit the highway. I stayed another night in their transient barracks and ate in their mess hall. The third day was like the first and second, so in the afternoon, I decided to turn myself in, before I actually became A.W.O.L.

Operations directed me to the Officer of the Day and I was feeling pretty low by this time. I had no idea what would happen to me. The Officer of the Day was a young Major, who was accompanied by an older Master Sergeant who sat at an adjoining desk. I approached the Major, saluted and stood there until he acknowledged me.

I told him I was there to turn myself in before I became AWOL, which I would be at 12:00 midnight. He didn't look happy as I told him my story, including I had been there three days and could not get back to my base, and I was without funds.

He replied, "That means I'll have to send you back to Biloxi with two armed M.P.'s . You will pay for their round trip fares, plus your own fare, and meal tickets for the three of you. This will come out of your future wages. In the meantime, I will confine you to the guard house."

I withered under this barrage of information. Standing at attention with my mind visualizing this trip, I wondered if I would be in handcuffs. I started to ask when the Master Sergeant interrupted by saying to the Major, "You can't do that, Sir."

"I can't? What do you mean 'I can't'?"

The Sergeant continued, "According to Army Regulations, if a soldier turns himself in before he's A.W.O.L. and declares he doesn't have the money to get back to his base, we have to provide the means for him to do that."

The Major wasn't liking what he was hearing and said, "Are you sure?"

"Yes, Sir, it's in the Army Manual. We have to cut him new orders in order to travel to his base, with a new timeline. Also, we have to provide him with a train ticket and meal tickets to get him back to his base."

"Who in the hell is going to do this on a Saturday afternoon when everyone in the office has gone home?" the Major demanded.

The sergeant stood and continued, "I would suggest we give him a three day pass and have him report here on Tuesday. By that time we can have the travel orders, train ticket and meal voucher ready for him and he can be on his way."

Resigned to the task at hand, the major said, "Take care of it, Sergeant." Angrily, he got up and walked out of the room. I stood silent, going emotionally from devastation to jubilation. I wanted to run over and hug the sergeant… but thought better of it. He motioned me over as he made out a three-day pass, and handed it to me with a smile. "See you in three days."

"Thank you, Sergeant. You saved my day."

He laughed, "I know."

I hitchhiked home… and surprised the family once again.

Eglin Field and My Discharge

I returned by train to Biloxi and life there was at a standstill. I returned to the Armament shop to supervise no activity. For lack of something better to do, we took inventory. When an opportunity arose to transfer to Eglin Field in Florida to defuse some large bombs, I volunteered as they offered me an early discharge in exchange for my services. It seems they had discharged everyone there who knew how to do it, and were looking for an Armament Specialist.

The job was a piece of cake… if you knew what you're doing. I studied the type of fuses they used and went to my textbook on fuses. The information I needed was there, as it was a standard delayed-action fuse. After I completed the job, they kept their promise and I was on my way to Camp Shelby, Mississippi for discharge. There is a saying in the Army when you want to complain about someone being slow. It's, "You'll be late for your own discharge." I nearly made that remark come true.

The last step before going through the discharge ceremony was a stop at a department having to do with legal matters such as G.I. Insurance, allotments, and disability pensions. Camp Shelby is a big place and buses were moving about a hundred of us about the base while we were being processed out of the Army. I got hung up at someone's desk while they were talking to me about insurance. When finished, I looked about and everyone was gone, including the buses.

In a panic, I got directions to the location of the next stop, the discharge ceremony and the issuance of discharge papers. It was a mile up a long hill, and I ran most of the way. I arrived at the formal ceremony being held in a large auditorium, completely out of breath. I rushed through the main door connecting me with the central aisle leading down to the stage at the precise moment the next name on the long list was called, "Sergeant McIntyre." Without changing stride I breathlessly shouted, "Here", as I huffed and puffed my way to the stage. The audience, mostly military, exploded into laughter, as they made the connection between the old army saying 'you're so slow, you'll be late for your own discharge' and what they were seeing transpire before their eyes. It was a good way to end my Army career remembering the old adage, "Always leave them laughing."

In no time I was on a bus, out the gate to the local train station, and on my way to California with a brief stop over in New Orleans. During that three-hour layover in New Orleans, I chose to take a walk to stretch my legs and also to enjoy my new freedom, even though I was still in uniform with a "ruptured duck", signifying my discharge, sewn on my blouse.

As I strolled along, a young woman approached me and asked, "Do you want to have some fun for a dollar?"

She had said it fast and low and I wasn't sure what I heard. "What did you say?" I asked.

She repeated it slowly and deliberately, "Do you want to have some fun for a dollar."

I had no trouble giving her a negative answer and continued on my way, but I thought, *that's the first time I have ever been approached by a prostitute… why now?"* Then I realized, *with a ruptured duck visible on my blouse, it was logical I would probably have a pocketful of money.* I wonder how many others have said, "Yes," and ended up being 'rolled' for their take-home pay?

ARRIVING HOME

The train ride home seemed long, and I was anxious to be a civilian. When it pulled in to the station in Riverside, California, Louree and her folks were waiting for me on the station platform. It was a happy reunion and one that wouldn't end in a matter of a few days, as my furloughs had.

Driving home, Louree and I sat in the back seat of her folk's car with my arm around her. Vida turned and asked over her shoulder, "What are your plans now, Harry?"

"I plan to get a job in construction while we wait for the baby to be born, and then start school in the fall. I'd like to use the G.I. bill to train to be an Architect. This is what Louree and I have discussed and agreed upon, and after a few days rest, I will be looking for a job."

And then the words to a song popped into my mind, *FREE AT LAST, FREE AT LAST. THANK GOD ALMIGHTY, I'M FREE AT LAST. Now I can get on with my life.*

Crew Members (Starting at top row, left): Gerber (lower-ball turret gunner), Harrison (radio operator/ left waist gunner, Smith (tail gunner), Hughes (engineer/ upper-local turret), and Fletcher (co-pilot). Lower row left are: Combs (navigator), Swisher (bombardier), McIntyre (Armorer/waist gunner), and Mitchel (pilot).

Roderick, the first of my three sons, was born in May just 87 days after my discharge from the Army. Louree and I were twenty-one years old, so we were a young family. Roderick, a healthy bouncing boy, was the first child born on either side of the families in a long time; consequently, he, Louree and I received lots of attention from both sides.

We lived with Pat and Vida, Louree's parents, for the first five months after my discharge from the Army since there were no rentals available. No residential building had gone on during the four war years as materials and labor went toward the war effort. Lots of people migrated to California during the war to work and servicemen and women stationed there returned or stayed because California had a lot to offer in the way of climate and job opportunity, thus causing an extreme housing shortage.

I worked at four different jobs while waiting to start college at the University of Washington in September. No one had a need for an Army-trained Armament Specialist or Aerial Gunner, so I dug ditches on construction jobs as a laborer and various other menial jobs to supply income while we waited for the birth of our son and the start of school. The menial jobs made me more determined then ever to go to college and get an interesting and challenging career. Finally during this transition period, I trained and worked for the Union Oil Company of California as a service station attendant.

Returning to the Northwest

The long awaited day arrived and we traveled to Bremerton from Fullerton in our newly acquired 1936 Ford coupe with all our worldly possessions in the trunk. Rod slept on the shelf below the rear window, and probably was the only one really comfortable.

We didn't spend money for a motel, but slept sitting in the car. It was probably a good thing we conserved what money we had as the two-hundred dollar check from my last employer, the Union Oil Company, which was to be there when we arrived, hadn't arrived, and it was our grubstake.

* * *

We lived a month, rent free, in a one bedroom apartment in my Aunt Hilda's daylight basement in the neighboring city of Bremerton. I had hoped to get a part or full time job there while I looked for housing in Seattle, enrolled in school, and looked for a part-time job in Seattle for the upcoming school year. Nothing worked: there were no jobs available in Bremerton due to the large lay-off after the war, the much needed check hadn't arrived, and there was no housing in Seattle for us although there were jobs.

Each day we drove across town to my Aunt Hesper's house anticipating the arrival of the overdue check; each day we were disappointed. We lived on very little during that month and considered selling the car, but determined it was necessary as a means to get to school, or a part-time job, or a means of escape out of our dilemma by returning to California. Each day brought us closer to that option.

After a month of trying to make things work, we grew totally discouraged and were out of money. We borrowed twenty-five dollars from yet another aunt and uncle to drive back to Fullerton, California. This was home for Louree and after five months living there, it began to feel like home for me.

Returning to Southern California for College

Upon our return, in four short months time, we were was able to get settled in an apartment, enroll in the local Junior College and get a full-time job that would become part-time when school started. And... I collected my two hundred dollar paycheck that was lying on an "inept" clerk's desk at the Union Oil Company's Los Angeles office.

Regarding our move to Washington to attend the University of Washington, we decided some things just weren't meant to be.

* * *

Fullerton Junior College, the oldest Junior College in the United States, was a beautiful and well-established school. The term *Junior College* preceded the now-used term *Community College*. The course I chose, Architectural Technology, was a two-year completion course and would result in an Associate of Arts degree and a certificate enabling one to be an Architectural Draftsman or a Building Inspector for a municipality.

I had lowered my sights regarding my career with the idea I'd try this for a year and then decide if I wanted to continue for the second year and completion of the course or go on to a four year school and earn a Bachelor of Arts degree. I had four years of training coming under the

G.I. bill, which provided tuition, books, and half the subsistence needed to live on. Therefore, a part-time job for me was necessary, as Louree was a full-time mother and homemaker, which is the way I wanted it.

Getting into the role of student wasn't an easy transition for me. I had a part-time job at the local Ford agency in their body repair and paint shop. Being a full-time student, and a full-time husband, and father, what I really needed was four more hours in the day.

* * *

I told Louree, "I enjoy my Architectural Technology course and the instructor, although it requires half of my school day. The other half is totally different consisting of English, Typing, and Art Appreciation."

"It really helps financially, your drawing plans in the drafting course that you're selling," Louree replied.

"Yes, isn't it great! By word-of-mouth people have learned what I'm doing, and they come to me to draw plans for a house they want to build, and so many want to build due to the housing shortage. They're looking for someone to draw their ideas, but can't afford an architect."

"Maybe you'll be able to quit your part-time job and we'd see more of you."

"Right now I need it, but my instructor is pleased with my ingenuity of selling my schoolwork; so he pays special attention to everything I draw. This assures my clients, and me, every plan will pass a city's building code requirements; it's a great win-win situation."

When my part-time employer decided they had to have a full-time employee, like I used to be… they fired me. At first it was a shock to my ego, but I soon realized it was to my benefit. There, I made one dollar an hour, but my drafting soon produced six dollars an hour. Now, I had some free time for my family and myself, and I was doing something, architectural drawing, which I really enjoyed.

One day at the breakfast table I said, "In June the school year comes to an end, but I think I should continue on through the summer so my G.I. bill stipend will continue."

"That sounds like a good idea. I'm pleased you like school and I don't mind skrimping by financially while you pursue your dream."

"I'm pleased you feel that way, Louree; it makes all the difference. Some of my friends are quitting school because their wives want more money, now!"

"We'll just look to the future when you have your degree."

"Going to summer school would give me the opportunity to take several difficult courses with more time to devote to them. One course I want to take is an advanced math course and the other a college level English course with Dr. Borst. He's like a mentor to me and he's caused me to like a subject I shied away from in high school."

Changing My Major

Taking and passing these two courses proved to me I was capable of succeeding at a four-year college. I needed this reassurance because I hadn't been a good student my last two years of high school. The reason was obvious. I left home at age sixteen, therefore needed to work part-time, and was a typical sixteen-year-old with little supervision and a new world to explore. Previously, I had been an above average student.

Even though Louree encouraged me to go on to a four-year college program, we weren't ready to give up our apartment and drafting income after our bad experience in Washington State. Deciding to stay put and continue on at Fullerton Junior College, I would take only college transferable credits as the school offered both types of courses.

When I started looking at four-year colleges in the general area of southern California I soon discovered I wouldn't have enough G.I. Bill time to get a degree in Architecture. It required five years of training and I had started with only four years of G.I. Bill entitlement. The last thing I wanted to do was end up short of my goal, which was a full-time job, doing what I wanted to do, with a living wage, and opportunity for advancement. Four-fifths of a degree wouldn't do it.

* * *

Before I gave up on my first choice I made an appointment with a leading Architect in Los Angeles. Barry Royal graciously gave me a half-hour of his time and I brought samples of my work with me. He looked at it carefully and said, "You have the ability to be an Architect, Harry, but do you have a working wife?"

That question took me totally by surprise. "No, we have a one year-old boy, so she's a full-time mother by our choice."

"If my wife hadn't mostly supported us for ten years, I wouldn't have made it."

I felt like a balloon that had just been punctured. "I guess that answers my question about continuing in this line of work." I thanked him for his time and his honesty and left his office knowing I had made a major decision.

I started looking around for a different major, one I could complete in the time I had left on my G.I.Bill entitlement. I'd always been interested in all types of sports: playing most of them; and the broad field of physical education. I could acquire the degree I needed to teach and coach at the junior high school level in the next three and a half years as I had one-half year of transferable credit right now.

An additional year was needed in order to be teaching at the high school level, which would be my first choice, but I could start at the junior high level and advance later with more training which I could acquire on my own. The important thing was to have a satisfactorily paying job to support my family and a job I enjoyed doing.

I came to realize attaining a Bachelor's Degree was the challenge I needed to make up for my "washing out" as a Cadet, ending my dream of being a pilot and an officer in the Army Air Corp. I was really motivated to succeed in college, and with my new major, Physical Education Teacher and Coaching, I started looking for a school as close to Fullerton as possible that had the training I was looking for.

Fortunately, such a school existed just eleven miles away in Whittier, California. Whittier College was a prestigious school with high entrance requirements, which I could now meet with my Junior College grades. That wouldn't have been possible if I had only my high school grades to offer. This meant we didn't have to move from our present home, as we were comfortable in our city-owned apartment reserved for low-income veterans.

We had signed up for a unit soon after reading in the local paper what the city was planning to do. Because we never took our name off the list when we moved to Washington State, we were one of the first to move in after our return to Fullerton. Things were definitely looking up.

Forty prefab apartments were moved in by rail from fifteen hundred miles away. They had been built as temporary war-time housing near a government Navy Yard and were no longer needed there due to the war's end. They were all identical one-bedroom units in four clusters of ten units each. We were the only student couple there, but all were young families who had a lot in common with us.

* * *

Roderick was a year old and had neighbor kids on each side of us to play with and help him learn to be a boy. Also, his grandparents and two aunts, Joyce and Patti, devoted a lot of time and attention to him. Louree often took him, first in his buggy and then in his stroller, the short distance to town to socialize with her friends and show him off.

School started in September and it was good to have a campus full of students and all the student activities we shared. Now that I had a new major to pursue, I spent more time watching the athletic program. I didn't have time to turn out for sports, but learning the game was important. I had played football and basketball in high school and understood the games. I made it a point to watch the track meets and made friends with several athletes.

My course work consisted of subjects such as English, History, Economics, Physical Education, and Theory of Teaching. I maintained a B average and continued to draw house plans at home. I knew enough about building codes now and always had a codebook at my elbow for reference.

I was asked to draw plans for a small motel by the parents of one of my school friends, which required some research on my part. My former Architectural Drafting teacher, Mr. Gallagher, was always willing to answer questions, although he didn't review my work now. I missed being in his class, but I had set my sights higher and he understood.

The school year went smoothly and Louree and I were able to attend the school's night football and basketball games since her parents were always willing to take care of the 'apple of their eye'. We also attended several school dances and an occasional movie, so life wasn't all work and no play.

As the school year came to an end, I looked forward to graduating with an Associate of Arts degree and admission to Whittier College, but at the sophomore level, as none of my Architectural Technology credits were college transferable. I knew this from the start, so I was prepared for the setback. I needed two and one-half years to finish my work at Whittier to obtain a Bachelor of Arts degree and I still had two and one-half years of G.I. entitlement so I was on target.

On to a Four Year College

That summer I didn't go to summer school so I looked for a job that would be a change from all that I had been doing and still bring in some money to supplement my occasional architectural drafting jobs. I found such a job one day when Louree and I were at the beach at Corona Del Mar. Parking was at a premium as it was mostly along a road that circled the half dozen businesses serving the beach crowd.

Corona Del Mar beach was not large as it was bordered to the north by a jetty and on the south by a run-out of rocks. The distance between was probably five hundred yards, but was excellent for body surfing and swimming with the waves coming straight in. Because it was popular, but small, this created the need for a commercial parking lot. One such potential site existed.

It was the only filled in lot that hadn't been built on, but had been covered with hardpan to accommodate a building; everything else was sand. On the weekends when the beach was crowded, cars had parked there haphazardly. Upon seeing the potential for a commercial parking lot, I inquired and discovered the owner had a small restaurant next door to the lot.

I approached him with my plan for a parking lot and we ended up with an agreement where I would run it on weekends, which was the only time there was the need for additional parking, and we would split the proceeds fifty-fifty. I now had a place to go every weekend, resulting in an additional source of income.

Louree chose not to go with me, as it would be too long a day for her and our two-year old son, Roderick. Also, she was pregnant with our second son to be born in the following March. I took two neighborhood teenage boys, Ronny and Donny Packard for company and when the lot was full they would watch it while I took a swim. They had two swims a day and I had one. I had an excellent tan when I started Whittier College in September.

* * *

Whittier College was a relatively small college with a population of two thousand students. It had an excellent reputation with a focus on Teaching, Social Work, Pre-Med and the Ministry. The college was founded and governed by the Quaker Church and one felt the church influence everywhere. There was no smoking on campus and everyone was required to attend a lecture each week dedicated to enhancing our spiritual values. At that time in my life, I was one of the smokers who lined the sidewalks surrounding the campus.

I took several courses in my new major, teaching and coaching, plus general requirements for the Bachelor of Arts degree such as history, Spanish, and Psychology. It was a demanding course load, but I also had to have a part-time job in order to support my family.

Being a Physical Education major, I was made aware of a job to work in the basket room in the gymnasium. I applied for and was awarded not only the job as listed, but being in charge of the basket room with three students working for me. The pay wasn't very good, but it was enough to meet our budget along with the subsistence paid me under the G.I.Bill.

In that position I got to know the various coaches and many of the players. It was a pleasant job, but I didn't have it long. I was in the coaches shared office one day when they were talking about a job opening for a part-time Physical Education teacher and a Wood Shop teacher at a local junior high school. It was only six weeks into the school year, but the present teacher had quit.

I spoke up and said, "I could do that."

The coach sharing the information asked, "How do you figure?"

"Well, I know drafting and I have construction skills through past experience. As for the Physical Education part of the job, I'm learning that now and I am a natural athlete."

"If you're really interested, I'll put you in touch with the Principal. He's a friend of mine; he was a star athlete here in basketball a few years ago."

"I am interested, if it can be worked out."

Teaching Half-Day on Emergency Credential

I interviewed for the position and convinced the Principal I could do the job. He said. "I'm offering you the position at six dollars an hour and I'll petition the State Department of Education for an emergency teacher's credential for you. Do you want the job?"

"Yes."

"Good! In the interim I'll hire you as a substitute teacher. How soon can you start?"

"I'll need a couple of days to arrange my schedule at school and find someone to take my job as the basket room manager."

"I'll tell the substitute teacher on the job now he has two more days. If anything changes, let me know. Otherwise, I'll expect to introduce you to your new class on Thursday at one o'clock."

I walked out of his office feeling like I was on 'cloud nine.' I found out later the students had literally run the teacher I was replacing off the school grounds. This would be a challenge.

The two classes I taught were in the afternoon, so I could drop one course in Physical Education and take my four remaining courses in the morning. The Principal convinced the State he couldn't find a certified teacher to do the job, so I was awarded an Emergency Teacher's Credential.

Now came the hard part. I was introduced to my students, forty, seventh and eighth grade boys. They were nice enough appearing kids ranging in age from twelve to fifteen. I was to be their Woodshop and P.E. teacher. Each class was fifty minutes long with a five-minute break in between.

The shop was fairly well equipped for bench work and drafting. The P.E. class had no gymnasium, but southern California had a moderate climate, so the class met outside most of the time. It didn't take long to determine who the leaders were and what to look out for. I told them what my expectations were, and what to expect if my expectations weren't met. They were impressed that I had been a sergeant in the Army, and I had a paddle.

The Principal instructed me to use a heavy hand as half of the boys were from the wrong side of the track and he would back me up. I did, and we had only one incident that I needed to share with the Principal. A smaller, but loudmouth kid bumped my arm when I was using the table saw one day, which is a safety violation of the first magnitude. I had a piece of board in each hand having just finishing cutting in half a piece of one by two, three feet long. Without thinking, only reacting, I reached out and brought the piece in my right hand down on his head. He ran out of the shop crying and saying, "My Dad will take care of you."

I shared this information with the Principal as soon as I could, and his reaction surprised me. He said, "Don't worry about it, that kid is always in trouble. His folks are fruit pickers and won't be up here complaining; they know their son.

My son, Jim, was born on March 3rd. and Louree really had her hands full now. It was a caesarean delivery and made it easier for mother and child, but created a large doctor bill to pay on and add to our monthly expanses. My teaching job made continuing in college possible.

As the school year progressed it became apparent the best athletes were also the leaders in the class. After shop class, I led my class in calisthenics each day and then team sports. It helped that I was stronger and faster than any of them, which they recognized and respected. But why wouldn't I be... I was driving back to the college each afternoon to run on the college's cross-country track team. I had decided I needed to be a letterman in at least one sport for my teacher resume.

The best athlete in the class and most prominent leader was a fifteen year old named Richard Rainier. He had an athletic build, excelled in all sports, and stood a little taller than I, as several of the boys did. I made it a point to get to know him on a personal level and discovered to my surprise he started each day by reading the morning newspaper from cover to cover. The typical fifteen-year-old doesn't do that.

He spoke like an adult and I discovered he lived only with his father. One day I asked him what he planned to do when he finished his education. He said, "I want to do what my father does."

"What's that?" I asked.

"I want to be a bartender."

I told him I thought he had the potential to get an athletic scholarship and get a college degree. He showed no sign of interest in that kind of thinking, so I dropped the subject. He evidently had already made up his mind.

The school year went fast and I learned as much as my students'... maybe more. The most important thing I learned was I didn't want to be a P.E. Teacher and Coach. I could see it was mostly about discipline, and I didn't want to spend my working time doing that. I shared this discovery with Louree and we had a decision to make.

She asked about the shop teacher role and I told her I could see myself doing that. It would mean changing my major again and finding a college that offered the course work, as Whittier College didn't offer that kind of training.

When the school year came to a close, my part-time teaching position had evolved into a full-time job. The principal took me aside one day and said, "I have to look for a certified teacher for the job and you're not going to have that certification for at least another year, so I can't offer you the position."

I smiled and said, "I understand, but I wouldn't accept the offer if you had made it."

"It hasn't been easy, has it?"

"No, there's nothing easy about that group."

"I appreciate your success in fulfilling the job for the school year."

"I've decided I don't want to pursue P.E. or Coaching. I like to play games and I understand and appreciate physical conditioning, but I don't particularly like to teach it."

"What are you going to do?"

"I'm looking into teaching shop, but I'd have to change schools."

"I think you'd make a good shop teacher."

"It's something my wife and I are discussing right now."

I excused myself and drove home, having finished the school year, both at the Junior High School and at the College. I wasn't going to summer school, so I needed to look for a summer job and a new school to pursue my new goal… shop teacher.

Changing Majors Again

After some research I found the best program was at a college in San Jose, California. Louree, the two boys and I drove to Avenal, California where Louree had a childhood girlfriend, Bobby, whom I met at our wedding. Bobby had married and encouraged us to visit. Avenal was on the way to San Jose, so I thought this would be a good time for me to drive on from there and spend a day visiting my potential new school and check out the housing and part-time work situation.

Avenal was two hundred miles north of Fullerton and San Jose was one hundred and fifty miles farther on. Louree enjoyed the visiting time with her friend and I did some important research. This was an important step for us to give up our apartment in Fullerton and to change schools and major course of study.

The school and program met my expectations, so I then checked out the housing and part-time work. That was discouraging. There was no available school housing and rentals were a premium as in southern California. Part-time gas station work was available so housing was the problem to be solved.

In the housing department at the school I noticed an advertisement for a caretaker for a forty-acre non-working ranch used by the owners as a weekend getaway. The work requirements were simple and the remuneration was a separate two-bedroom house available, rent-free. It was located at Morgan Hill, a small town thirty miles south of San Jose and on my way back to Avenal. It was worth looking in to.

After a phone call, I met the lady of the house at the ranch and she showed me around. The separate house was actually part of a barn like structure, but it was adequate. The ranch was mostly pasture with no animals. There was a small fruit orchard, a chicken house and pen with a dozen chickens for eggs and a large a two-story farmhouse the owners used on weekends.

The work called for taking care of the chickens, help harvest the few fruit trees, and oversee the property to prevent vandalism, etc. I could have the job if I wanted it, but they wanted someone now. Knowing there were gas station jobs available, I was tempted, so I called Louree. She told me to use my own judgment, so I did and said, "Yes." I told her it would take me a week or two to make the move and she agreed to that.

I returned to Avenal and shared my new information. They thought I had accomplished a lot in one day. I hoped they were the right moves… time would tell.

In two weeks time we had the use of a pickup truck belonging to one of Louree's uncles, sold some of our furniture, and were packed and on our way to Morgan Hill. It was the middle of June, so we would move in, I would get a full time gas station job until September and I had been accepted as a student at San Jose State College majoring in Industrial Arts. I had a year and a half of G.I. Bill entitlement left and that's what I needed to graduate and have my major fulfilled.

Moving to Central California

Louree's parents drove the pickup truck with our worldly belongings in the back while we led the way in our '37 Ford sedan with Louree and me, our two sons, and my 14-year- old sister, Sylvia. Mother had recently married and asked if Sylvia could live with us for a while to give her and her new husband some time alone and to get their lives together.

I hadn't lived with my sister for ten years, but she was more adult than most fourteen years olds, and she was good company and helpful to Louree with our two young sons. She joined us just before we moved, so all of us were experiencing change in our lives. I felt better about moving Louree to a ranch out of town with Sylvia there because I'd be gone all day working somewhere.

It was an all day trip to Morgan Hill with one flat tire en route. I put the gas on my credit card for both vehicles plus the new tire for the truck, so I'd have a bill to pay and money was scarce. I found a job in a gas station, but not in San Jose, or Morgan Hill; it was in Gilroy located ten miles beyond Morgan Hill, which made it forty-two miles from San Jose. That meant a lot of driving when school started.

The weather was warm, as it was summer in central California. We soon adjusted to it and enjoyed the weather. Each day I gathered eggs from the hen house and saved some for the owners. As the fruit ripened, I would help the lady of the manor pick fruit and take several flats to the buyer in town.

Roderick and I would tramp over the forty acres looking for rabbits to shoot when time allowed. I had traded our couch and chair in Fullerton for a high powered twenty-two rifle with a telescopic sight. This was to expedite the move that was going to be in a pickup truck with limited space. I had never owned a gun before even though I was an expert with a fifty-caliber machine gun. There is a world of difference between the two guns, so the rabbits were relatively safe.

I worked ten hours per day, six days a week at the gas station, so with the one hour per day commute, I was gone from seven-thirty to six-thirty each day. Louree didn't complain, but what was there to be happy about. Her only social contact was a fourteen-year-old girl, and I at the beginning and end of each day.

As the summer wore on and the beginning of school grew closer, we could see the handwriting on the wall. If this were a lonely, unsatisfactory life for her now, it would be more so when school started. Once again, we had a decision to make. Because I hadn't burned my bridges behind me and checked out of Whittier College, I was still enrolled and could continue there, but with yet a different major.

We studied all the options and I decided I wanted to teach, but the only option that accommodated the entitlement time I had on the G.I. Bill was to get an Elementary teacher's certificate and my Bachelor of Arts degree. This enabled me to teach from grade one to eight. I could envision myself as an elementary school teacher, so that's the choice we made.

Returning to Southern California

I had been saving during the summer so we had enough for the move and a new beginning around Whittier. I rented a one-way haul trailer and the five of us headed south. We arrived at Fullerton and stayed the night with Louree's parents. I found a rental, so we could unpack the trailer and have a place to put our things. Sylvia was still with us, but Mother and her new husband arrived one day after we left Morgan Hill and had to journey an additional three hundred and fifty miles south to catch up with us and take Sylvia home with them to Washington State.

San Jose turned out to be a repeat of the attempted move to Seattle, but on our return to southern California things began to break for us as it had after our return from Washington State three years previous. I signed up for college housing a year earlier when I first started attending Whittier College and now our number came up. We were overjoyed and made a quick move into school housing. They had twenty Quonset huts, which were two bedroom duplexes. They were small, but efficient and the rent price was right. Actually, it was fun living among only college students who were married veterans with children.

I obtained a part-time service station job and school started in a matter of days after our return to southern California. We had everything we needed except a couch, chair, and breakfast set, which we soon replaced.

We were now expecting our third child thirteen months after the birth of our second son. Louree really had her hands full, but I learned all you need to know about washing clothes and changing diapers.

School was demanding, but I was able to do my homework during my evening job at the gas station. My time with the family was mostly during the day when I wasn't in class. I worked Saturdays, Sundays, and holidays in addition to the evening hours, so I went a year and a half without a day off. However, I was making my grades and staying buoyant financially.

Our third son, Tom, was born in April and Louree had all three home with her. However, a good climate provided for lots of time for our children to play outdoors with the neighbor kids. We bought a washing machine and had the drying lines full of diapers located next to our Quonset. On Saturday and Sunday evenings I was home after working the day shift at the gas station. This was special for me, and I would drag out my ukulele and sing my three sons to sleep on those nights.

* * *

I could no longer participate in track because of my work schedule, but I had earned my letter and it wasn't important on a resume anymore as I had changed my major to elementary teaching. The school year went smoothly, and I was maintaining my B grade average. I had a mentor in my Psychology professor, Dr. Baldwin. He took an interest in my life's journey and was my faculty advisor. After all, he hadn't had a student at my age with three children before. He became like a second father to me and was much appreciated. Seeing a problem coming up for the next school year, he alerted me to it.

If all went well, I would graduate in the middle of the next year at the same time I exhausted my G.I. entitlement. However I would have to petition the Dean of Education to take four credits above the maximum to have that happen. He knew from past experience the

Dean would probably grant my petition if I gave up my part-time job. That got my attention, as I needed that money.

Louree and I pondered this and I suggested curb-stoning cars. This meant buying and selling cars from your house, usually using the newspaper for advertising. The idea was to buy a used car at a good price, clean it up by detailing it, and selling it within two weeks so you wouldn't have to change the title or pay tax. I'd had some experience in this when I worked for the Ford Motor Company as my first job when I started college three years prior.

The school year came to a close and I was now within a half year of my graduation goal. I was still working at the gas station and went full-time on the day shift. The station was located at a very busy crossroads on Whittier Boulevard, so I decided to try curb-stoning a car or two that summer and started with my own '37 Ford Sedan. I parked it on the parking strip and sold it within several days.

I had another car in mind and made a purchase of a Mercury Club coupe. This was definitely a young man's car, and I liked it so well I kept it. Evidently, I was still a young man at heart; I had now reached my twenty-fifth birthday. However, I could see the feasibility of this way to earn money for the last half-year of college and still satisfy the Dean. With an active used-car market and my car detailing and selling skill, I could make it work.

* * *

When I registered for school, my advisor, Dr. Baldwin, was right on target. I quit my service station job and lived off of savings until my G.I.Bill check came for the first month of school. I bought and sold cars at a pace of about one a month; if I sold more often I would need a business license. It was legal to sell five cars per year in California at that time without a license, and I had four and a half months to cover financially. My goal was to make one hundred and fifty dollars on each transaction.

Student Teaching

This school year was different; I spent half of the school day 'student teaching'. That meant I was assigned to a teacher in a surrounding area school and started out as an observer, than worked slowly into teaching the class under close supervision for a few days at the end of the quarter.

Each of the two quarters remaining in my senior year would find me in a different school with a different teacher, at a different grade level. My first assignment was at the fifth and sixth grade level, as this was a combination class of forty-five students. I think the teacher was really looking for team teaching as she was overloaded with students and at two grade levels. California schools were bursting at the seams in those days with the big influx of people after the war.

Fortunately, and perhaps not by accident as I had nearly a year of teaching at the junior high level, it really did become a team-teaching situation. However, I learned a lot from a skillful teacher. I was pleasantly surprised how much I enjoyed teaching the students and felt I had made a good choice with my major change.

The second quarter found me in an eighth-grade class with a normal sized class of thirty and an excellent teacher for me to emulate. Here again, I enjoyed the students and the process of teaching. When I compared these students with my previous shop and P.E. students, I realized that had been an unusual class, not the norm… thank goodness!

I was taking care of my afternoon classes and enjoyed the extra time I could spend in the library studying. Home, with three young children in half a Quonset hut, was not conducive to studying. We had the money needed to make ends meet and the end of the school year was close, so I started looking for a teaching job.

I answered to a sixth grade position advertised in Anaheim, California, which was only four miles from Fullerton, our hometown. I had an interview and was offered the job, if I could start right away. They wanted me to start January fourth, immediately after Christmas vacation and my college courses continued on for an additional three weeks. I asked them to let me talk to my college advisor and determine if something could be worked out; they agreed.

My advisor and I explained this to my instructors and they agreed to allow me to miss class as long as I took the final tests on the third Saturday proctored by Dr. Baldwin. I started teaching on January fourth, and I finished college, officially, three weeks later. I was very busy during those three weeks: teaching a new class of wonderful kids; keeping up on the reading assignments of my classes, and preparing for the final tests.

I passed my tests and Louree and I both breathed a deep sigh of relief.

Graduation and My First Teaching Job

My first class was a well-behaved group of sixth graders who had an excellent man teacher I was replacing in the middle of the school year. He was leaving because of a promotion to a principal's position in a new school in Anaheim. I felt challenged to fill his shoes, as he was not only a skilled teacher, but the students loved and respected him. He came the first day and introduced me to the class and then said goodbye.

In a matter of a few weeks, for all intents and purposes, the class was my class. Because I was young and full of energy, I soon felt a strong relationship growing with each student. My previous teaching experience and my two practice-teaching assignments my senior year gave me a big step-up in the process of becoming a teacher.

The class was made up of twenty-one girls and fifteen boys, that made it an average class, number wise. One third of the class was Spanish or Mexican heritage, the balance was Caucasian. Students were not allowed to speak Spanish at school, so they mixed well. I never detected any racial problems.

No one is an instant good teacher; I made my share of mistakes, but I learned by doing and the other sixth grade teacher and the principal were a big help to me. Miss McDonald, the principal, never failed to seek me out a few days before payday and ask if a twenty-dollar bill would make the end of the month easier…it did.

At first I actually made less money as a beginning teacher than I did as a student on the G.I.Bill and working part-time, and this was dividing my yearly salary by less days, meaning there would be no summer pay for me. I would need a summer job, for sure. In fact, I needed a summer job for my first eleven years of teaching, but I'm getting ahead of the story.

When you are a journeyman teacher, if I can use that term, you make a good wage, but it takes ten years to get there; it's a system that needs modifying. In addition to being a bulwark against starvation for the McIntyres, the principal determined I would have no extra duties, like lunchroom or playground supervision. I appreciated this and had her permission to leave the campus during the one-hour lunch period. I later determined this was to accommodate the rest of the staff to give them free run of the faculty lounge. They were all woman who liked to take off their shoes during lunch hour, put on their slippers, and let their hair down, so to speak… and it worked for me.

I drove to a walnut grove area about a mile from school and ate my sack lunch in my car enjoying the solitude the area provided, as thirty-six kids even if they are well behaved, take a lot of energy. I had no idea that particular walnut grove was to be the future location of Disneyland.

Each day began with the salute to the flag followed by two songs. We had songbooks and I would let the boys choose one song and the girls another. I soon learned I had to be selective or the boys would choose the Marine's Hymn every day. *Oh, the way boys choose to show their masculinity.*

Two specialists visited and taught the class in vocal music and art every other week, which I enjoyed as much as the students. Both specialists were woman and they took great effort to get me into the middle of the presentation, sometimes to my embarrassment. For example: in art I would be draped with an oversized man's white shirt, put on backwards simulating a painter's smock. Then directed to lead the students in applying watercolors to paint a picture under the direction of the specialist.

* * *

One morning before school Miss McDonald came to my classroom as I sat preparing for the day. She smiled and said, "Harry, I have a favor to ask."

"What possible favor can I do for you?" I disbelievingly replied.

"I have a new sixth grade student coming today and although it's Mrs. Brown's turn to receive the new student, I want him to be with you?"

"I don't understand." I was instantly flattered, but bewildered.

"He's a bigger, older, Mexican boy who has just been kicked out of the parochial school. That spells trouble and at the least calls for a man teacher. The sisters have given up on him."

I felt flattered by her request and not being inclined to run away from trouble, replied, "Of course I'll take him, what's his name?"

"Lupe Guadalupe."

"Wow!" I sat back in my chair and smiled, "That's a name for you." Then dealing with the reality of the situation, said, "I'll need to have the janitor bring in a large desk and put it at the back of the room."

"Thanks Harry, I'll bring him in after he arrives and the janitor has brought in a desk."

* * *

Fifteen minutes after class began Miss McDonald came to the door and motioned me out to the hallway. I left the room and, behold, there was Lupe Guadalupe... not the typical sixth grader. He was tall for his age and well built, an honest, open face and one that someday would be handsome. We shook hands and I could tell he liked my man-to-man approach. Miss McDonald excused herself with a knowing smile, and I led Lupe in to the classroom.

Interrupting their studies, I said, "Class, this is Lupe, Guadalupe a new student." I could tell by expressions some of the students knew him. Several of the taller, more mature girls exchanged knowing and appreciative glances. Lupe said nothing and acknowledged no one. I led him to his desk, which had a stack of textbooks on the desktop. He sat down and it fit, thank goodness. I then went to the front of the room to start our English lesson for the day.

At recess I called him to my desk, and we talked briefly. I said, "Lupe, I know you had problems at your last school, and we don't want that to happen here. I will never put you in a situation embarrassing to you, and in return I will expect the same amount of effort and conduct from you as I do any of my students. In the future, if we need to talk about anything, let me know. Does that sound fair?"

"Yes, Mr. McIntyre."

"Then I'm happy to have you as a student, Lupe. Now go enjoy your recess."

He walked out of the room with an aura of light heartedness about him and a spring to his step.

I soon learned he had an artistic talent and I exploited it at every chance. Lupe and I did many of my weekly bulletin board changes together. He reached his zenith when I asked him to do the office bulletin board when our turn came up. In the four months I had Lupe as a student I never had one negative incident with him. At the end of the school year he collected money from the other students to buy me an end-of-the-year present. It was an attractive sport shirt that I proudly wore for the class picture and the last day of school.

Teaching at Newport Beach

I knew I wouldn't be coming back to this school in the fall because I had applied for and was awarded a better paying position in Newport Beach, California, teaching seventh and eighth grade math at Horace Ensign Junior High School. It would mean a move before school started and after I finished with my summer job, which was back at The Union Oil Company as a service station attendant.

Louree and I started looking for a rental in nearby Costa Mesa where the rents were less expensive. We answered an advertisement that sounded interesting. It was a two-bedroom farmhouse within three miles of the school. It seemed right for us and we moved in just before school started. Roderick would be starting school this year and a bus came nearly to the door. The house sat on the northeast corner of forty acres of black-eyed peas with a large barn fifty yards away from the house and several out buildings including a garage.

Only the house and garage were for rent, which was all we were looking for, as I was no farmer. The barn contained privately owned riding horses, which were boarded there and a corral for them. An acre of tomatoes separated us from the barn and corral. Consequently, we had all the tomatoes and black-eyed peas we could eat.

The father of the landowners, known as Mr. Tommy, had a pony ring he took to a mall on weekends for kids to ride. He kept his ponies there at the farm and Roderick and Jim loved to watch them and occasionally get a ride from their owner. Mr Tommy said he loved to watch Jim come to the corral each day. If he fell down catching his toe as he ran through the downhill tomato patch, he bounced up without a whimper or a scratch, as he was a sturdy boy.

The locals sought after these tomatoes for their high acid content. When the tomatoes came to a certain stage of their development, Mr. Tommy stopped watering them, causing the acid content to become very high with the help of the hot August and September sun. This made them desirable for making catsup; the locals came and bought them on a "U-pick" system.

It was an interesting place to live for the five of us, but after two months, when the weather turned cold, we moved. The single wall construction of the house and the fact it stood on short posts and pier blocks three feet off the ground for ventilation, made it difficult to heat in the winter. With two young children crawling around on the floor, it was an unhealthy situation and Tom and Jim had continual colds. We found another house that filled our needs closer to school and also close to Roderick's school.

* * *

I reported to my new school several days early and met the staff including the principal, who had been one of the two men interviewing me for the job. The other interviewer was the superintendent of schools, Horace Ensign. The principal was a younger man, in contrast to Mr. Ensign who was one year from retiring. In the interviewing process, they each asked me questions. One in particular was they wanted to know what my philosophy of grading was. I replied, "I believe each student needs to be judged on their own merits and I don't use grades as a threat." I then asked a question of my own, "What is your philosophy of grading?"

The principal told me later, "It was at that moment you had the job, if you wanted it." I was surprised by this shared information. I did want the job and was assigned to four math classes and one hour of lunchroom duty each day. Therefore, I had a free period instead of a fifth math class in which to eat my lunch; everyone else had returned to class. I, obviously, was the new kid on the block to get this unpopular lunchroom assignment. However, I liked it and used it as an opportunity to talk to the students informally.

Because of the mild climate and the fact I was alone, I took my sack lunch across the street to sit on a bluff giving me a view of the city of Newport Beach, Balboa Island, and an unlimited view of the Pacific Ocean. On a clear day I could see forever, or was that Santa Catalina Island. The view made a good lunch partner.

I had two eighth grade and two seventh grade classes of general math and it took awhile to readjust to junior high students after my well-behaved sixth graders. I was tested by that element in a class that wanted to run things. I walked a line between stern and friendly, resulting in a good learning environment.

I had a couple of natural stand-up comedians in one class and I gave them the the other students the last fifteen minutes of Friday's class to tell jokes, if we'd had a good week. They along with others lived for those fifteen-minute joke periods. I didn't sensor the jokes ahead of time, which would kill the spontaneity, and only regretted my procedure a couple of times. Surprisingly, their peers censored them on the spot.

The make up of the student body was unusual; they were in two groups: the "haves" and the "have-nots." The original town of Newport Beach was built on a sand spit of land a mile long. The houses were small; beach-type homes occupied by the working class, mainly commercial fishermen and their families. The new part of town was the choice beach property and the high bluff property overlooking everything. That's where the wealthy lived, including a lot of "Hollywood" people, and Horace Ensign Junior High School was there on the bluff overlooking the town and the Pacific Ocean.

Subsequently, school clothes became and issue. The solution was a uniform adopted with the girls wearing dark skirts, white blouses, and dark cardigan sweaters four days a week with Wednesday a free choice day. There was no need for a uniform for the boys, as they always wore the same thing. But they did have to wear shoes in addition to their usual denims and T-shirts. I had to remember, this was a beach town.

* * *

One day after school a fellow teacher, Dick Sweet, asked, "Have you done any sailing?"

I told him, "No, I had an outboard motor and fourteen foot open fishing boat as a boy, but no sailing."

"How'd you like to crew out on my brother's thirty six foot racing sloop? The boat requires a four-man crew, and he's short one man for this Sunday's race."

"Let me run this by Louree as it's my only day off since I'm working part-time on Friday evenings and all day Saturday for J.C. Penney in Santa Ana. She may need to go somewhere."

"Let me know by tomorrow, as I have to get a crew member to qualify for the race."

I went home that afternoon and told Louree of my invitation to sail.

"Do you want to do this?" she asked.

"Only if it doesn't keep you stuck at home all day; you need to get out too."

"If I drop you off at Dick's house and keep the car, I can take the boys to visit my parents in Fullerton; and we'd all have a good time."

"It sounds good to me. Call your parents so they'll be expecting you and I'll tell Dick I'm ready for a new adventure."

We boarded the boat about ten o'clock for a race starting in five-minute intervals at eleven o'clock. There would be nearly a hundred boats in the race and the course would do a horseshoe turn in the Balboa Bay turning basin and then out the jetted entrance to the ocean and north twenty-five miles to Long Beach for the end of the race. The crews would travel home by automobile and the boats would stay there for the week until the next race back.

The race was a disaster. Before the race the boom swung over and hit the skipper on the head causing a wound that needed stitches. He left the boat bound for the doctor and said he'd try to board us during the race on the way out the turning basin. He did this successfully by leaping off a dock as we swung out of the course line and he landing in the middle of the boat's cockpit.

We were in third place in our segment, and as we were leaving the harbor between the two jetties of riprap rock the size of jeeps, the strong wind blowing up the coast hit our sails full blast. Because we were winched down taut for speed, the top twelve feet of the mast snapped off drowning us in canvas and rigging. That was the end of the adventure for us. We limped back to port and called it a day.

At the end of the school's basketball season it was traditional to have a faculty-student basketball game. Because we were a staff with many young men including three coaches, I didn't expect to get much playing time. Basketball, unfortunately, had become a tall person's sport. My opportunity came in the middle of the second half of the game as I played a guard position bringing the ball down the court.

No one was free to receive the ball, so I continued on in to the basket, but was blocked from taking a regular lay-in shot. Instead, I continued on under the basket and out the other side, putting a one-hand, over my head behind me shot going away from the basket. It hit the backboard sharply and directly into the basket. An unbelievable shot, and when I left the game I was satisfied with my performance and with the appropriate applause and comments; I just had a moment to remember.

A Working Summer's Vacation

The school year came to an end and Louree and I decided to spend the summer in Bremerton to see if that is where we wanted to permanently live. It was my hometown and I always had a desire to return home to a simpler and slower-paced life. Being young, we threw caution to the wind and sub-let our house for three months, loaded up the sedan and headed north with no job and no place to stay.

We arrived at my aunt and uncle's house and discovered the two-bedroom house next door was for rent. It was furnished and within our price range, so we hurriedly closed the deal… so far so good. A conversation over a cup of coffee with a friend of my aunt's the next day led to the needed job. She'd heard the county assessor was hiring a temporary staff to re-evaluate the entire county for taxing purposes.

I called for an interview that afternoon and was surprised to learn the assessor was Harry Maston, the father of a friend of mine. Also, I knew Harry because I used to pick up my route newspapers daily in front of his business when I was eleven years old. I had the interview, and I was exactly what they were looking for. I knew construction, read and drew house plans, and had strong math skills.

I was hired on the spot and started the next day using my own car for transportation moving from one site to another. I was assigned mostly rural property to assess and had three wonderful months doing a job I enjoyed and getting re-acquainted with my former hometown, friends and relatives. The weather was ideal that summer and we decided to move to Washington.

I had a contract to fulfill in Newport Beach, so we returned to our rental home and my teaching job. As I think of that summer now, I'm sure my guardian angel was working overtime.

* * *

The school year progressed pretty much as the first year and I really enjoyed the faculty, students, and administration. It wasn't easy, thinking about leaving, but I'd never get over the desire to return to my hometown unless I did it this. The administration was satisfied with my work to the point they suggested I take a year leave of absence so there would be a job waiting for me if we decided to return.

I wrote to the Bremerton school district and asked for a job application, so I would be going to a job with them if they chose to hire me. Teachers were in short supply all over the United States; so they sent me a contract, without an interview, sight unseen. I was eligible to teach in a junior high school or an elementary school and they would put me where they needed me, in elementary school. That was fair enough; I was flexible.

At the end of the year the faculty gave me, and one other teacher who was retiring a going- away party. Louree and I rented a one-way U-haul trailer and headed north in June hoping to find a rental, a summer job, and settle in before school started.

Return to the Northwest

There was a two bedroom house across the street from my aunt and uncle's home, which was ideal for us. I found a job in a Union Oil gas station and the summer went by quickly. To my surprise I was assigned to teach a sixth grade class at Marion Avenue School; I expected a junior high school assignment. The school was within walking distance of our home, which meant Louree had a car at her disposal every day.

I figured I'd work there for a year and ask for a junior high school assignment the second year. That, of course, depended on our decision to stay in Washington instead of returning to Newport Beach. I had taken a twenty percent cut in pay to come to Bremerton, so it had one strike on it before I even started to teach there.

There were two sixth grades at the elementary school and when the students heard there was to be a man teacher, many of the students wanted to get assigned to the *man's* class. This caused some embarrassment for the elderly woman teacher of the other class. Ironically, she was one of the elementary teachers when I was in elementary school as a student.

I met my class of thirty-six students and they were a great bunch of kids. I met many of their parents at the first P.T.A. meeting and I had known several of them from the past.

The faculty was older than my last assignment, but the principal was a man who became one of my best friends.

One of the fifth grade teachers taught her students to square dance as part of her physical education program. One day she suggested we combine our classes and she would teach my class a round dance. My students were all for it, as some of them had been in her fifth grade class and missed not having dancing as part of their curriculum.

This was all new to me, but I accepted her offer. To make a long story short, it went so well, I learned round dances and square dancing and discovered I had a talent for calling square dances. Before long I was asked to take my class to another school and teach them some of the things we had learned to enable them to start their own program.

Some of the mothers got together and made colorful skirts for the girls with white blouses and western cut colorful shirts for the boys to go with their Levi pants. I'd never seen anything snowball like this. We were invited to perform at an adult square dance club; that's like bringing coals to Newcastle. I had to be careful it didn't overshadow what school was all about… the basic curriculum.

* * *

At the end of the school year when I intended to ask for a transfer to the junior high level, I enjoyed what I was doing, so I stayed put. We bought our first house just three blocks from the school and I enjoyed the walk. Rod and Jim attended Marion Avenue School and Tom would be following soon.

I stayed for three years and finally decided it was time to move on. I applied for the junior high school level and was hired as a teacher of English, Social Studies, and Reading, called a core teacher. This meant I had two different groups of students for three hours each day. It was a good curriculum, I was comfortable teaching these three subjects, and soon became active in after-school activities such as roller skating and social dancing.

A professional dance teacher from Bremerton came in to teach our students ballroom dancing and she used me as her partner. Several hundred students took part and after the students gained a level of dancing skills, we had after school dances regularly. My two core classes often sponsored these dances and we had a school jazz band for music.

The roller-skating meant busing several hundred students two miles to a roller rink. I had skated in rinks since I was a teenager, so this was enjoyable for me and I was an active chaperone. There was no formal instruction here, but most of the kids knew how to skate. The rink owner's daughter was one of my students, and she became my teacher showing me how to waltz on skates.

At the end of my fourth year as a core teacher, I was eligible for a sabbatical leave as I had been in the school district seven years. This meant I could step out of teaching for a school year at half salary and pursue more training. I applied for, and was accepted in, graduate school at Washington State University as a student to train to be a public school counselor. The school was located several hundred miles away on the other side of the State.

My three sons were devastated to think they would have to leave their school and friends for a year and move to a new city. Everything had been arranged for this to happen at the end of the school year when, unexpectedly, the assistance superintendent approached me after school one day. He needed a counselor for the next school year, and the job would be mine if I wanted it. However, I would be expected to get the training needed after-the-fact and pay for it on my own.

After discussing it with the family, I accepted his offer and declined my scholarship. It wasn't an easy decision to make, as I needed that training and the Master's Degree that went with it for further advancement. However, it made the family happy to stay put, and that meant a lot to me.

A New Job in Education

I began the school year as the boy's counselor at Coontz Junior High School, and it was an on-the-job learning experience. I had a successful first year and needed a summer job to earn money for more training. I had always wanted to try my hand at commercial fishing and with the summer off from school, this seemed the time to do it.

I saw a newspaper advertisement listing a 25-foot troller-style fishing boat for sale, fully equipped, and for a price I could afford… if I was creative. I made an appointment to look at the boat located in the town of Winslow, Washington, which is on Bainbridge Island fifteen miles north. On questioning the owner, Jack Watkins who was deputy sheriff on the island, he said he would consider a time payment, of limited sorts.

We met at the Eagle Harbor Marina in Winslow and walked out on the dock to the boat's slip. I was immediately impressed with the boat. It was a double-ended, converted, navy hull and looked to be in good condition. It had a stand-up, open-in-the-back, hurricane bridge, which I liked. The cabin, forward and lower, consisted inside of an enclosed head, plus two stacked bunks on the port side and a closet, oil cook stove, and cupboards with counter space on the starboard side. The bottom bunk doubled as a place to sit while one ate. All in all, it was cozy, complete, and nautical.

The hurricane bridge area contained a wooden and brass mariners wheel, two Captain's chairs elevated, so you could sit or stand, and comfortably see through the high windshield. Below the windshield was a panel of switches and gauges, a compass, counter space for maps and charts to be spread out, and a removable five-gallon container of stove oil along one side. Side windows added protection from the elements, and the back was open for easy access to the commercial fishing equipment.

Jack said, "This was designed as a one-man boat, but two would be better; one to handle the fish gear, and one to handle the boat, as it doesn't have dual controls in the stern cockpit as most trollers do.

The trolling poles go up each side of the hurricane bridge and are connected to a center mast with a yardarm where trolling poles are attached when you're not fishing. When you are fishing, the poles are lowered in position about 8 feet above the water at the tips with two steel fishing lines running from each pole. One line is located near the tip of the pole, the other about half way down the length of the pole. Each line will have six spreads and a 10 to 15 pound sinker to take it down. A float bag will be attached to take the outside lines forty or fifty feet beyond the stern of the boat, then down. The inside lines go straight down from the poles, and all four lines are brought in by electric reels."

"So that's how a troller works," I replied.

"As you can see," he continued, "The reels are centered in the cockpit at the stern of the boat where you stand as you work with the four lines and each of the 24 spreads."

"What's a spread?"

"A spread is six feet of heavy fishing leader with a clamp and swivel on one end, and a lure of some kind on the other. These are clamped onto the steel line at one fathom intervals, and you can legally have only six spreads on a line, and believe me that's enough."

"I can see it would keep you busy, especially when you're catching fish."

"The boat had been freshly painted inside and out, and all of the fishing equipment was in good repair."

I was impressed, so I took the next step, "I won't stand the expense of hiring a surveyor to checkout the boat, but I want to see the bottom of the boat out of the water."

We agreed to meet the next day at low tide at the marina and Jack would have the boat on a grid located there. The bottom would be high and dry so I could check for dry rot, worms, blisters, and damaged planks. Jack was an amiable sort of a guy and easy to talk to. He appeared to be about ten years my senior, or roughly fifty years old. He was strongly built, a little short of six feet tall, and had a full head of thick pepper and salt hair topped off with a modest mustache. Some would say he was handsome with a devil-may-care attitude, which could spell either fun or trouble.

I arrived at the appointed time and Jack and I watched the tide as it receded enough for me to get underneath the hull in a stooped position with a sharp, long bladed pocketknife. I checked the hull for dry rot and bruised planks, then the rudder, prop, and drive shaft for corrosion, looseness of fit, and any irregularities of shape. Everything checked out and I was ready to talk money.

I proposed, "I'll pay you your asking price, if you'll take one third down and the balance at the end of the fishing season. Also, the commercial fishing license goes with the boat, you help me move it to the commercial fishing grounds at La Push, and check me out en route on how to handle the boat and all of the commercial gear. I felt like I had stated all my terms in one breath, and now I took time to breathe deeply.

He smiled and said, "Agreed, Harry, if you will do one thing… bring along a case of beer as it will take three days to get there, and I have a hell of a thirst. Being the sheriff here means I can't drink on the island."

"It's a deal," I replied, "but I'll need a couple of days to get the down payment."

"This is Saturday; I'll want the money by Tuesday and I'll need a notarized contract." he countered.

"You put together the contract and I'll see you here Tuesday after school… say about five o'clock, and I'll have the money." We shook hands and I departed, leaving Jack sitting there watching the tide come in. His closing comment was, "How come I get to do all the fun stuff… like watching the tide come in?"

Driving home I felt flush with the excitement of the deal and realized that finally my dream of commercial fishing was about to come true. All I had to do was figure out a way to get the down payment.

Looking for a boat when I didn't have any money may sound irresponsible, but I had a scheme in the back of my mind and now was the time to bring it out and test it.

I was a member of a faculty investment club at the junior high school where I taught. We were told to look around for investments that the club might consider. The next day, Monday, I asked the members to meet after school. I presented the fishing boat deal with me as skipper, adding, I needed the money by tomorrow. I felt I had done a good job of presenting the proposal, and the fact I once sold new and used cars was in my favor.

However, they voted and turned it down saying they wanted the club's ventures to be less risky; I accepted that decision and mentally shifted gears. However, Ted Brinkman, one of the club members, stood up and said, "I would like to go into it as a silent partner with Harry if nine other members would do the same and each would contribute one tenth of the down payment."

I was stunned by the suggestion and even more so when, suddenly, there were nine other guys ready to give me a check Tuesday so the deal would fly. These fellows were also members of a monthly poker club to which I belonged, so we knew each other pretty well.

The next afternoon I had ten checks and on my way to Winslow to consummate the deal. Jack and I went to his lawyer's office and I was in for another surprise. I gave him the money and he handed me the title to the boat. I stammered, "I didn't expect the title until the boat was paid for in full."

His lawyer explained, "Jack doesn't want to be liable in any way concerning the boat so a promissory note due September first for the balance will solve the problem."

Everything was in my name including the promissory note, so I really had ten very silent partners. If this adventure went sour, I was the only one liable. Well, faint heart never won fair maiden as I'm prone to quote at times like this… so I signed the note.

Jack and I agreed on a date to take the boat the 150 miles by water to La Push after school was out and I was free for the summer. La Push is a Quileute Indian village on the coast of Washington State with a marina for commercial fishing boats. Actually the marina is up the mouth of the Quileute River about 300 yards, which provides safe moorage and a place for the fish buyers, Butts and Pattison, to buy the commercial boat's catch for the day.

Commercial Fishing

We met at the boat with our gear and provisions for the three-day trip plus one case of beer. Jacks eyes lit up when he spotted the beer. We said our goodbyes to our spouses and headed north around Bainbridge Island into the Straits of Juan De Fuca on our way to Port Angeles, our first port of call. It was a lovely June day and the water was relatively flat. Jack offered me a beer and helped himself to one.

I only had two swigs from my stubby when I noticed that he was reaching for his second stubby, and so it went. By the time we had rounded Point-No-Point the weather began to turn bad and Jack was feeling no pain.

We were now in the Straits of Juan De Fuca and by the time we passed Foul Weather Bluff I knew why it was so named. I had taken the controls from the very start and Jack had now gone below to sleep off his drunken state. The waves became higher to the point I called to Jack to come up and assess the situation. Jack was dead to the world. I knew the straits had a reputation, which included swallowing of a navy destroyer some years back. Now the wind was blowing off the tops of the waves filling the air with spray and spindrift.

The farther north we preceded the higher the waves became. I later learned the original rudder on these converted navy hulls had been taken off and a much smaller rudder installed so they would be less cumbersome backing up in tight quarters, like in a marina. However, the smaller rudder didn't give the proper steerage in heavy weather like I was experiencing.

The waves built up to a height, which looked to be twenty feet high with a long run off. As the boat slid down the spent wave, the stern started to come around to starboard, which had to be stopped to avoid a rollover at the bottom of the trough. This meant I was fighting the wheel to starboard to straighten out the path of the hull. Then, as soon as I was at the bottom of the wave with the hull straight, the next wave was waiting for us. The boat rose to meet the rising onslaught and broke through the top third of the wave with green water, not spin drift, going right over the top of the hurricane bridge. As soon as I was through the top, the boat started down the steep slope to the next wall of water.

At first I found myself cursing each wave silently, then in desperation, aloud. However, after a series of these monsters hadn't defeated me, I found myself laughing, half-hysterically, at the onslaught and shouting challenges at the demon waves. Adrenalin had kicked in big time, and I was on an emotional high.

* * *

This went on for three hours until I was able to hide behind Dungeness Spit, which is just a few miles from our first night's destination, Port Angeles. I was exhausted from the ordeal and realized that I hadn't even had time to light my pipe in that three hour period. Thinking back now, I recalled only one word from Jack. He said, "Jesus," as he flew out of his bunk and lit on his back in the middle of the cabin floor. That was the same wave impact that flipped the five gallon stove oil Jerry can out of its' holder into the air doing a full loop, ending up in the fishing cockpit at the stern of the boat.

I grabbed a beer and was taken aback by how few were left. I had never experienced a drinker like that. No wonder he was unconscious. I sat on the roof of the cabin as the boat idled out of gear, and ate a sandwich, drank my beer, and pondered my next move. I could drop the hook here and wait out the storm or I could get back into it and make Port Angeles before nightfall. I decided on the later course and from a distance of a half-mile the waves looked like they had slacked off some.

I found out distance is deceiving. As soon as I was out of the protection of Dungeness Spit, a mile long spit of land thrusting out from the west side of the Straights Of Juan De Fuca, I knew I was in the same game as before. However, this time I knew the boat and I could stand up to the storm as long as it didn't get any worse.

Fortunately, it didn't, and an hour later I pulled into the lee of the breakwater, Idez Hook, at Port Angeles and immediately enjoyed slack water. A forty-foot troller was idling along testing his engine as I overtook him. He shouted over to me, "Did you just come out of that slop?"

"Yes." I replied.

"Nobody should have been out in that slop." I couldn't have agreed more; however, it gave me some comfort to know the captain of a forty-footer thought it was a bad one, too. I cruised in at four knots, which is harbor speed. I could see open slips ahead at the transient pier and quickly chose one. I then slipped the engine into neutral, coasted in and stepped ashore to secure the lines fore and aft. And wouldn't you know, Jack awakened and was ready for shore leave.

We exchanged forced pleasantries, as he knew I was less than satisfied with his performance. However, he informed me he was off for the night and would see me at 8:00 A.M., ready for another day. I could only surmise that Jack had a girl in every port and Port Angeles was no exception. No wonder Jack was willing to escort me to La Push; this was his no-holds- barred vacation. He took his shaving kit with him and walked up the gangplank into the night… sober.

I took stock of my cupboard and chose an easy dinner out of a can plus the last bottle of beer. Can you believe that a case of beer disappeared in one day and I had only three? I turned in early and slept the sleep of the innocent.

* * *

I awakened to bright sunlight and no wind, a beautiful combination. It was 7:00 A M. and the harbor was awakening. I just finished a big breakfast when Jack came sauntering down the dock. Surprisingly, he didn't look any the worse for wear with a grocery bag cradled in each arm and a broad smile on his face. I greeted him and asked, "Have you eaten breakfast? He had, and set his two bags down on the deck in preparation for coming aboard. I could see into the open bags and they were full of stubbies of beer. Jack acknowledged my greeting and looking at the bags, stated, "These ought to get us through the day."

Half-heartedly I told him I thought they would. We soon were under way and glided effortlessly at four knots out to the entrance to the marina and the harbor. Today was the exact opposite of yesterday, weather wise. The straights were as calm as I have ever seen them. We sucked in the warmth of the day and I had a return of my former optimism. Our goal for the day was to reach Neah Bay, an Indian village and marina on the most northern tip of the state of Washington. I suggested we fish for a while, but Jack disagreed. He thought as long as the straits were so unpredictable, weather-wise, we had better keep our speed and make for Neah Bay.

We followed that plan because it made sense, and I put aside my need to catch a fish. This was my boat in every respect as far as Jack was concerned, and being a passenger he was free to open and down stubby after stubby of beer and sleep at will. I didn't indulge in even one stubby of beer thinking it might have some positive effect on Jack, but not so. Jack just enjoyed the ride and toasted the day… repeatedly. Jack was a good storyteller and kept a running monologue going most of the time. He worked his way into a nap shortly after lunch and that accounted for the rest of the afternoon as far as Jack was concerned. I followed my Texaco automobile road map and continued north.

I made a 90-degree turn to port just before we got to Tatoosh Island and started the long protected run into Neah Bay. Water traffic was light, but I did notice an open, dory-type boat being fished as we passed on the way to the marina. What really took my eye were the two fishermen aboard. It looked like a grandfather/ young grandson team and both were burned mahogany by the sun. They had no protection from the elements and their skin showed it. The grandfather was old, tall and lanky, with long silvery hair falling to his shoulders. The boy looked to be about twelve years old, a younger version of his grandfather. They fished with hand gerdies mounted on the gunnels, which is commercial fishing at its' most primitive stage. We subtly acknowledged each other and soon they were just a speck in the distance. I thought to myself *they're wise to stay in protected water with their open boat, but I wonder if they can make a living at it?*

I awakened Jack as we approached the marina because the boats were tied up "piggly wiggly" (first come first serve and rafted together due to a lack of dock space). He said, "That's to be expected. We need to choose an outer boat to tie to, which hasn't moved for a while."

We chose one and walked across the inboard boats and onto the dock. This enabled us to get to a gangplank, which put us up on the pier after a relatively steep climb. Jack assured me we could get out in the morning as long as we let anyone wanting to tie up to us know we were leaving on the morning tide. That shouldn't be a problem because I would be aboard. As for him, he informed me that he was on his way to hitchhike out of town.

This took me by surprise, but his explanation was quite simple. Neah Bay, being an Indian reservation, could not sell alcoholic beverages and since we were out of beer, he would hitchhike off the reservation to the nearest watering hole, which was 15 miles down the road. He said he would see me in the morning, as he had friends there who would insist he spend the night. I didn't spend much time wondering if these friends were male or female. One thing had to be said about Jack, he had a strong constitution.

* * *

I saw him head for the highway out of town and decided to treat myself to a restaurant meal. There was only one choice in the vicinity of the dock and it fit the surroundings... tacky. The outside hadn't seen a coat of paint in a long time and the ambience inside was a close match. A huge, older Indian sat on a stool at the counter. His ample bottom hung over on both sides of the stool, and he was very inebriated. I thought this strange because the Indian reservation was supposed to be dry, and he was drunk. Because of his verbal bantering with other fishermen, he provided the entertainment, while I ate my hamburger steak. He knew everyone in the restaurant but me, and evidently sensed I wasn't his type as he talked over and around me. I took this more as a compliment than a put down; I enjoyed my anonymity.

He spoke in a loud, slurring voice with his mouth full of food. It was a disgusting sight and combined with the tackiness of everything in sight, I couldn't help wonder if my destination, La Push, would be like this, as it ,too, was an indian reservation village.

As I slowly walked back to the boat, a feeling of depression came over me. I was beginning to wonder if I had bitten off more than I could chew. Very few of the boats looked prosperous and the village was extremely primitive, by my standards. However, I came to fish, make money, and have an adventure, I rationalized. I'd feel better after a good night's sleep and I would stick to my own cooking in the future.

The night passed slowly, and I was even happy to see Jack swagger down the gangplank in the morning. To my surprise he had no beer. I asked him about that and he informed me his wife was picking him up that afternoon at La Push, so his partying was over. Consequently, the day was the best day of the trip, and we took time to put out all the gear. He showed me how everything worked and it was a hands-on learning experience at its best.

We arrived at the jetty entrance to the Quileute River early in the afternoon of the third day and Jack took the controls as we threaded our way between the wash rocks at the foot of James Island and the rock jetty just a short forty yards away. This made for a very narrow opening to escape the surf of the ocean and into the smooth current of the Quileute River. The marina was 300 yards up river and a welcome haven from the relentless ocean waves.

After securing the boat in a vacant slip, we walked to the fish buyer's office where Jack introduced me to one of the owners. He explained I was the new owner of his boat and wanted to set up an account with them, which would include moorage, gas, groceries and chandlery items, such as fishing gear. This meant I could charge these things until the end of the season and, in turn, sell my fish to them at market price. At the end of the fishing season my daily fish slips would be compared with my expenses and a money settlement made. No money changed hands until then. Actually, it was a pretty good system, as most fishermen had little money to support their fishing needs. I fit that profile to a tee.

* * *

Jack's wife arrived and I said my goodbyes just as my oldest son drove up. Rod was 18-years-old, strong as an ox, fresh out of high school, and raring to go for an adventure. He would be my fish puller and constant companion for the next three months. I had to take a quantum step back into my usual life with the arrival of my son. I was once again a father and teacher who happened to be trying to make a living during the summer months.

I was no longer the carefree adventurer in the company of a highflying rogue. This realization settled over me as Rod and I walked around La Push to get the lay of the land and a feel for the place. The marina piers accommodated about two hundred commercial fishing boats of every description imaginable. The village comprised of two-dozen, one-story houses, a meeting hall, and a small grocery store. All of which were badly in need of repair. The fish buyers, Butts and Pattison, owned the gas dock, fish buyer's barge, grocery store, chandlery, and restaurant.

The coast guard station consisted of one large building that housed men and boats. It was a reassuring sight to know that there was someone close by that could be called on in an emergency. The loud sound of breaking waves was a constant reminder the Pacific Ocean wasn't always peaceful, but it was always there. La Push had a wild, rough appearance that was foreign to me. *I'll adjust to all this in time*, I told myself. Frankly, I was having a hard time staying optimistic about this whole scheme. *If I've bitten off more than I can chew, I will soon know it.*

Rod met a young fish-puller from two boats away affording him some companionship in his own age group; I met Bundy. Now to say Bundy was a salty old fisherman was putting it mildly. Bundy was about as profane a man as I've ever heard. He was a retired tugboat captain and neat as a pin. His boat was spotless, the trailer he lived in was spotless, and he was, if not spotless, a whole lot tidier than most of the fishermen I had seen. The appearance of the boats usually reflected their owners. Some looked well cared for; others looked like floating Spam cans.

My meeting with Bundy came about when Rod and I had to be towed in by the Coast Guard one afternoon. This experience resulted in feeling both embarrassment and total relief. We had gone dead in the water in the mouth of the river with wash rocks on one side and the jetty of rocks on the other. It was the worst of all places for this to happen since five minutes out of control could put you on the rocks, and five minutes on the rocks meant you just lost your boat.

I jumped up on the roof of the hurricane bridge, ripped off my shirt, and started waving it as a flag of distress. This got the attention of two coastguardsmen cruising the ocean's breaker line off-duty fishing in an open dory-type coast guard boat. They immediately cranked in their lines and powered over to get between the jetty and our boat. They expertly took our lines for and aft and towed us out of our dilemma.

The coastguardsmen accepted our enthusiastic appreciation and shrugged it off as all in a day's work. Towing us to our slip, they cast us free to tie up to our mooring cleats. At that moment Bundy appeared.

He was a slender-built man of retirement age who reminded me of Popeye, the cartoon character. He inquired, in his own inimitable way, what the matter was and I told him I didn't know except I lost all power just as we were returning from a day's fishing.

He seemed to take a liking to my son and me and offered to get his boat testing-equipment and trouble shoot the problem. I'm sure a part of his motivation to help was because he recognized us as two green horns who were trying to make a go of commercial fishing.

He soon reappeared and in time determined one of our two alternators wasn't working. Consequently, both of our storage batteries were dead. Because we had electric gerdies, we had to have two large storage batteries. These needed to be constantly fed electricity from the alternators running off the engine and it wasn't happening.

I bought a new alternator, had the two batteries charged, and we were back fishing… thanks to Bundy. He acted as if what he did was the natural thing to do when you're in the fishing fleet.

Bundy intrigued me with his rough talking manner and his knowledge of the sea. He was a good fisherman and taught me a lot about the fishing waters off of La Push. I spent many evenings at his boat or trailer helping him drink the bottle of Scotch I gave him for solving our boat problem.

One day he discovered I was a teacher, a fact I hadn't shared with anyone, and had sworn my son to secrecy. A former student spilled the beans by recognizing me when I was talking to Bundy on the boat dock. Bundy incredulously asked, "You're a (expletive) teacher? You know… being a teacher would be a pretty damn good racket, if people would just keep their goddamn kids home." He would make remarks like that and never crack a smile, but his eyes gave him away. You could see a faint sign of laughter in his eyes, if you looked closely.

I met two other fishermen that I became friends with, Harvey and Sluggo. They were both native americans and their boat was an ancient, metal-patched affair, but they caught more than their share of fish. Harvey was stocky, about five feet eight inches tall; shy, but with a quick and easy smile. His head was misshapen due to a forty-foot fall off a water tower roof onto a dock when he was a young man. He never married, and I guess it was because of his odd appearance.

Sluggo, the opposite of Harvey, was taller, darker-skinned, slender, and some would say handsome. He earned his name by constantly getting into fights when he and Harvey went drinking, which were fairly often. They taught me how to alter the end of my fishhooks so I would stop losing fish. This, of course, is crucial. I never was sure how or why I was attracted to these offbeat characters…maybe it was because there was so many of them at La Push. Or maybe I needed some levity in my new life.

I soon learned the fishermen inhabiting the two hundred boats in the marina had their own law. The State Patrol would swing through La Push once a day, but it was a token visit. When a fisherman was found floating face down in the water beside his boat, the investigation was very short when it was discovered he was a thief. Stealing is not accepted in the fleet and a fisherman would lay his gear on the dock to work on it, walk off and expect to find it there when he returned.

The big motivation for my son to go fishing was to make money so he could go to Australia. His high school girlfriend was an exchange student from Australia and had just returned to her home after spending her senior year in Bremerton. This meant I had a motivated fish-puller on board.

* * *

Daily fishing fell into a routine: up at four, put on the coffee pot, dress, wash, start the engine, untie the lines, back out of the slip, and cruise the river channel down three hundred yards to the ocean.

The first day out Rod asked, "Where are we going to fish today, Dad?"

"I think we'll go south and watch where the other boats put out their lines and follow suit."

We traveled south for about five miles and found other boats trolling in a long line spaced about a hundred yards apart. "What do you want me to do, Dad?"

"Let down the trolling poles and attach the stabilizers to take the roll out of the boat as the water has rollers about five feet high. When you finish that, take the wheel while I put out the four steel lines and prepare to put on the spreads."

"What's a spread?"

"A spread is six feet of heavy leader connected to the steel line by a clip with a swivel at one end and fresh or artificial bait on the other end."

"Wow, suppose we had a fish on every hook?"

"Theoretically, you could, but that never happens, I'm told." As time went by we discovered we would be lucky to have even one on at a time. Some days the water was like a millpond and some days you had to hold on to keep from going overboard.

"How do you know when you have a fish on?"

"You listen for a bell to jingle. You're not waiting for a tug on the line because the gear is too heavy and indirect for that. Where the line attaches to the trolling pole, a sheep's bell is fastened so that a fish on the line will make it shake and you can start taking the line in. Each line has a different size bell so you can soon distinguish by the sound of the bell which line has the fish on. As the line comes in, the spreads pop out of the water every fathom and you quickly detach the spread and attach it to a place on the stern out of the way, trailing in the water. This is done without stopping the line until you come to the spread with a fighting fish on the hook. As you yard it in, hand-over-hand, you gaff it and hoist it aboard. Then, you hit it on the head with the back of the gaff and throw it in the kill box."

"Wow! So we're actually listening for a bell to ring, not a tug on the line."

"Yep, just like a prize fighter. The back of the gaff is actually a club, which is shaped like a small baseball bat with a gaff hook sticking out the other side. Later, usually on the run home, we'll clean the catch, leaving the head of the fish on for economic and cosmetic reasons. When we arrive at the buyer's barge, we'll use a pew stick to hoist the fish into a weighing pan that has been lowered to us."

"A pew stick, what is that?"

"A pew stick is a pole with a sharp metal tip used to spear and lift the fish individually into the weighing pan. The weighing pan is a round convex metal pan about 30 inches across that is attached by three strands of cable to a single cable, which is controlled from above on the buyer's barge. You put the Kings in one pan, the Silvers in another pan, and the Sea Bass (brown bombers) in another pan. These are hoisted aboard the buyer's barge, weighed, and a fish slip is filled out and lowered to us. This slip tells the amount of each type of fish we sold and at what price. The price changes daily based on the law of supply and demand."

"How did you learn all of this so soon?"

"Jack Watkins is more than a great drinker, he's a great teacher."

* * *

Each day of the three-month season was different depending on the weather. Some days we fished in the fog. We nearly collided with James Island a couple of times. It's a thrill to break out of the fog and look up at a 200-foot cliff of granite you're approaching rapidly. Our navigation system consisted of a portable, three-band radio where you needed to have silence to be able to hear the ping of the beam emanating from the top of James Island.

To attain this silence, I had to shut off the engine, lay a ruler over the top of the radio, and turn the radio in a radius to pick up the center of the beam, or I should say the loudest ping. With the help of our navigation map of the area I could determine where we were headed… sort of. Of course this beam brought us right to James Island, it didn't tell me how far we were from it. This was primitive navigation, to say the least.

* * *

One day we came upon a huge gray whale basking in the summer sun. We never saw its tail or head; just the middle which was about forty feet long. We decided not to disturb it, as one whale had confused a fifteen-pound lead sinker for something to eat and had ripped the whole trolling pole right off the side of the fishing boat. We sneaked away as quickly as we could because we were pulling four such sinkers.

At the end of each day we would come to the buyer's barge situated about a three hundred yards upstream from the mouth of the river. We would wait in line, (no simple task) tie up to the barge, and unload our catch. Many days it was hardly worth the effort.

* * *

One day I looked up at the pier beside the buyer's barge and there stood two of my silent partners grinning down at me. The fact they recognized me was a surprise because I had a week's growth of beard, a deep tan, and a bandage above one eye with traces of dried blood down the side of my face.

I had made a mistake that day bringing in a salmon by grabbing the line above the flasher instead of below it on the salmon side of the flasher. When I hoisted the fish high over the gunnels, he was thrashing wildly, which is par for the course. However, the flasher was moving right along with him. This was all about face high to me and the flasher slashed me above the left eyebrow.

I separated the salmon from the hook by running the Swedish gaff down the line to the hook and gave it a sharp twist. As the fish fell to the kill box, I ended the fight by hitting it soundly on the head with the rounded side of the gaff. Rod handed me a large bandaide and we went on fishing.

My silent partners wanted me to take them out fishing that evening, which I did, but my heart wasn't in it. I had already spent twelve hours on the water and… they caught no fish.

* * *

Each day we went out optimistic; most days, we returned disappointed. Eventually our optimism turned to skepticism, and finally the fishing season came to an end. We fished hard, but the fish just weren't there. Only ten percent of the boats made money that year. All-good-and-bad-things come to an end, and I decided fishing fell into the later category. Rod and I came to terms with Butts and Pattison financially in order to head for home.

By the time we paid for our gas, moorage, fishing gear replacements, groceries, and restaurant bill, not only we hadn't made any profit; I had to write them a check. However, one can be philosophical about such things as money… I'm told. This didn't help much when there was a boat to pay for *immediately* and an airplane ticket to Australia to buy. This meant the boat would have to be sold as soon as possible.

The first port of call on our trip home was Neah Bay and we searched for a boat to tie to as the customary crowd was there rafted together, although we were hoping for the impossible… open dock space. As we glided along, suddenly Rod, standing near the bow, shouted, "Hey Dad, there's open dock space coming up." This was unheard of, but who was I to question a miracle. I shifted to neutral and coasted by the open dock space to look for 'keep off" signs or whatever. No signs appeared, so I put the boat in reverse and backed in.

We quickly tied our lines and waited for a voice to tell us we were in someone's private parking space. Nothing happened. Rod and I looked at each other and did an enthusiastic high five. Then we noticed something we hadn't seen before. Over the stern of our boat two poles about two inches in diameter sticking out of the water several feet and about three feet apart.

"What the heck is that?" exclaimed Rod.

I followed the poles down underwater to their source and sighed, "You're not going to believe this, Rod. We're sitting on stop of a sunken troller and those are the tips of its trolling poles. No wonder there's forty feet of open dock space."

Our hopes of a free and clear berth dissipated quickly. We had hoped for a miracle to have moorage next to the dock in order to leave the boat there for sale and go home for a few days of rest. Because I had decided to sell it to pay off the note and to pay what was left to my ten silent partners, the boat was more apt to sell in Neah Bay than in our homeport of Bremerton. Therefore, I needed this dockside space desperately in order to be able to leave the boat and to advertise it for sale.

Then creative genius kicked in. I studied the water carefully and checked the tide table in order to determine, as best I could, the distance between our keel and the sunken boat's cabin top. "Rod, I think there is a chance we can sit on top of this sunken boat even at low tide and have a couple of feet of water between us. You hitchhike back to La Push and get the car. We'll ride our boat down to the low tide level, which should happen at approximately 2 a.m., and if we have water between us and the sunken boat, we'll secure our lines and go home."

Rod was happy to be off the boat and have the adventure of hitchhiking across the remote part of the Olympic Peninsula to La Push. Also, he was looking forward to getting home as much as I. Meanwhile, I took two white flashers and painted' FOR' on one in red letters and 'SALE' on the other. I then used fish line and strung them in a banner fashion across the inside of the windshield of the hurricane bridge. Next, I made a list of the boat's equipment and salient selling points finishing with our phone number, address, and selling price. I put down the same price I paid for it even though it was no longer a freshly painted boat with an abundance of fishing gear. We had lost gear, which I hadn't replaced, bounced off creosote poles and docksides, fished for three months and showed it. Because I thought I bought the boat at a low price in the beginning, I felt the price I asked for was possible to attain. My goal was: not lose any more money on this venture.

In an amazingly short time Rod returned with the car, having immediately caught a ride with a logger who was going directly to La Push, and Rod was all smiles with the prospect of going home. We cooked dinner, turned in early, and I set the alarm for one o'clock. We slid into our sleeping bags, we hoped, for the last time.

The alarm went off, I dressed in the dark, and went topside to check the lines. We were within one hour of low tide and still had three or four feet of water between us. Walking the dock helped me stay warm, and finally it was two o'clock. Anxiously, I hung over the stern of our boat using my strong flashlight beam for visibility. Hurrah! We were't sitting on top of the sunken troller. I determined we had about two feet of water between us. Quickly awakening Rod, I told him the good news. We stuffed our sea bags with clothing, clean and dirty, and any other valuables, grabbed our sleeping bags and headed for the car and home.

* * *

It was good to be finished with fishing… an experience I needed to do only once. The next day at home I received a phone call from someone who had seen my boat in Neah Bay and wanted to take a ride in it. After questioning him at length I determined he was a qualified buyer and agreed to meet him at the boat at 12:00 noon the next day. I needed a little rest before I hit the highway back to the Olympic Peninsula and the Indian village of Neah Bay. I asked Rod if he wanted to go with me. He just smiled and shook his head and mouthed "No way."

I arrived at the appointed time with my fingers crossed. I quickly parked the car and walked the length of the long dock to the mooring site. As I approached the boat, I couldn't believe my eyes. I saw an old man with long white hair that hung to his shoulders and a young boy, both burnt the color of mahogany by the sun, standing at the edge of the pier looking down at my boat. It was the same two I had felt sorry for because they had to fish in an open dory-type boat with hand gerdies when we first arrived at Neah Bay three months earlier. They were there to buy my boat.

Suddenly, I grew apprehensive about the money part of the deal. I pointedly asked him, "If you decide to buy my boat, how do he plan to pay for it?"

He replied without hesitation, "Cash."

Well, it's hard to argue with cash… so we went for a demonstration boat ride. I explained carefully every step necessary to start the boat and get it under way just as if he had already bought it. I put out all of the fishing gear and went into great detail regarding the idiosyncrasies of the boat. The old man seemed to like everything about the boat and without any dickering said, "I'll take it."

We returned to the dock and walked up to the post office to close the deal, I with a spring in my step. The necessary forms for the State of Washington and the Coast Guard were there to sell a boat and transfer title. We quickly filled out the paperwork and I produced the title. Then we came to that crucial moment, the time for the pay-off. He reached into his bib overall's large breast pocket, pulled out a roll of bills that filled his hand, and peeled off the hundreds, one at a time, until he reached the magic number.

"I guess that does it," he said. We shook hands and returned to our own individual lives.

On the return trip home in the car, I burst into the song, "Oh what a beautiful morning." I was euphoric having so many burdens removed by the sale of the boat. When I told this story to my ten silent partners they eagerly asked if there was any money left on his roll when he finished paying me.

"Yes, he did what I didn't do, made money fishing." I paid off my partners, then Jack Watkin's promissory note, and the adventure was over.

A friend of mine later remarked, "You seem different somehow after your fishing adventure, Harry. You seemed so self-assured. Did you have a successful fishing season?"

"You can't lay your life on the line as many times as I did this past summer and not come out different," I replied. "I don't hold so tightly on to life now, and I'm more optimistic about everything. Considering all things, I guess I did have a successful fishing season."

The John Wayne Marina

This ended one summer's adventure. Every summer was different and when I talk about thirty years of teaching, counseling, and administration, I also remember the thirty summers that were an important part of my life.

* * *

Another summer that stands out in my memory is the one when I traveled about in my pickup and camper enjoying the Pacific Northwest. I was on my way to my son Jim's home in Port Angeles and I ambled into the waterfront cafe at the John Wayne Marina, located on the Straits of Juan de Fuca near Sequim, Washington, looking for food and the John Wayne Museum in that order.

Seating was no problem as I was the only one there except for the unseen person rattling pots and pans in the kitchen. I seated myself at one of the half-dozen tables making up the cafe, selecting one with the best view of the marina. This particular table gave me a close-up look at the working end of the marina. Below me lay the boat ramp for the sport fishermen, the gas dock, and two, one hundred-foot long docks for loading and off-loading people and cargo. The far dock had several workboats and a pleasure boat with a "Coast Guard Auxiliary" banner tied across each side of the cabin. The closer dock had two workboats moored along one side; one was in the process of being unloaded.

A young, blond waitress appeared, took one look at me in my western outfit and said, "Hi honey, where'd you tie your horse?" She smiled down at me with the impudence of the young and beautiful. At my age one doesn't take offense at being called honey by a young, pretty female. I laughed at her attempt at humor and familiarity. "I left Paint home today and decided in favor of my pickup truck and camper." I responded by refusing the menu offered and ordering coffee, a hamburger deluxe and a side order of fries.

After serving the coffee she disappeared into the kitchen. It was then I realized she was also the cook. I leisured over my coffee smiling to myself, *these duds have stood the test of time. The western hat, lizard-skin boots, faded levis, hand-made brass buckle for my tooled-leather belt, and soft-plaid western cut shirt have been worn by me over the years.*

Today I'll revisit my boyhood hero via the small museum right here in this building. Even though it isn't large, the Duke would approve. He kept his converted Navy minesweeper here, as he loved this part of the Northwest. He also has a home in the area, and rumor has it some of the family still live there.

As I gazed down one story to the water level, my eyes settled on the near dock. A well cared-for workboat was being off-loaded by three strong-looking young men dressed in gray and blue sweats, as though this was the uniform of the day. They carefully lifted large, blue, plastic containers the size of milk crates out of the boat onto the dock where a fourth man slid and stacked them four high until 32 crates of something, neatly stacked, waited to be taken somewhere.

When the cook-waitress returned with my lunch I asked, "What are in those blue crates down on the dock?"

"Geoducks," she replied matter-of-factly.

Geoducks?" I gasped. I guess that was probably the last thing I expected. Geoducks, up until now, had never played much of a part in my life's story. Oh, I saw a picture of one once…ugly things; a big clam with a long tapered neck. A sight that really doesn't do anything for you. *I wonder what The Duke would think of this geoduck harvesting going on in his marina?*

"Yep, geoducks," she repeated, seeming to savor the word. "They fly them to China."

Well now, a statement like that has enough going for it to get my attention; even if I didn't care much for their appearance.

"China?" I asked incredulously. "Why China?"

"Big money. The Chinese don't have any 'cause geoducks only exist in the Puget Sound area of Washington State and somewhere in Australia. They like the taste and texture and make sushi out of it."

"Really? I had no idea Washington waters had such an exclusive crop; and you say they eat them raw?"

"The Chinese and the Japanese like 'em that way. Personally, I don't go for that raw fish stuff." She turned and walked away before I could ask any more questions. I finished my lunch and bought my way out of the place, my curiosity aroused to the point I had to look up close at those ugly geoducks that were going to be flown to China. *Hell, I've never even flown to China.*

As I approached the dock, the boat that had been unloading pulled out leaving the dockside man to move the crates by a hand dolly up the ramp to a waiting truck. After he finished loading the thirty-two crates, I approached the muscular, young man, "Where you taking those geoducks, pardner?"

"Sea Tac," he replied. "That's over by Tacoma; it's an airport." He had no way knowing I lived twelve miles from that airport. "They are to be flown to Vancouver, British Columbia, then on to China."

"That seems like a lot of trouble and expense to sell a geoduck," I replied. "What do they bring?"

"They sell for five dollars and fifty cents a pound at the dock here and twenty-eight dollars a pound there."

"Good grief, now I can see why they're flown there. How many pounds do you have in your truck?"

"Twenty-two hundred," he replied matter-of-factly.

"Wow! If my eighth grade arithmetic serves me right, that's over $60,000 for a day's catch. Is that possible?"

"It sure is, but you have to remember that it takes big money to do it," he replied. "I'm outta here, mister; I'm due at Sea Tac in three hours."

Walking back to the main building of the marina, I reflected on this conversation. The Duke's museum would have to wait for a little while, as I had a whole lot of unanswered questions going around in my head. I stopped next at the harbormaster's office as a possible source of information. The harbormaster was a handsome young man, which didn't fit the appearance of any harbormasters that I had run across in my earlier boating days. *Do you suppose he's one of The Duke's kin?* He was just locking his door to leave, but graciously gave me a few minutes of his time. I asked him about the scene I had just witnessed.

He smiled and replied, "It's big business this time of the year. The commercial boys only have a couple of months to harvest their crop. The Indians spread out their harvesting all year."

"The Indians do this, too?"

"Oh, yes," he continued. "They get the right to harvest half of all seafood that comes out of Washington's waters."

"No kidding? Why?"

"According to a treaty the United States and the Indians agreed to about a hundred and fifty years ago. At that time the Indians agreed to turn over their claim on the land, and in return they were to have the right to harvest half of the food that comes out of the sea."

"Thanks for the information," I tossed at his back as he hurried away to tend to business on the dock. As I walked toward the museum, I noticed that the other workboat at the dock was being unloaded in the same manner as the first one. I decided since I still had some unanswered questions, maybe the crew would help me. The truck driver was wheeling the crates up the ramp as the other crewmembers off-loaded the crates onto the dock. One fellow had a ponytail of which most women would be envious.

All three of the men were young and strong but dressed helter-skelter. I guess they didn't have the team spirit like the other crew. Later I found out this was an Indian boat and the other a commercial boat. This was not an occupation for the weak or faint-hearted I learned as I watched them work. I patiently waited until the boat was unloaded before I collared Mr. Ponytail. I walked up to the crates and inspected the contents. The geoducks were lined up neatly in rows with a wide, blue, rubber band stretched around their middle. "Why the rubber bands?" I asked.

"To keep the shells from opening up so they'll live longer. With the rubber bands they'll last three to five days."

""They're alive?" I gasped.

"Yep, and they'll be alive when they arrive in China because they are air-freighted." "Where do they go from here?" I asked, thinking I was confirming information I had already been told.

"Sequim. We pack them for shipping there and then take them to Sea Tac. That's an airport near Tacoma."

"Yes, I know," I replied. "Did that other truck stop somewhere for them to be repacked for shipping before going to Sea Tac."

"Yep, they stopped at Poulsbo."

"Why not Sequim?"

"Because we're tribal at Sequim and they're commercial at Poulsbo."

"Oh!" Just then an old, rusty, fastback coupe pulled up driven by a slender, young, thing that held out a lunch sack for Mr. Ponytail. He took the extended sack and after a few words beyond my hearing, kissed her lightly and she was on her way. By the looks of the car, I surmised that not much of the profit in a geoduck found its way into the pockets of this young man.

He excused himself with a, "Gotta go; the tribe is waiting."

I walked away still not knowing how geoducks were harvested. I returned to the dock area and saw two older men hunkered down inside of the Coast Guard Auxiliary boat to get out of the offshore 15-knot breeze. As I approached their boat, they stepped out onto the rear deck to intercept me.

"Is that a geoduck boat tied up behind you?" I asked.

"Yes, that 's what it is," replied the younger one of the two. They wore identical jackets and caps with no signs of rank on their shoulders, but this one seemed to be in charge. I'm curious; how are geoducks harvested?"

"Well," replied Mr. In-Charge, "They use divers who descend no less than 18 feet nor more than 70 feet under water in areas that have been designated by the Bureau of Natural Resources to be harvested and marked off by buoys. The divers use a water hose similar to a fireman's hose and literally wash them out of their holes. "

"Really? Are they monitored by the state when they're doing this?"

"Yes, the Department of Natural Resources sends scuba divers down to be sure they stay within the boundaries and that they take all of the clams they wash out. This results in there being three grades of geoducks for the market. Prime goeyduck are 8 to 10 years old and nearly white in color. The old, dark ones are up to 140 years old and can weigh up to twenty pounds."

"I had no idea that it took that long for a geoduck to mature," I replied.

"Most people don't have a clue about this business," he assured me. The commercial companies bid on the right to harvest geoducks just like timber companies bid on the right to cut trees. They then have a designated time in which to harvest. The Indians can take a similar number of geoducks due to their treaty, but they don't have the same time restraints."

"How much are these things worth?" I ask innocently, in an attempt to substantiate my already acquired information.

"Oh the skipper gets five to six dollars a pound, but geoducks sell for twenty eight to thirty dollars per pound in the orient, I'm told."

"Thanks for the information, Captain."

I turned and walked back to my truck and trailer to get out of the wind and to think over all I'd been told. As I walked up the ramp from the water to the parking lot, my mind began to sift through the newly acquired information. Perhaps it was time I talk to someone who actually harvests the geoduck. However, I really needed to be one my way, but I was determined to return and get the rest of the story.

* * *

Three weeks later I returned on my motorcycle, an 1100 c.c. Honda Shadow, to get the rest of the story. Out of the corner of my eye I could see a lone worker finishing folding a water hose over one corner of his boat's transom. He was a medium-built man in his forties, with the quick movement of one who is in excellent physical condition. I asked, "Are you a geoduck harvester?"

He looked up from his chores giving me a friendly smile and said, "Yes, I'm a cowboy."

This took me by surprise. "Your a cowboy? Is that what a goeduck harvester is called?"

"Those of us that aren't Indians."

I could see the humor and the reasoning behind the term. To encourage him to answer my questions, I told him years ago I had been a commercial fisherman with my own troller out of La Push, Washington one summer.

He responded by asking me questions about my fishing experiences and we became brothers-under-the-skin, so to speak.

"Tell me about your diving…do you use scuba gear with an air tank on your back?"

"No, we have direct air from the surface at all times."

"Really? Do you have gear like a deep sea diver?"

"No, we use a dry suit similar to theirs, but better fitting and a mask similar to a scuba mask. It has a larger faceplate and outlets for air and phone.

"You're on constant air supply from the boat and in voice communication?" Is that right?

"He hears every breath I take," he laughed. He was apparently enjoying sharing his unique job with me. He sat on his haunches on top of the main hatch cover and allowed me to continue my line of questioning.

"I'm curious…how do you see down there? I would think if you're using a water hose to blast the geoduck out of its home, the surrounding water would be filled with silt and sand."

"We use the water current to clear the water for us. We anchor upstream of the current and work down stream as far as our three lines will allow us. This way the current is always moving the silt and sand out of the work area. We work our way in a straight line toward the boat."

"How do you actually get the geoduck from its resting place into your bag?"

"You grab the geoduck by the neck, which is protruding out of the sand, and put the water hose, which has been reduced to a metal wand, down the hole and trigger a blast of water. The sand moves away from the stream of water and up comes the clam.

"Wow, that's quite a technique. How do you stay down? I would think that you would tend to float to the surface when air is being constantly pumped to you."

"I use a seventy pound weight-belt and ten pounds of weight on my shoulders," he grinned as he verbally painted this picture of himself underwater.

"How do you get back to the surface with all that weight on you?"

"I climb the air hose hand-over-hand," he laughed anticipating my surprise.

"Well that does create quite a picture. After all that, do you mind if I ask how much you get for a pound of geoduck at the dock?"

"About eighty-five cents."

"Good grief! You are being swindled," I blurted out. "If the Orientals pay twenty eight dollars a pound, how come you only get eighty-five cents a pound?"

My sponsor, The Alaska Fish Company, keeps eighty percent of the dock price to pay the Department of Natural Resources for the privilege of harvesting. I get twenty percent, which is eighty-five cents per pound right now."

"Well, Pilgrim," I drawled in my best John Wayne voice, "I think you're being had."

He laughed good-naturedly, "Hey, this is a great life, I make a good living and a day out here geoducking beats any day in an office."

I could buy into that Duke, but I wonder if I would want to spend three to four hours a day under 18 to 70 feet of water pulling clams by the neck out of the sand.

* * *

In September, I returned to my job as boy's counselor at the junior high school where I had previously taught for four years. It was a challenging job and totally different from teaching. I not only worked with students with problems individually, but I was in charge of, and administered, the standardized tests for the entire student body. I also made presentations to eighth grade English classes starting a unit on choosing a vocation, which led to research and writing a term paper on their chosen vocation.

I attended two summers of school at the University of Washington to get the needed training for the job I was now performing, and at my own expense. I had planned to attend a third summer and get my Master's Degree, but the family budget didn't allow it. Instead, I taught summer school at the elementary school level in the morning for six weeks and the high school level U, S. History class for five weeks.

Returning to Graduate School

I continued in this counseling job for six years, and due to my limited attention span, I needed to move on to a new challenge. I decided to ask for a sabbatical leave, but a half year this time as I had no scholarship to help with the finances and I wanted a new job, principal, which required more specific training and a Master's Degree.

I had already completed half of my graduate work at the University of Washington, and by changing schools to the University of Puget Sound in Tacoma, I could cut down the long four hour commute to Seattle and accomplish my goal in eight months. A half-year sabbatical and one summer school would do it.

I made the necessary applications, both at the district lever for the sabbatical leave and at the University of Puget Sound for their graduate school Master's Degree Program. I was accepted by both and left my counseling position to return to teaching until the middle of the year when my sabbatical leave would begin. It was easier to replace a teacher in midyear than a counselor. This change of schools cut my commute time in half, but increased the cost, as U.P.S. being a private school, was more expensive.

Rod, in the Air Force now, had left his car, an M.G. convertible, for me to fix up and drive while he was overseas. I sold the family automobile to help meet the family budget and Louree accepted a part-time job at J.C. Penny's Department store. She had always been at home when the kids needed her, but Tom, the youngest son, was seventeen-years-old now and had his own part-time job.

* * *

Graduate school was a challenge, but I applied myself and made my grades. U.P.S. was a small Ivy League type college and everyone there wanted you to succeed. This was different from the large State University where you seemed to be only a number, not a person. The classes were small and the teachers personable. I made a few friends in the master's program and even worked in a game of tennis occasionally on warm summer days.

I was one class short of graduation at the end of summer because the class hadn't been offered, but it would be offered on Saturday for those in the Master's program during the next school year. This worked for me, since I had to return to the Bremerton School District and teach for a year as required by the terms of the sabbatical leave. I was given a fifth grade class to teach for that year, which surprised me, but I guess that was where their need was.

The school year was relaxing after what I'd been doing for the past ten years and I really enjoyed the students. Rod was still in the Air Force; Jim was in his first year of college, Tom, a senior in High School, and Louree had a full time job now as a secretary for the federal government at the Keyport Torpedo Station.

As the school year came to an end in June, I graduated with my Master's Degree and began looking for a job outside Bremerton since the promotion ladder there was jammed for years to come. Only fifteen percent of the teachers with principal's credentials obtain that coveted position, so it was a formidable task.

I took the first job offered, a position in a rural eastern Washington community, Almira, as a combined Junior and Senior High School principal. It meant selling the house to support the move and still be able to keep Jim and Tom in college. Rod had just received his discharge from the Air Force and also started college. So, Louree and I had our three sons in college at the same time, a formidable task, but Rod had the G.I.Bill to pay his way.

First Principal Position at Almira

The house sold and we moved a week before school started to this high plateau, wheat community of four hundred people. However, the school district was two hundred square miles in size, so the school was accommodating several hundred students. Our house was a two-bedroom, older home just a block from the school. It was not as nice as we sold, but homey and comfortable.

This new location was quite an adjustment for us: we knew no one within eighty miles, our home was empty of sons for the first time in twenty-two years, I had a new type of job and Louree was home alone.

After a month Louree was offered a job as a teacher's assistant, and took it gladly. She would be helping a second grade teacher who was "overloaded" with twenty-three students; the average class size in the elementary school in Almira was thirteen. In contrast, I'd never had a class less than thirty-six students.

This really helped Louree survive in Almira as the women of the town, as a whole, didn't accept outsiders easily. It was easier for a man, especially if he was principal of the high school and a member of the only men's service organization; the Lion's club.

I soon discovered a high school and junior high school principal in a rural setting wore many hats: public relations, curriculum development, staff supervision and evaluation, finance officer, disciplinarian, supervisor of school events, supervisor of transportation, counselor, director of athletics which required representing the school at county level meetings for scheduling athletic contests, plus attending all athletic and social events of the school.

When the school year started I was short a half - time teacher in order to meet the curriculum needs determined by the State. Therefore, because it was my job to make things work, I taught a social studies class for the junior / senior class, a science class for the seventh / eighth grade students and a physical education class for the freshman / sophomore girls. A senior girl, age twenty, took care of the locker room in that class for me. Only the social studies and girl's physical education class met every day, so I made it work.

In the office I had seven junior and senior class girls who each spent one period each day as school secretary. They all had previous experience at this and did a fine job. It was a win-win situation because they were learning office skills, and we had a well-staffed office for our size and needs.

If you looked at the school annual you'd think, *this has to be a big school.* We had athletic teams for all major sports for boys and girls; only we played eight instead of eleven-man football. We had a band, orchestra, and choir; all the high school required academic classes, including home economics and business courses, and an active social calendar. However, it took a seven period day to do it, while most city schools have a six period day.

The school year sped by, and I enjoyed most of it; I can't say the same for Louree. We left town nearly every weekend to visit relatives in Wenatchee, or Spokane, or occasionally back to Bremerton when we had longer than a weekend to be away, like at Christmas. When it came time to consider signing a contract for next year, we decided I should go job hunting.

Through the employment office of the Washington Education Association, I saw a job advertised in Federal Way, Washington for a high school counselor. Administrative jobs were scarce and usually rural. The cities had internal promotion and it was hard to get a foot in the door. I applied for the Federal Way job and was accepted. I was still putting my master's degree to work, as I had a double major in administration and counseling.

Return to High School Counseling

Jim spent the summer with us and we traveled to Ashland, Oregon in our sixteen-foot travel trailer so I could attend a class offered in English pertaining to the Shakespeare plays. I needed this credit to attain the next step on Federal Way's salary schedule. Money was important, as Jim, who was still in college and needed financial support. Tom had dropped out of school after the first semester, deciding he wasn't ready for more formal schooling at this time. He joined the Army for two years and was sent to Germany in the army of occupation. Rod had married and was in his second year of college and self-supporting.

When school started in the fall we had rented a two-bedroom house on high bank waterfront and were happy to be back in suburban life. I was assigned as a counselor to one of the two high schools in Federal Way and soon felt at home there. I was assigned to the sophomore class numbering about four hundred students. I would move with them as they progressed to the next grade at the end of the school year. Therefore, I would do the same in their senior year and be with them for three years; it was a good system for the counselor and the students.

I found the job more demanding than I expected, as suburban students were nearly invisible in the community and had more temptations, which created problems like drugs and alcohol. Also, the Supreme Court had taken a stand against schools dictating a dress code for students. Later it was determined students are better behaved if they are well dressed, a fact educators had learned a long time ago. After several years the Supreme Court backed off silently and gracefully and gave back some power to the school's staff.

The drop out rate was higher than I had experienced in the past and was a constant problem. Eventually the trend was reversed through counseling and an enhanced curriculum. The staff at Federal Way High School was excellent and I soon felt a part of a team with a common goal… student success.

Principal Position at Sacajawea

In the middle of my second year an administrative position as vice principal of a relatively new junior high school was advertised internally and ten applicants, including myself, were interviewed. I was chosen for the job, as I was the only one who had previous administrative experience. My year at Almira High School gaining experience paid off.

I said goodbye to my counselees, who were now in their junior year, and to the staff I enjoyed being a part of. As vice principal at Sacajawaya Junior High School, I not only handled the discipline problems, but also oversaw the athletic program, the after school program, and evaluated twenty of the forty-member staff.

Tom, our youngest son, returned from his enlistment in the Army, married and was in college. Rod had moved on to the University of Washington, and Jim was a senior at Western Washington State University. Louree had returned to work for the Federal Government as a secretary in Tacoma. We bought a house our second year in Federal Way, as we wanted to be permanent there.

Sacajawaya Junior High School was very modern in architectural style and in new ideas in teaching. The school a one story, flat roof, patio style school had no inside hallways, was very spread out, and lockers were in horseshoe shaped bays, locked in off-school hours.

The curriculum was departmentalized, so each department had a lead teacher overseeing the other teachers in that department. Some team teaching was done; volunteers from the outside were used for one-on-one teaching with slower students. Classes varied in size, depending on the activity going on, and some rooms were capable of expanding or decreasing in size with moveable walls.

Like all curriculums, it had pluses and minuses. However, the campus design created problems traditional schools didn't have. Locker bays gave opportunities to have a quick smoke with the help of a lookout. Being spread out with open halls, it was harder to monitor student activities between classes. The vice principal, whose place I was taking, had asked for a transfer when he found the discipline part of the job too demanding for him… I had my work cut out for me.

At the end of two and a half years, I welcomed a transfer to another junior high school in Federal Way since a new principal was coming in and wanted to bring a former colleague with him as vice-principal. I moved to a traditional junior high school with a principal I knew and liked. It was great being his assistant, and I stayed there five years before I once again became restless.

Rod was in his last year in college, Jim stayed on an extra year to be in graduate school, and Tom had divorced and was in his junior year at Western Washington State University. Louree transferred to the Federal Building in Seattle and was promoted to a managerial position in the Social Security division.

I had two more years in education before I was eligible to retire and after seven and a half years as a vice principal, I was ready for a change. It was apparent there was no advancement in the offering, so I asked myself, *where was I happiest in my twenty-eight years in the field of education?*

The answer was simple, "In the very beginning… in teaching elementary school." So I resigned my principal's position and asked for a sixth grade elementary teaching position where another friend was principal. My request was granted and I enjoyed returning to the classroom in a less stressful job to finish my last two years in education.

It had been a satisfying career, but, ever looking forward, I was ready to move on to a second career. Ironically, at this time Louree and I divorced after thirty-three years of marriage. I guess we were both ready to move on in our personal lives, also. I was fifty-five years old with thirty years of service in education and now on a pension, which was sixty percent of the average of my two highest paying years. It was important that I continue to work and earn money, since Louree and I shared this pension equally. She continued with her Federal job and I looked for a second career.

* * *

Roderick, Jim, and Tom, all married, graduated from college, with careers and now had children of their own, ultimately making Louree and me a grandparent seven times over.

Retirement, Divorce, and a New Partner

I took a new woman into my life after the divorce, Joyce Ray, a nurse in the Federal Way School District, who was divorced, and with three grown sons. After a brief courtship, we decided to live together without the formality of marriage, since we both previously had long marriages. Because there would be no children, due to our ages, and a pre-nuptial property agreement, the formality of marriage didn't seem to be important, at least at this time.

We bought a view condominium at Brown's Point, overlooking Commencement Bay and the city of Tacoma, and we both were employed. Life took on a normal routine and our grown children were compatible when all were together. We enjoyed a new social life, with mostly her friends, and I introduced her to some of my outdoor activities. Skiing was one and I'll now insert a story I wrote as a memoir in a writing class years later.

"The Longest Day"

I awoke with the sun on my face. The room came into focus and I became conscious of Joyce lying beside me, breathing softly, still in sleep. I looked at the clock on the dresser; it was eight o'clock. Today was to be a repeat of last Saturday with one exception. Tonight was New Years' Eve so we would stay longer after dinner at the Alta Vista Inn and celebrate the beginning of a new year. *I wonder what the New Year will bring?*

Last Saturday had been a day worth repeating except perhaps for the display of temper I had shown when I got us lost on our drive to Crystal Mountain Ski Resort. I had purchased a package of private ski lessons for Joyce as a Christmas present, so she could share the joy of skiing with me. Her first lesson last week was a success and she was so proud, as she had me follow her down the beginners' slope showing me what she had learned.

The gourmet-type dinner at the Alta Vista lodge on the return home had been a surprise bonus and we lingered over coffee nudges in the upstairs lounge. The mental picture I have of the two of us with our stocking feet propped up on the free-standing open fireplace listening to a local entertainer sing and play his guitar is vivid.

The breathing beside me became irregular. Joyce rolled on her side and looked at me with one eye open. "What are you doing lying there awake?" she said in a teasing voice. "You looked to be a million miles away."

"No, only sixty. I was thinking about last Saturday and looking forward to today."

"Well then, let's do something about it." She slipped out of bed with the ease of a ballet dancer and headed for the bathroom. I followed suit and soon breakfast was over, and we were locking the door to our condo heading for a day on the slopes.

The Volvo turned out of the driveway and down the winding road looking out on to Commencement Bay. *We really have a lovely set-up,* I thought to myself as I maneuvered the car down the hill. *Joyce and I share our beautiful condo overlooking Tacoma and Commencement Bay, we both have our careers, our families are grown, and we care deeply for each other.*

We purchased the condo two months after my divorce was final. Divorce had been a tough thing to experience after 33 years of marriage. Basically, it was just a matter of two people who had grown so far apart there wasn't enough left to meet either of their needs.

"Oh, look at the mountain with the sun on it," she cooed. Everything was beautiful to Joyce. She ended her 30-year marriage four years previously and was ready for a second marriage when we met. We talked of marriage and decided when I'd had a little more time and distance from my previous marriage, we'd make a decision. Right now we were satisfied to buy a condominium together and build a relationship.

The road left the bay shore and cut across the Puyallup valley to the foothills that nestle in the shadow of Mt. Rainier. I glanced over at Joyce snuggling into the seat beside me. Her straight chestnut brown hair was cut in the style of the day; one length to the nape of the neck and it swished as she walked. Of course Joyce didn't walk much. She skipped, bounced, or jogged, but her effervescent energy didn't allow for much walking. She looked small sitting there beside me and she always seemed shorter than the five foot two inches she claimed to be. Her bright blue eyes and fair English complexion completed the picture. I felt lucky to have this pretty, petite lady as my partner.

We entered the freeway maze separating us from the foothills and wouldn't you know it, I got lost again. I declared, "Well, at least I didn't make the same direction mistake twice, and I choose not to get angry this time."

"Marvelous," she exclaimed as she clapped her hands together in delight. "Good for you honey."

I did a U-turn a half-mile down the road and found the elusive exit to take us to the Crystal Mountain Ski Resort. The car leaped forward as it responded to my toe, anxious to be on its way. The wooded terrain turned into small farms as we ascended the top of a plateau. Mt. Rainier dominated the mid-horizon and it was easy to understand why the local Indians called it "Mother Mountain."

"You know, Joyce, it would be fun to live out here on a small farm after we retire. The grandchildren could have a pony and we could have chickens and a garden and maybe raise our own beef."

"Yes," she said dreamily, "that would be nice."

We left the small farms after a few miles and once again were driving through timber. The road became steeper and the trees taller. The mountain was lost from view now. "Greenwater is up ahead; would you like to stop for coffee and a stretch?" I asked.

"No, I don't think so. My coffee didn't go down right this morning. Just excited, I suppose. Oh, I can hardly wait to have my second ski lesson."

After ten miles, a bend in the road revealed the parking lot first, then the lodge complex at the Crystal Mountain Ski Area. The parking lot was three-fourths full by noon and the surrounding snow pack looked good. It had evidently snowed during the night and the ski runs would be fast. I drove past the condominium area and on to the parking lot maze on my way to the unloading area near the day lodge. "I'll unload you and the gear so that we won't have to work so hard. Then I'll park the car on the lower lot and join you," I stated matter-of-factly.

"Sounds like a good idea, Sweetie; there is a lot of gear to carry."

"Hey Hon, look up there ahead of us. There's a vacant parking space just a hundred yards from the unloading zone." I quickly turned into it and went about unloading the Volvo. "I'll carry that gear for you, if you'd like."

"No, I can do it."

"Well, you take your skis and poles and I'll carry your boots, with the yellow bottoms, yet," I teased, "and I'll take my gear and the equipment bag."

"Oh, it's going to be a great day; I wonder if Mike can give me my lesson right away?" Joyce exclaimed.

"We'll soon find out," I puffed, showing signs of strain from the load. I could see out of the corner of my eye that Joyce was beginning to show some signs of strain, too. "Let's stop for a minuet. Boy, it sure takes a lot of work to have fun."

After a brief rest, we found our way into the locker room. Joyce sat with a quick drop to the bench; her gear slipping from her hands to the floor. "Wow, that was a load. I'm all in," she puffed.

"You sit there a minute," I suggested, "and I'll go get the lift tickets. Mike said that you would graduate to the lower chair today. That will be much easier than the rope tow."

I returned in a few minutes and found Joyce sitting pretty much the way I had left her. "Here, let me help you put your boots on." I got down on one knee and eased each of her stocking feet into her new boots.

Joyce sighed, "I hate to say this, but I feel like an old woman."

I looked at her in surprise. I had never heard a remark like that from this positive, full-of-energy lady. As I looked up into her eyes I could see fatigue I hadn't seen before. The bronchitis she had that last week of school before the Christmas vacation had been hard on her. I encouraged her to take it easy, but being a school nurse, she felt responsible to be available to the school children when they needed her. Also Christmas baskets for less fortunate families were one of her crusades and she loved delivering them herself. Some of the children's gifts in the baskets, along with the food, were paid for by her, anonymously.

"Look Hon," I stammered, "why don't you sit here for awhile and I'll go see if Mike's around."

"O.K. that would be good."

I returned ten minutes later and informed her that her lesson was set for one o'clock. "Are you sure you're up to it?"

"Oh, yes. That will give me plenty of time to finish dressing and I'll just take it easy. You go on ahead and ski. I know you're anxious to begin and we'll meet at Mike's ski hut after the lesson."

"Well, O.K. if you're sure. I'll meet you at the hut at two o'clock, and we can take a few runs together; you can show me what you learned."

She looked at me with those blue, blue eyes and managed a smile. I leaned over her as she sat on the long bench and she seemed so small. I kissed her softly. "See you later," I promised. I turned and walked out of the door.

I located my skis and poles in the rack outside the lodge where I had left them and headed for Chair One. I shared the trip to the top of the mountain with a middle-aged member of the mountain rescue ski patrol. Our conversation got around to how some people rebel at what the ski patrol sees as its job on the mountain. My companion went on to tell me about a lawsuit pending because the parents of a teen-ager didn't like the way their son had been handled when rescued.

"I'm surprised," I injected, "that anyone would sue the ski patrol for the manner in which they were rescued, as long as they were rescued."

"Yes, it's a crazy world sometimes," he replied. "Well, here we are at the top. Have a good run."

I surveyed the sweeping panorama before me as I adjusted my goggles for the anticipated run down the mountain. *What a marvelous place to ski, I wonder what's in store for me today?* I soon began to feel comfortable as I wound my way down the mountain snowfields and trails. The snow was fast and the day was sunny for the most part and clear. The trip down took less than ten minutes. I looked at my watch; it was 1:05 p.m. *Joyce would just be starting her lesson*, I thought to myself as a strong urge swept over me. *Maybe she wouldn't mind if I watched part of her lesson.*

I found myself turning off the trail I had been on and onto a trail that returned me to the lodge and the beginner's slope. I skied up to Mike's hut, but was informed that he had just left with a student for a private lesson. *That would be Joyce.*

I skied over to the rope tow to catch up with them when I noticed a crowd of skiers on the far side of the tow near the bottom of the beginner's slope. As I approached I saw that someone was lying down in the center of the crowd. All I could see was the bottom of their boots; they were yellow. At that instant my body stiffened. The impact of what I saw hit me. Then a man stood up and looked my way. It was Mike. I fought to get off my skis and under the rope tow to get to Mike and to the center of the crowd.

"It's Joyce," Mike blurted.

"What's wrong?" I screamed.

"I'm not sure," he retorted. "She complained of feeling ill and collapsed."

"My God," I stammered, "it's her heart."

"Has she had trouble before?" he asked anxiously.

"Yes," I replied, fighting to keep control. "Eight years ago she had a heart attack."

"Did you hear that, Ken?" Mike exclaimed. "You were right to give her mouth-to-mouth resuscitation." A woman was desperately trying to find a pulse at her wrist. The crowd's face was one of anxiety.

I sank to my knees and grabbed hold of her booted feet in an attempt to make connection with her and yet stay out of the way of the experts. I did the only thing I could do; I prayed like I had never prayed before. "Oh God, please don't take her. Joyce, don't leave me."

A voice from a young man from the crowd said, "I am an emergency-room doctor, can I help?" The crowd parted as he made his way forward.

"Yes," Ken gasped. "This isn't working. We've got to get her to the infirmary. We have a respirator there and everything you will need, doctor. I've sent for the toboggan litter."

"Here it comes now," yelled Mike. "Move back folks and let it through."

Joyce looked so small lying there in the center of that circle of well-wishers. All were strangers except Mike and myself and yet each person there was linked together with the single purpose of bringing her back to life.

The crowd stood back as the ski patrol members carefully lifted her onto the toboggan. The snowmobile eased the litter easily over the snow, and I had a difficult time keeping up as I half ran and half stumbled behind it. Once inside the infirmary another doctor and nurse joined the team and the ski patrol members withdrew to the perimeter of the drama. I had repositioned myself at her feet and held onto her ankles as I watched, in shock at the scene before me.

The doctors and nurses worked rapidly and expertly as they tried one procedure and then another to get Joyce's heart to take over again. Nothing worked!

The emergency room doctor took me aside and said, "It doesn't look good. We're going to keep trying, but if we are not successful in the next five minutes, there's no hope."

He was telling me what I guess I already knew. I thanked him and returned to my vigil. Ten minutes later they stopped. Everyone left. They were beaten and it showed in their faces. I moved to Joyce's side, laid my head on her chest and sobbed, "Don't leave me, Hon." But I knew she already had. I looked at the wall clock. It was 2:05.

A member of the ski patrol called the mortician in Auburn, Washington and he was on his way. Mike said commandingly, "I'm not going to let you drive home alone, Harry. I will drive you and my brother-in-law will follow and bring me back here."

I sat there, emotionally spent and nodded my head to the affirmative. I was in a state of shock and everything seemed unreal. The trip home was a never-ending one. Mike tried to make conversation with me and I tried to do my part, but it was painful for both of us. Eventually we arrived, I fixed a hot drink for them, thanked them profusely for their kindness, and then they were gone, but not before my son from Bremerton had arrived. I had called him from the ski lodge at the suggestion of Mike, and he arrived just minutes after we had reached the condo.

The people around me were rescuing me… and I needed rescuing. First Mike, then my son Rod, then the minister and his wife stopped by on their way to celebrate New Year's Eve. I then called my mother who said she would be ready to be picked up the next day and would stay with me as long as I wanted her to.

I called each of Joyce's sons soon after I arrived home and broke the tragic news. It was one of the hardest things I ever had to do, but I felt some relief from having done so. I guess it's true, misery likes company. We agreed to meet the next day at the mortuary in Auburn at a specified time.

The wheels were in motion ending this segment of my life…

A Second Marriage

I remarried, three years later, to Selma McGuire, a divorcee with four grown children and nine grandchildren. Thus, the family tree grew by leaps and bounds; Louree never remarried.

I worked three years at several jobs in the motivational-training field before I trained for a position as a vocational rehabilitation counselor. I counseled injured workers assigned to me from the Department of Labor and Industries. Being a private contractor, I chose to have more time off. I casually mentioned to my ski partner, Pat Lettenmaier, I had always wanted to go to Baja, Mexico.

His comment was, "Why don't we do it?"

Surprised by his apparent eagerness I asked, "When is a good time to go?"

"How about October? It's too early to ski and I don't have anything else going then."

A Trip to the Baja

That's how it started; it was now late August and I had to make sure the truck and camper were up to the seven-thousand-mile trip. The truck and camper were older, but so were we. I went through the camper and the truck with a fine toothcomb looking for potential problems. I did some cosmetic and mechanical work, bought extra parts for the truck that might possibly be needed, and waited for the date of departure.

We left during the second week in October and had an uneventful trip through the states of Washington, Oregon, and California. By that time we were used to traveling in a truck and camper and had the bugs worked out as far as sleeping, cooking, and housekeeping duties were concerned. A seasoned traveler, Pat is a good traveling companion, having gone around the world once and taken a solo two months, hiking trip in Nepal shortly after his retirement as a Boeing engineer. In other words, he's smart, an outdoorsman, and a good camper. I've too have done my share of traveling and camping, but never wandered as far or as often as he.

After three days driving 1400 miles south, we crossed the border into Mexico at Tijuana. Immediately we knew we were in a second or third world country. Most things seemed tacky, run-down, and in need of repair.

We drove a hundred miles south of the border and made our campsite at an advertised, but deserted, campground a half-mile off the main road and three hundred yards from the Pacific Ocean. In addition to a half-dozen cement pads for trailers or campers there were a dozen beach-type cabins, which appeared to have no connection with the empty pads. Some were cabins were vacant, some permanently lived in. They all appeared to be poorly designed and built.

We took a walk to the beach to stretch our legs, look at the ocean, and try our hand at surf fishing. I was wearing a Panama hat, which immediately blew off my head and into the surf. It never looked the same after that. I think using a three-pound coffee can to block it so it could dry was mainly responsible for its new shape. We caught no fish.

It became apparent that not many people lived along the beach in this part of the world. The locals lived closer to the main highway where living was easier. When I say main highway I really should say only highway. The Baja has a two-lane blacktop highway from Ensenada south to the tip, Cabo San Lucas. There is a sign by a stoplight south of Ensenada that reads *this is the last stoplight you will see for 1200 miles.* That gives you an idea of the change of pace that we are experiencing as we travel south.

A local man stopped by our camper before dinnertime and offered to sell us a fresh caught fish. It solved our menu problem for the evening meal. It is a white fish, about two pounds, which he offered to clean for us. We agreed on a price of two dollars. "Is that pesos? I asked.

"No senor, dollars."

It is apparent that our American money will spend easily south of the border. We soon learn to buy pesos, as they will go farther. Our fish cost us more than it would have if we had traded in pesos. However, the fish was delicious and a nice change from our regular fare that relied on being packaged or canned. We turned in early and slept well with no disturbing night noises. The preceding night we had chosen a campsite too close to a busy freeway near San Diego, and sleep had eluded me, but not Pat, who is a wonderful sleeper.

We were awakened the next morning with the loud braying of two wild donkeys that chose to mate across the dirt road from our campsite. Two middle-aged women who lived in one of the broke up the romancing with hurled stones. Pat chastised them for being unrealistic. I stayed out of the discussion, as I felt I had no expertise in this area.

Later we saw one of these hefty women in the bow of a sixteen-foot open boat equipped with an outboard motor that was shooting the surf line head-on in order to get out to the fishing waters. I was amazed at her courage to sit in the bow of the boat giving it ballast, so her male partner could aim the boat directly into the breaking surf. They were successful and soon were out of sight. Pat and I walked the beach for several miles to take in its beauty and get the exercise needed in order to spend the bulk of the day driving.

As we were about to leave, a local citizen stopped his pickup truck behind our camper blocking our exit. He informed us in a courteous way he owned the property we were camped on and the tariff for staying the night was five dollars, American. He explained that he moved his trailer park to this higher ground because several years ago a Tsunami wave had wiped out his larger trailer park plus private beach cabins that had occupied the land closer and lower to the beach. We had no problem being assessed five dollars for our night's stay.

"That bathroom across the road is mine," he said. "If you used it, I hope you put the used toilet paper in the box instead of flushing it down the drain."

We were taken aback by this information, yet we assured him we had, which wasn't true. We took this as a lesson learned.

He explained, "This is a general practice in the Baja because of our inadequate septic tank and drain field system."

We paid him and he backed out of our way. As we traversed the narrow, single-track dirt road back to the main highway, we passed many acres of truck gardening. It was apparent this was the main industry in the surrounding area. A variety of crops included beets, lettuce, celery beans, tomatoes, and sweet potatoes. Irrigation was going on and it was a lovely sight to see.

The few houses we passed were in good repair, colorful and with well-tended yards. The houses were small and seemed to surround a public school, like chicks sitting around a mother hen. You sensed the school was the center of life in this small village. The few businesses were strategically placed on the main highway, which bordered the edge of town to serve the villagers, tourists, and those living in the outlying areas.

We stopped at one of the small stores (there were no large ones), as I needed a tube of liniment for a sore shoulder. Each store seemed to be a specialty store. If you wanted meat, you went to one store. If you wanted groceries, you went to another store. If you wanted pharmaceuticals, you went to still another store. I entered the pharmaceutical store, which was one room about ten feet by twenty feet in size. The shelves were made of single rough lumber boards that I might use for shelving in my shop back home. The merchandise, such as it was, was neatly placed one or two deep. It was immediately apparent they had a limited selection of everything and not much depth in their inventory.

A middle-aged woman appeared from the rear of the room and asked in Spanish if she could help me. I couldn't think of any Spanish words that would convey to her what I wanted. I then tried my hand at charades, but this got me nowhere; however, it did bring a smile to her face. Finally I resorted to surveying the shelves until I came to a tube of liniment. I had no choice as to brand or scent. They had an inventory of three, so she was still in the liniment business after my purchase. I had the feeling I had overpaid with my American money, so we resolved to go to the bank and buy pesos. There was no bank. We proceeded on our way, determined to buy pesos before the day was out.

It was nearly noon, as we had a late start due to our morning beach-walk. We looked for a turnout or a park or someplace to pull over and fix lunch in our camper. It took a while, as there are no rest stops in the Baja. Finally we picked up signs that we were approaching a town of some size. The sign said San Quintin. "I thought San Quintin was an island prison in San Francisco Bay?" I said.

"That's spelled San Quentin," replied Pat. "This has the letter' I' instead of an 'e' in the middle of the word, so it's probably pronounced differently."

We stopped for gas although we still had nearly a half tank. The scarcity of gas stations and stores of any kind made us decide on the 'side of caution'. We pulled over to the side of the station to park and fix our lunch. It wasn't what I consider a great picnic sight, but if we didn't concentrate on the outside view of dirt, plastic bags, scrub cactus, and more dirt, it was okay.

It became apparent to us that most of the gas stations were built from the same set of plans and were painted the same gaudy orange and blue colors. We found out later they were government owned and strategically placed so tourists wouldn't be stranded between the far-distant towns. I'm sure they were attractive when they were new, but they looked like they had been thirty years without maintenance. They had dirt driveways, no landscaping, and the bathrooms were a real challenge for the senses. They had two types of gasoline: Ethel and Regular. The Ethyl was comparable to our Regular in the United States and their Regular was something less. We made the mistake of buying the Regular gas once and the truck ran 'sick' until we added some octane-booster. Fortunately, I was prepared for this emergency.

Traffic is never heavy in the Baja. We were stopped once for an hour while they were resurfacing the road and only a total of a dozen cars, trailers, motor homes, and campers sat waiting. As we waited we soon realized that resurfacing meant less than what it means in the States. It became apparent that both lanes of the road ahead of us had been oiled, and we thought we were probably waiting for a machine with a gravel spreader that would soon appear around the bend a quarter mile ahead. A power roller to pack down the gravel into the fresh oil would probably follow this. We soon found out our assumption was wrong.

A one and a half ton truck with stake sides soon appeared filled with crushed rock and four workers armed with shovels stood in the back of the truck. Two workers were shoveling gravel out the back end of the slow moving truck; the other two were the reserve team who took over in a few minutes to take their place at the back of the truck shoveling for all they were worth. It was heavy, fast work and I can see why they had two shifts.

Another truck and crew replaced the first truck as soon as it ran out of crushed rock. After three turn-arounds like this, they finally got to us. We then proceeded over freshly graveled and oiled road for about a mile. We could only imagine the long process of road refinishing in the Baja. Several of the locals, instead of waiting in line, went off the road and drove parallel to the road until they passed the road repair crew. The condition of their cars looked like they had done this before.

We came to the border separating the states of North Baja and South Baja. There was a monument and a sign informing us of this fact. Because the Baja is so long, I guess they thought it warranted being two states. We soon came to our second night's destination, Guerrero Negro, which in English means 'Black Warrior'. The town was off the highway about a mile, but we stayed in a trailer park at the junction of the main high way and the road running into Guerrero Negro. The complex consisted of a dozen motel cabins, a dozen trailer pads, a restaurant and a bar. This was the only establishment at the junction.

We had been six days on the road from our beginning in Federal Way, Washington, so we decided to treat ourselves to' dinner out.' It was cozy and clean and the food was excellent. We had Mexican dinners and washed it down with a bottle of Dos Equis beer, as we weren't drinking the water to avoid Montezuma's Revenge.

We took a short walk after dinner and turned in early. The next day we drove the mile into Guerrero Negro and were pleasantly surprised by the quality of the homes and businesses. We went to the bank first and bought pesos. The lady behind the teller's cage was not friendly at all. Maybe she was put off by our use of her native tongue. We needed to replenish our larder and stopped at a fairly good-sized grocery store. An elderly gentleman's job outside the store was to sweep the area clean so customers wouldn't track sand into the store. The roads in the town were not paved and there were no sidewalks. The price of groceries seemed to be similar to prices in the states. The selection was limited, but we found everything we needed.

Guerrero Negro's chief industry is processing salt from the Pacific Ocean. The flooded low, flat fields held salt water forming drying ponds for evaporation that left the salt, which was then collected and ended up in bags of varying sizes to be sold locally and elsewhere. No town the size of Guerrero Negro could use that much salt. The town seemed prosperous by Baja standards and probably had a population of several thousand people.

We retraced our way back to the highway and headed south. Pat and I took turns driving as we had from the beginning. This gave us plenty of opportunity to study the terrain of low rocky hills dotted with cactus. Cactus comes in a variety of sizes and shapes, but the Sorrero cactus is prevalent here. Once in awhile a single-track dirt road would branch off from the main highway, wander through the terrain, taking the course of least resistance, and disappear over a distant hill. I wondered about the occupants who might use this road to their house and marveled at such a remote way to live.

The next stop would be Rosaria. I think the Mexicans like this name as I found it used three times on our map. We were still close to the Pacific Ocean side of the Baja so we looked for a trailer park before approaching Rosaria. Sure enough there was a sign that advertised "Honey's Ocean Front Trailer Accommodations." This sounded like just what we were looking for. Here again, it was only a sign and a road leading off the main road in the direction of the ocean, which you never saw unless you took a side road. It seems the Mexicans don't want to look at water. The towns up to this point in our trip were near the water, but not on the water.

Following the road about a mile, it did a ninety-degree turn south and ran parallel to the Ocean. We came to "Honey's" and were shocked to find that we were the only rig there. Again, it was about three hundred yards to the ocean, but no other houses or trailer parks were to be seen. I had a strange feeling of emptiness and taken aback by the vastness of the beach area, minus people.

We drove up to the house, which was the only building except for a couple of small sheds in back. I knocked on the door and a young Mexican woman appeared. Behind her stood an inquisitive, but shy, young boy. The woman greeted me in Spanish. I returned the greeting and asked about trailer space. It was obvious they had plenty of space. The sites were sort-of-level with some utilities, but no lots were paved. A man appeared in the background, but made no attempt to communicate with us. It became apparent that this couple and their son were off-season caretakers.

Again, the fee was five dollars, American, or fifteen pesos. We paid, but there was no sign-in procedure. We selected the most level site and hooked up to electricity and sewer, but not the water. We were apprehensive about using the local water so we limited our drinking and cooking to our 30-gallon tank that we had filled before crossing the border. We washed our clothes and our rig using the local water. We boiled local water for dishwashing and drip-dried the dishes in a rack. Pat and I were both health conscious.

We prepared lunch and then took our fishing gear and headed for the beach. The weather was a pleasant 80 degrees so we wore only bathing suits, sandals, hats, and a T-shirt tucked in our swimming suit waistband at the back. We were ready for some surf fishing, swimming, and beach walking. We got all three, but no fish. Not even a strike. We watched some young men with a long gill net bring fish in, so we knew there were fish there.

The five young men had suddenly appeared in a dilapidated, old pick-up driving up the beach and stopped just beyond where we stood in the surf. The waves were gentle and the breaker line was a long way out, coming in over a fairly flat beach. Standing knee deep in the fairly warm water, we soon were occupied watching these five work. They stretched out a long net that looked to be six feet wide and one hundred feet long.

This procedure was accompanied with much laughter and clowning around. Grabbing the end of the net, one young, strong-looking man walked into the surf taking the end of the net with him.

Each man spaced himself anequal distance along the net and grabbed onto it. They then walked into the surf perpendicular to the waves. Eventually the one in the lead was swimming with the net for a short distance. After a few minutes they reversed the procedure and brought the net in with fish trapped by their gills in it. This is gillnetting without a boat. They obviously were not satisfied with their catch, so they rolled up the net, put it in the bed of the pickup, climbed aboard, and went hooting and hollering up the beach. This show ended our stay at the beach.

* * *

Driving on south, we passed a man walking shortly before noon. Even though it was an isolated area, we decided not to pick him up because of stories told back in the States about bandits in the Baja. He didn't appear to be that type, but we chose to be cautious. After all, he would have to sit up front with us in a two-person cab or back in the camper out of our sight with all of our personal items. Passing him by, we felt pangs of guilt even though he hadn't tried to thumb a ride.

Looking ahead we saw a turnout, which would make a suitable lunch site, and parked near the biggest Sorrero cactus I'd ever seen. Other people stopping here had chosen to carve their initials in its tough skin. *People aren't that much different are they? Or maybe it was gringos from the States like us.* By the time we had finished lunch our hitchhiker caught up with us. Pat flagged him over and offered him water. He quickly drank a pint of water and said, "Gracious."

He was a slender young man who spoke no English and was poorly dressed. He had evidently walked twenty miles and was going to Mulege, which was another twenty miles ahead. We gave him another pint of water, but did not offer him a ride. Both of us struggled with that decision, but we chose the side of caution again. Our consciences were soothed somewhat knowing we had given him a quart of our precious water, which he obviously needed. The fact he never asked anything of us…maybe that was the hardest part of all.

* * *

Mulege was a pleasant surprise. The highway ran alongside the water; this time the water was the Sea of Cortez, not the Pacific Ocean. We had crossed the Baja Peninsula from west to east because that's where the only road goes. Besides Tijuana, Mulege was the largest Mexican town we came to with a population of around 3000 people. The main street ran at right angles to the highway with a pretentious citylimits sign welcoming us. While driving up the main street, we were stopped by a local policeman as were all other cars entering town. Pretty girls, colorfully dressed, went to each car and extended a small bucket for donations for some local charity. We were surprised by this, but donated a peso to 'something'. There was a festive mood about this transaction and the girls and the policeman gave us 'gringos' a big smile.

Pat said, "I want to make a phone call to the States and let people know we're okay." This took some doing. He finally accomplished this after three or four dry runs; cell phones were still in their infancy stage.

The town consisted of two main streets and four or five minor cross streets. As we walked along the sidewalk from business to business we replenished our supplies of food. There seemed to be a lot of ironwork on the buildings similar to the French quarter in New Orleans. Also the vegetation was very tropical. Date palms were prevalent and Bougainvillea hung from the balconies, as most downtown buildings were two stories high. The two main streets were paved, but the minor streets were not.

However, the real show stopper was a church in the middle of town made of steel and glass. It was of European architecture with a high steeple. A reader board told us it was designed by a Monsieur Eiffel and was a gift from the Republic of France to Mexico. This same architect had earlier designed the tower in Paris bearing his name. The church stuck out as a rose among brambles, looking so different from any building in town; perhaps any building in the Baja. France gave the United States the Statue of Liberty and Mexico the steel and glass church in Mulege; an unusual gesture by today's standards.

The phone call completed and the larder replenished, we started looking for a place to spend a night or two. Someone made us understand there was a state park on the south edge of town on the water. I can't remember who this saint was or how they got that information across to us, but sure enough, it was there. We found a vacant campsite, which bordered a lagoon.

"Hey Pat," I called out, "this should be worth a three day stay."

"This does look like paradise, doesn't it? You get us registered and I'll set up camp."

I walked to the campgrounds office passing the public bathrooms on the way. The smell of the outdoor privies caused me to register for only one night. I figured we could decide tomorrow if we wanted to stay longer. There were about thirty campsites and I felt fortunate we had one so close to the water.

On returning to our campsite I brought Pat up-to- speed regarding my decision for one night and then decide; he agreed. It was about five o'clock and we had time to look around and socialize before settling in for the night with dinner, cribbage, and lights out. An Englishman, who had been there two months, occupied the campsite next to us. I was impressed until I found out why he had been there so long. It seems his automobile, a Mercedes Benz, had a serious engine problem and he looked locally for a mechanic to fix it.

In the Baja any man with a half-dozen automobile wrenches calls himself a mechanic. Our new neighbor had turned his car over to a so-called mechanic and lived to rue the day. Six weeks later the Mercedes was worse than ever. He had his car towed to a honest-to-goodness garage that's had it for two weeks, waiting for parts from Germany. Fortunately, he was retired, had no family, lived in a tent trailer, and had a paddleboard and bicycle to get around on, plus I might add, a magnificent tan. He seemed resigned to his fate and was making the best of it.

* * *

It was Pat's turn to cook dinner, so he excused himself and I wandered to the water's edge. It was a picture postcard setting. Sailboats swung to their anchor buoys spaced a hundred yards apart. The water was crystal clear and warm for swimming, snorkeling, and fishing. I slipped off my sandals and standing ankle deep in water, let it caress my feet. A fourteen-foot aluminum boat pulled to shore near me and a deeply tanned caucasian man jumped out, tilted the outboard motor up, and pulled the boat on to the sandy beach beyond the tide line. He had a slender, but muscular, build and sun-bleached hair that hung halfway to his shoulders. Turning toward me he said, "Hello, Amigo."

"Hello," I replied. "By the looks of your bootie in the bottom of the boat, I see you have been snorkeling for shells. I offered my hand, I'm Harry McIntyre from the States."

He returned the gesture, "Just call me Dave. I'm originally from Canada, but I've been here in Mulege five years."

"Really! If you don't mind my asking, how do you make a living here, or are you independently wealthy?"

"Doing what you see me doing right now. I just dropped off a client I took out for the day snorkeling to view the tropical fish and gather shells. It's a full day as we eat lunch on the beach."

"Fantastic! Tell me more." Just then a young Mexican man approached us and spoke to Dave rapidly in Spanish. It was apparent they were close friends, and Dave answered him in fluent Spanish. I had no idea what they said except *hello* and *goodbye*. Dave laughed at the surprised look on my face.

"As you can see, I'm not a gringo anymore; I'm one of them. I came here five years ago to recover from a nasty skiing accident I sustained near my home in Canada. I liked Mulege so well, after I recovered, I stayed. Up until then I had been a professional skier; not much chance to put my skills to work here, so I bought this boat and motor and turned a newly acquired hobby of collecting shells into a business."

"That's a great story, Dave. How much do you charge for a day on the water? Maybe Pat and I could go out tomorrow."

"I get eighty dollars a day including lunch, but I only work every other day, so tomorrow is out."

"Why only every other day?"

"That's all the money I need to meet my needs."

Just then Pat called and informed me dinner was on the table. I said goodbye to my new friend and I told him I'd try to see him tomorrow. Dave walked off toward a nearby restaurant where he was soon joined by a couple of female friends. So *much for mad, impetuous youth.*

On my way back to our campsite, I became aware of being attacked by an army of small gnats. Back home we would call them "no see-ums." I quickly closed the screen door behind me and was thankful all the windows in the camper had screens. Pat had a wholesome meal on the table, which we did justice to.

"Why don't you take a walk while I do the dishes," I suggested. "Then we can continue our cribbage tournament."

"Good idea, McIntyre. I need to get out of the kitchen. By the way, have you checked out the bathroom and shower area?"

"Yes," I replied, but I chose not to elaborate on my findings.

I had barely finished my kitchen chore when Pat returned swearing and brushing off his clothing with flailing arms. "Damn no see-ums and what a smelly bathroom and shower area. I suggest we move on tomorrow, as we don't need this; I don't care how pretty it is."

I stepped outside to check the evening air and the lagoon view at night. In about two minutes it was I standing in the camper flailing my arms around my head and shoulders to eliminate any no see-ums. "I wonder if this is a nightly thing or a rare occurrence? I'll ask our neighbor in the morning, since his lights are already out. Is it your deal or mine?"

* * *

Just as I was getting to sleep, an eighteen-wheeler came down the hill bordering the park. The cowboys of old in the Baja have a counter-part. They drive eighteen-wheel trucks and are equipped with air brakes. Most areas in the States outlaw air brakes because of the excessive noise they make when applied, not so in the Baja. Truckers like to use them to save the hydraulic braking system as running against the engine is acting like a brake. The noise they make will bring you right out of your bed, and that's exactly what happened. I jumped out of bed looking for the train that was about to run through the camper.

Needless to say, between the gnats, odors, and air brakes, we knew we weren't going to stay there another night. Our neighbor with the sick Mercedes informed us this was a nightly occurrence. We told him we were looking for a nice, quiet piece of waterfront to spend a couple of days as we had been traveling steady for ten days. He told us if we were going north instead of south there was such a place called Punt Chivata just thirty miles up the coast. He described it in such glowing terms that we made a major decision. Instead of going further south, as we originally planned, we would call Mulege the end of the line and turn north to Punta Chivata. This turned out to be a good decision as it was all our informant said it was.

The road north ran about ten miles away from the Sea of Cortez, so we turned onto a secondary road to get to our destination. In places this secondary road was little more than a flash-flood riverbed. After traveling only ten miles the first hour, we began to wonder if we had made the right decision. However, all the apprehension vanished when we reached the crest of a hill and could see the Sea of Cortez lying out before us like a beautiful, blue, jewel necklace.

We shifted to a lower gear and crawled down the rutty single-track road until suddenly we saw a few houses and a small grocery store. The road branched and to one side was a small airplane landing strip, and a storage yard with boats, motor homes and trailers. Along the water's edge were about twenty rather nice, modern homes leading to a one story rambling hotel with a dock and accommodations for seaplanes.

The other branch of the road took us down to the water's edge and a state park with about fifteen campsites, each with a palm frond umbrella, fire ring, and space for camping.

At first glance we could see empty spaces, so I backed into one in order for our camper door to open to the white sandy beach and surf beyond. The park had outdoor toilets and showers without a roof, but reasonably clean and no repulsive odor. What more could we ask for?

The water wasn't heated, but it didn't need to be because the water pipes ran close enough to the surface of the ground creating water warm enough for a prolonged shower. The source was artesian. Therefore, the water was free of the parasite responsible for 'Montezuma's Revenge.' We had rationed our water for the past week allowing ourselves only two gallons per day, and suddenly we had all the good water we could use, and did we ever use it. In fact, we even washed the camper and truck before we left three days later.

Punta in Spanish means point or cape so we were in a cove formed by the point of rock for which it's named. The Point was flat rock rising about twenty feet above the sea, triangular in shape, and about the area of two football fields. On the north side was our campground; on the south side was a beautiful swimming beach. The north side had a reef about a hundred feet off shore, visible at low tide, which provided a safe harbor between it and the beach for the small fishing boats owned by the campers.

The Sea of Cortez has about a four-foot tide, which reminded us that we were on salt water. It is three hundred miles long and a hundred miles wide in places. It always appeared peaceful to us, but we were told it could give you a fight for your life, if it chose to. The water temperature was delightful and we stood in it for several hours at a time, fishing. There was very little surf and the water was crystal clear.

After a leisurely lunch Pat suggested we split up and explore the area. I think he needed some alone time after ten days and nights with me. He went south and I headed north. The north end of our cove stopped at a promontory of rock that jutted out into the sea a hundred feet. I climbed over it watching for creepy crawlers as I went hand over hand up the rock edifice. On the other side was another cove more beautiful than ours, but only because it was totally uninhabited. The waves came in gently, and there was not a footprint or human mark of any kind. It was a thrilling experience, except for one thing; there was no one with which to share it.

At the far end of that cove was another promontory of rock, which was higher by far than the first one. Feeling a need for adventure and exercise I climbed to the top of it and stopped dead in my tracks. There before me was a cross, decorated with artificial flowers. A subscription on a wooden plaque read: "To My Beloved Juan." Here, in the middle of nowhere was this tribute to a man, presumably by a woman who loved him. How many pairs of eyes have seen this? *Not many.*

Looking to the north from this three hundred foot promontory, I could see cove after cove before they dissipated into a long straight beach. I headed back to our campsite to share my adventure with Pat and to hear about his. I wished I had brought my fishing pole from the camper as the rock formations below the surface of the water at the promontories showed underwater caves and shelves where fish could live.

Pat and I returned to the camper at the same time, which proves that our attention span is very similar. He said, "There's a swimming beach and relatively new houses lining the beach to the south. Each lot appears to be about a hundred feet wide and located on a rock shelf about twenty feet above the water."

"We'll have to try that beach out."

"Good idea. The homes reflect North American taste more than Spanish, so I'm guessing Americans own them."

Our immediate neighbors were friendly, but it was evident there was a "clique" who'd been here for long periods of time. They had their own happy-hour starting about four o'clock and ending when it got dark. This included a half-dozen couples with permanent set ups, even to the extent of having dug sanity pits for their gray and black water. They'd planted flowers, and even built temporary decks with harbors. Every afternoon and evening, their talking and laughter filled the air. Most permanent campers had twelve to sixteen foot fishing boats anchored in front of their space protected from the surf; what a perfect set-up.

One older couple lived at Punta Chivata in the park year around. They kept in touch with their family by phoning the States each Sunday from the hotel for twenty dollars for five minutes of cell phone time. Another couple lived in the Park six months out of the year, and then went north to Portland, Oregon to sell pots and pans at home demonstration parties for six months to support their life style. Pat and I agreed, it's different strokes for different folks.

* * *

The second day there we took our snorkel gear and headed for the swimming beach. We had a grand time searching out and watching the beautiful tropical fish. It was an unusual experience swimming along with a school of fish. They seemed to enjoy our company as much as we enjoyed theirs. The water was comfortable and we stayed in for about an hour.

We decided to treat ourselves to a night out at the hotel as we had been told they had a good restaurant. We walked the half-mile to the restaurant and were pleasantly surprised to have outdoor dining with a million dollar view of the Sea of Cortez by sunset. We were surprised the waiters wore tuxedos and everything was first class. We asked our waiter how Punta Chivata could qualify to have such luxury dining. Because he had few customers, he seemed to enjoy leisurely answering our questions.

He said, "Once the hotel attracted the world's rich and famous who were interested in catching trophy fish. They flew in, landing at the adjacent airstrip, or arrived by boat to fish the local waters for some of the world's best fishing. Consequently a hotel and restaurant was built to accommodate them in a style they were used to, along with a fleet of charter boats for fishing. Unfortunately, just as everything was in place, the fish decided to move several hundred miles south. What we were experiencing that night was the leftovers from a short era of prosperity. The food was delicious, the service was excellent, and we extended ourselves on the size of the tip.

The next day was spent, hiking and fishing the different coves, and viewing the dozen very nice homes along the water between the Point and south to the Hotel. Several were under construction and we inspected them to compare construction techniques between the States and the Baja. There were no differences we could determine except the extensive use of stucco for their exteriors. The workers even had boom boxes turned up loud, but the lyrics to the songs were beyond our understanding.

That evening after dinner, with our housekeeping chores complete, we sat for our usual two games of cribbage. Suddenly there was a knock on the door. Pat and I looked at one another registering surprise. I was closest to the door, opened it and stood frozen looking into at least twenty pairs of eyes focusing directly upon me. Then came a sound, somewhere between a yell and a scream. "Trick or Treat' was discernable from the cacophony of sound. Pat stood behind me now and we both burst into laughter…it was Halloween, even in the Baja.

We had a three-pound box of cookies we used for tribute. As each child came forward they said "gracias" in soft, shy voices. Some wore simple costumes... others did not. Behind this group of small children stood a half dozen smiling mothers. Somehow it felt like home wasn't very far away.

* * *

The morning after the Halloween episode we washed the rig and headed north. There comes a time when you know a trip is over and it's time to go home. The first day of the return trip brought us back to Guerra Negro and the same campgrounds where we had stayed on the way south. We treated ourselves to a meal at their restaurant and much to our surprise, the couple at Punta Chivata who sold pots and pans six months out of the year, were having dinner and on their way back to Portland. They parked their thirty-two foot Airflow trailer in the storage lot at Punta Chivata so were traveling light.

That night a barking dog, which had been locked up in a car interrupted our sleep while its owners were having a late party at the restaraunt bar. Finally, in desperation, I went to the owner of the establishment and complained. The problem was solved as the dog stopped barking. We pulled out the next morning and headed back to Honey's R.V. Park for the second day of our journey home.

A stop for lunch in a quaint Mexican town with a town square and a very large Catholic church held a surprise for us. We toured the church, as it seemed the thing to do, and returned to the square to eat our lunch in the camper. As we sat eating and looking out the window at the park and the passing social scene, two very pretty young senoritas stopped near our rig. They sat on steps leading up to the park and seemed to be preening themselves, like male peacocks do. They stayed during our entire lunch break and were there when we left. As we drove away I saw them follow our departure with their eyes. Then the thought came to me, *just possibly, these ladies are there to conduct business with two old gringos.* I mentioned this to Pat and he said, "Get real, McIntyre."

We arrived at Honey's early in the afternoon and decided to go clamming for Pismo-type clams. After borrowing two small shovels from the caretaker of the R.V. Park, we walked to the beach, then each set off in different directions in search of the ever-illusive clam. When we returned to our starting point, Pat had one clam; I had none. We asked the caretakers at Honey's if clams were that scarce. She was able to get across to us in broken English, that here husband brought home over 50 that day. Obviously, we didn't know how to find and dig the Pismo clam. We used our stateside technique of digging razor clams, which was totally wrong.

The secret is to walk barefoot in knee-deep water at low tide and feel with your bare feet for a lump in the sand. When you discover a lump you are standing on a Pismo clam. You then scoop down with your shovel and bring the clam to the surface; live and learn. If our only source of food on this trip were the ocean, we would have died of starvation.

The next morning we headed for Tijuana and the border crossing. As we got in line with our rig, street vendors took this opportunity to sell the gringos one more thing they didn't need. I was interested in a blown glass sailboat, but the line moved forward, and so did we. The vendors were like carnival hustlers, which made the waiting in line anything but boring.

The border police inspected our camper, but mostly spent their time reading our facial expressions. After a cursory search, they waved us on and we were back in our native land. There is something exhilarating about returning home. We felt like we belonged; a feeling we hadn't had for several weeks without being conscious of the fact.

We stopped for the night at campgrounds in Escondido, a few miles north of the border and paid twenty-five dollars for the privilege, not the five dollars we paid everywhere in the Baja. However, the conveniences were as different as night and day: clean restrooms, showers with hot water, level paved parking spaces, and for an extra dollar, cable T. V.

Day four on our trip home was spent traveling as many miles as we could before evening. This took us through most of the state of California. We stopped at the town of Mount Shasta, California and awoke to ice on our wastewater bucket the next morning. It was November; and we were entering the Siskiyou Mountains from the south. The change in weather was shocking, as we had become accustomed to eighty-degree weather in the Baja. That evening I started to turn on the furnace in the camper, but Pat was reluctant to have me do so, as it was old and hadn't been used for a long time. He was afraid of being asphyxiated in our sleep. He loaned me a wool stocking cap, which helped get me through the cold night.

Day five was spent like day four with the goal of covering as many miles as possible since we had already viewed this scenery just three weeks prior and we were anxious to get home. By nightfall we entered into Washington, but it was difficult finding a campsite for the night. We drove about five miles out of the way to find a very secondary campground. However, we were in Washington, our native state, and we would be home in Federal Way tomorrow.

We arrived in Federal Way shortly after noon, as we didn't stop to eat lunch. I took Pat to his home where we shook hands, congratulating each other on a successful three week's round trip to the Baja.

We discovered the Mexican people were soft-spoken, smiling, and friendly. Also, we learned arid country has a beauty of its own and everyone in the world doesn't want to live on the water's edge. Well-meaning friends asked me if we carried a gun with us.

"No, we never felt in danger," I replied. "Well, maybe for a brief moment on Halloween Night."

Vocational Rehabilitation Counseling

The job of Vocational Rehabilitation Counselor was helping injured workers set new work goals, plus getting the training to be employable at these new jobs that accommodated their injuries, and getting them employed. It was a demanding job, but always rewarding. I traveled to my clients, to training sites, and potential job sites, so I did a lot of driving. Therefore, I chose to have a Corvette as a company car. This made the job even more rewarding.

I worked for four different firms during my twelve years of employment and moved on for four different reasons. The first firm went broke six months after I started, but that gave me time to serve a necessary apprenticeship to learn how to do the job within the confines of the State Department of Labor and Industries. Of course they hired me because of my master's degree in counseling.

The next firm I worked for sent me over half the State of Washington near the end of my four-year stay there with clients spread out in the rural areas. Politics pays a part in this industry and my boss got on the wrong side of someone and lost his State license. In my travels I was helping him shut down outlying offices to accommodate the States decree. Prior to that I carried a full load of twenty clients in a concentrated area near my home.

The third firm was a one-office firm in Ballard run by a former State senator. He had three different businesses under one roof and I was his only vocational rehabilitation counselor. He paid me half of what I brought in through my billing the State for my hours and travel. He provided the license, office, and office support. This worked well for me, as I was one the road three days per week and two days in the office. Unfortunately, a professional in the field told him I was making too much money, so he suggested I work for a smaller share. I declined, as I was ready to move on due to the historic length of my attention span.

The last firm had an office in Tacoma I worked out of and did most of my work on the road or home. With the aid of a fax machine, I reported to the office once per week for signing of documents and a meeting with the boss. This lasted four years, and as I approached my seventieth birthday I decided it was time to retire…again. It had been a challenging, interesting, and workable second career and I appreciated the opportunity.

Alone in the
San Juan Islands

As a vocational rehabilitation counselor I interspersed my work with short trips by land and water. This was often solo, as Selma didn't like 'roughing it'. Another trip that comes to mind is one to the San Juan Islands for five days by boat.

The boat and trailer behind my truck looked enormous as I traveled north, but a boat always looks much bigger out of water, especially on a trailer, and especially on the freeway, moving through Seattle at highway speed for passenger cars. Actually "Kitchen Pass" was a twenty-two foot Sea Ray; a fisherman's boat in a classy sort of way.

It had a 350 c.c. inboard engine plus a small outboard for trolling that slept two in a cuddy cabin, and seated four topside with seats that broke down into beds to accommodate two sleepers under the Bimini canvas top. Mostly, it looked like a day-cruising speedboat capable of handling rough water; which is true. People don't sleep in a cuddy cabin very often; it's just a place to get out of the weather. However, on this trip I would be sleeping there for the next five nights.

At five-thirty I pulled into the Skyway marina at Anacortas, Wa., which, I discovered, was one-half hour after they shut down the boat hoist for the day. However, I persuaded the departing marina crew to launch me for fifteen dollars, which included parking for my truck and trailer. If the marina never saw the money resulting from that transaction, I was not going to worry about it; I was on my way.

The immenseness of Rosario Straits struck home as I headed off across the eight-mile width of the straits. A wave of anxiety passed over me when I saw I was the only boat in sight and I could see for at least twenty miles. In addition to this anxiety, there was a three foot high wave pattern, I had no moorage for the night, and nighttime wasn't that far away. I quickly rationalized the anxiety away by concentrating on the rugged beauty surrounding me on all sides. After all, I was alone with a powerful boat under me and heading for five days of no planned activity. Feeling better, I now decided to head for Rosario. With a little luck they would have what I needed, moorage, gas, a store, and people; in other words a mariner's haven when there is a fifteen knot wind and you're losing visibility rapidly because of darkness.

I checked and rechecked my chart to determine exactly where I was and the best route to Rosario. Finally, I saw a ferryboat far ahead weaving it's way through a narrow passage off to portside. That had to be Thatcher Pass formed by Decatur Island to the south and Blakely Island to the north. Traveling thirty miles an hour at 3500 r.p.m. soon put me through Thatcher Pass, a quick 90 degree turn to starboard and there, approximately 10 miles ahead, lay a familiar and welcome sight, Rosario. It looked like a snug harbor for the night. *In fact it looked like the only harbor before nightfall.*

As I glided through the narrow opening of the marina I knew if there was an open moorage it would be to port as that is where the slips were for the smaller vessels. It was seven o'clock now and too late to be moving on to another marina, if there was nothing here. I knew the chances were slim since it was August, the height of the tourist season, but--- aha!---one beautiful open berth. With a little careful maneuvering and line tending from a helpful fellow boater, I snuggled in like a chick next to its mother hen at night. I stepped onto the dock, tied my lines after setting the bumpers, and walked to the harbormaster's office to register for the night.

Dinner was simple, I warmed up leftover pork roast slices, and new potatoes and gravy. This was accompanied by gazpacho, {a cold salad comprised of sliced tomatoes, onion, bell paper, and cucumbers swimming in vinegar and spices.}, sour dough bread, and a glass of burgundy wine. After a hurried clean up, I took a walk around the grounds at Rosario, which takes a half hour at least if done properly. Rosario formerly was the estate of a shipping magnate named Moran from the Seattle area. Today it is a full-blown resort with probably a hundred units to rent, three restaurants, a grocery store, spacious manicured grounds, two outdoor pools, and of course, the marina. I guess I should also mention that they have three bars and a nightclub, too.

The night was long as I relearned the gentle art of sleeping aboard a boat in a sleeping bag on a series of cushions for a mattress in a confined space called a cuddy cabin. However, all good and bad things do come to an end and at 8:30 a.m. I awakened to the roar of the propeller of a boat coming to life not too far from my head. It took awhile for me to figure out where I was and what that awful sound was. I poked my head out the companionway and discovered the boat ahead of me was just about to cast off. The two fellows on board thought it was hilarious that they had awakened a late sleeper; I didn't share their mirth.

After a breakfast of hot lemon water, cold cereal, and coffee I made my way out of the marina with the help of the fellow boater from the night before. I asked him if he was leaving that day. He informed me he and his wife reserved a berth for a week each summer at Rosario. They then motored there in their boat if the weather was agreeable, sat for a week, and then motored home. To each his own, I thought. I guess it's like pitching a tent for a week in a state park.

I headed east back into Rosario Straits only now I'm ten miles north of where I left the straits the evening before. I was headed for fishing at Point Lawrence, which is the most easterly tip of Orcas Island. The trip was smooth and fast as I clipped along at 30 miles per hour. I drank coffee from my quart thermos filled from left over breakfast coffee and watched the sky slowly break up from overcast to sunny and clear. I passed a pod of Orcas or" Killer Whales" frolicking like children in a pool. They came up on each side of my boat and raced me for a while, but soon tired of the game.

Five other boats shared the fishing grounds off Pt. Lawrence and though we all worked hard at fishing, I saw only one ugly red snapper boated. I did bring up one five-pound dogfish, but cut him off, leader and all. After a dog fish's teeth rake a leader you might as well throw the leader away because the next fish on may be a fighting salmon and you wouldn't want to lose him because of a faulty leader.

The electric downrigger soon became defunct when the 10-pound sinker, snubber, and lure hung up on the bottom. After much tugging on my part the line broke and I lost my only set-up for the downrigger. This didn't end the fishing; it only meant I would just be using a sport pole.

After four hours of no action after trying every lure in my tackle box, I cranked in my line and headed for Friday Harbor. This is a half hour run in a fast boat like Kitchen Pass. The boat got her name from the original owner. He was a building contractor in southern California who took his workers fishing around Catalina Island when work was slow. Occasionally they were late in returning which caused unhappiness on the home front, especially if the wives hadn't been told about the fishing trip. The owner, tired of taking this heat from the wives, made a rule that the worker had to prove that his spouse knew where they were and what they were doing. Therefore, he named the boat Kitchen Pass because of this process of having a pass, so to speak, from his wife who runs the kitchen and wanting no meals ruined because of a delinquent husband. I know it's a stretch, but that's how the boat got its name.

Friday Harbor is a busy place in the summertime. The marina was full and boats were on the hook between Brown's island and San Juan Island upon which the town of Friday Harbor is located. Friday Harbor is a quaint little town sitting on a hillside and makes its way down to the water's edge. It's a busy harbor with a state ferry docking every hour during the summer months on the way to Victoria, B.C. or returning to Anacortes. It also has a marina accommodating 600 boats, a seaplane slip, a custom's dock, a fuel dock, a shipyard, and a University of Washington Sea Laboratory.

The town was named Friday Harbor because, years ago, some island workers in the San Jeans spent the weekend, starting with Friday, celebrating the completion of a week of work in a remote site... like an island in the San Juans. Of course in the summertime every night is Friday night. If you add 130 transient boats in the summer, that adds up to a lot of people and I became one of them. The harbormaster directed me to a berth and I tied up for the night. Going ashore for groceries gave me an opportunity to stretch my legs after a day's confinement to a boat. Most important was a shower located under the harbormaster's office, which sat high to oversee the marina. I had been 36 hours without a shower, so need I say more?

I cooked a meal very similar to the preceding night, because it was already precooked. After a filling meal, I cleaned up the dishes and took a leisurely stroll on the marina walkways. I alway like to look at the different boats, maybe to find my next boat. *There is always a next one for a sailor, isn't there?* One commercial fishing boat took my eye when I saw the skipper showing off a forty pound salmon to a crowd of boaters who broke into applause at the sight of the fish. Where else could a dead fish be applauded except here in the northwest?

Naturally everyone wanted to know where, when, how much lead, what kind of lure or bait, and how fast was he trolling? He was extremely vague with his answers, so that we only knew he caught it at daybreak, somewhere in the straits of Juan de Fuca, on commercial gear.

I stopped in for a nightcap at a local restaurant with a cocktail lounge overlooking the harbor. There was a fifty-fifty mix of locals and summer people. How do you tell them apart? The summer people are better-dressed, deeper tans because they work at it, and usually have a more prosperous look about them.

I sat looking at the day go away, sipped my Drambuie, and listened to the chatter. A local woman had the floor and was telling all who wanted to listen how she had quit her job that day, was tired of being island-bound, and was headed for Seattle the next day. Her friends wished her well, and she went out into the night.

Returning to Kitchen Pass, I reluctantly climbed into my sleeping bag and hoped for sleep. Exhaustion won out and I slept most of the night. I awakened to the sounds of a marina coming to life. A boat in the distance coughed, then another and another. People were walking their dogs ashore to do what dogs do and return for a day on the water. A tremendous blast of a boat horn told me the Washington Ferry System was still in business. I looked at my watch; it was 7:30. I needed coffee and something besides cold cereal. I quickly dressed, as the temperature, even in summer, was in the fifties.

I remembered that the restaurant-bar of last night had a breakfast menu, so I made my way to the public restrooms under the harbormaster's office in order to make myself presentable for the restaurant crowd. I found a seat by a window and soon had a cup of steaming coffee in front of me. The whole waterfront was coming alive now, and the shipyard off to my left and below me became my focus of attention. I guess I enjoy watching other people work.

The waitress interrupted my people-watching to ask for my order. Pigs in a Blanket are one of my favorite breakfasts and it was on the menu. I settled back with my second cup of coffee and my gaze settled on Brown Island across the bay, just a few hundred yards. Some people call it Friday Island, but not so. It's hard to believe that just 30 years ago this heavily inhabited island was for sale for twenty five thousand dollars because it had no water. Today it is divided into eighty, one acre parcels with water piped from Friday Harbor and twenty five thousand dollars wouldn't go far towards the purchase of one of those eighty lots now.

The waitress brought my breakfast, a third cup of coffee, and the check. I am amazed how good the food tastes, which indirectly tells me my cooking isn't that great. I paid my way out of the restaurant and pushed off for Roche Harbor. It lies on the northern part of San Juan Island, which is a half hour run, if you don't stop to fish. However, I did stop, which is a nice way to waste an hour or two.

The trip north was very scenic and the ferry plowed by every so often on its way to Victoria B.C. or on its return trip to Anacortes by way of Friday Harbor, Orcas Island, and Lopez Island. The passengers on the ferryboat usually wave and I always return their salutation.

Entering Roche Harbor is by way of either West Pearl Island Passage or East Pearl Island Passage depending on the tide and the draft of your boat. With my planing hull, I can go either way at any tide. The complex of Roche Harbor Resort dominates the entire eastern shore of Roche Harbor. Many large boats are anchored out, some to buoys, some just on the hook. Part of the marina is built to accommodate the type of yacht you would expect to see off the Greek Islands; the other part of the marina is where I headed. They had a spot for me, as it was early in the day. I fixed a simple lunch of soup, chips, and beer. Actually, I was really more interested in sight seeing than eating; especially after that big breakfast.

Roche Harbor is touristy in a historic sort of way. The hundred-year-old grocery store is charming and has what you need if you are on a boat. I learned the Catholic Church on the resort grounds is the only privately owned Catholic Church in the United States. It also served as a school a hundred years ago. Roche Harbor is formerly a company owned town, but today it is privately owned. Quarrying of limestone was its industry, with housing, school/church, company store, hotel and docking facilities provided by the company. After a leisurely walk around the area I decided to treat myself to dinner at the hotel restaurant. Again, we are talking about the hundred-year-old Haro Hotel and Restaurant.

I found shower facilities next to the grocery store and prepared myself for a night-on-the-town, that is to say, dinner out and a leisurely after-dinner drink. I dressed for dinner, clean levi's and a polo shirt, and strolled the length of the large boat section of the pier. The boats were backed in so I had the feeling I was a part of a half-dozen cocktail parties in progress being held in the open back deck area of these palatial yachts. I graciously declined an invitation to one of them because I don't mix easily with strangers, especially if they're rich.

The restaurant was like a large gazebo attached to the hotel and the food was excellent. As I lingered over a cup of strong coffee I became aware of some sort of commotion on the dock below me. What I was about to witness was the evening ceremony of lowering the American flag at sundown. I later learned this was a tradition here and part of the show for the summer trade. Young people in their teens, who worked for the company, were dressed in red, white, and blue sailor-type blouses. They marched down the dock in military style and "struck the colors" accompanied by appropriate music coming from a P.A. system. It was impressive in a fun sort of way and all activity stopped while it was in progress. The evening dock strollers, the cocktail parties, and the diners all applauded at its conclusion. Somehow you felt like this ceremony was appropriate here and that it brought forth the feeling of one belonging to something much larger than these surroundings; in a word, patriotism.

I bought my way out of the restaurant and headed for my boat, which was only a hundred yards down the dock. I was beginning to feel a need to talk with someone, but there was no one to talk to, so I went to bed. I remember a friend of mine being asked if he ever slept in a sleeping bag. His reply was, "No. But I spent a night in one once." I guess that best describes the first half of each of my nights. Finally, fatigue stepped in, and I slept.

The morning sun was just showing over the trees as I dressed, grabbed my shaving kit and headed for the shower facilities. So did a lot of other people who did not live on those big yachts, so I dutifully stood in line and waited my turn. I did strike up a conversation with the fellow ahead of me. Breakfast was simple, which consisted of coffee, juice, and fruit. I stowed my cooking gear and pushed off for my next port of call, Sucia Island. I slowly worked my way out of the crowded harbor and followed a line of other boats looking for a day on the open water. All of them were pleasure boats; Roche Harbor is not a place for workboats.

Being at the most northern part of the American San Juans, Sucia lay about 15 nautical miles due east, which is a half hour run at 30 knots, but I had to try my luck in the pursuit of the ever elusive salmon. I tried herring, hoochies, lopacs, and plugs at varying depths, at varying speeds, but no fish. Unless of course, if you count dog fish.

Sucia is a horseshoe shaped archipelago, mostly a marine state park. It is composed of Sucia Island, Little Sucia Island, Harnden Island, and Ewing Island. The small islets, North and South Finger Island, are privately owned. The rest is state park.

I approached Sucia from the south, as there is no entrance to this horseshoe shape of islands from any other direction. Once inside, the water is as smooth as liquid glass and an interesting shoreline beckons to be investigated. Moorage lies a half-mile ahead at the end of the bay. There are about twenty boats at anchor and a few lucky ones on park buoys. Lucky, I say, because a wind from the south can give you a lot of anchor-tending duty during the night. There is no dock here, so you must have a dingy of some type to go ashore, unless you like to swim. I have a rubber dingy, which is blown up with the aid of a foot-operated pump.

After carefully setting the hook, I decided to go ashore, stretch my legs, and investigate the immediate land area of Sucia. The trees obviously were second growth timber; first growth stumps were evident as I followed the single-track path to the other side of the island. After a walk of five minutes I came to a beautiful cove on the north side of the main island. Several sailing-type boats in the forty-foot class lay at anchor. Several children were playing on the beach, but no adults were in sight. A dingy was at the water's edge, so I assumed that the children belonged to one of the sloops. I thought how lucky these children are. It was a beautiful day, with the July sun directly overhead, a few horsetail shaped clouds seemingly motionless in the sky, and the temperature a respectable seventy degrees.

I was anxious to get back to the boat as my stomach told me it was lunchtime. I quickly walked back to the dingy and to my surprise I discovered that it was not plump with air as it had been when I left it a few minutes earlier. The foot pump was on board the boat so I could either take my chances on an under inflated dingy, wait to be rescued by a passing stranger, or swim. I chose the dingy.

I carefully pushed it into deeper water, mounted it as gracefully as I could and held my breath hoping it would bear my weight. I had a few inches of freeboard, thank goodness. I carefully paddled the distance from shore to Kitchen Pass sinking lower in the water with each stroke. I reached the swim step at the stern of my boat and gingerly stepped off. I secured the half inflated dingy to the deck cleat and sat down to enjoy the welcome security of the boat.

I pulled out the food box, the propane two burner stove, and a pot in which to heat soup. The coffee pot filled the other burner and soon I had a simple lunch of soup, peanut butter and jelly sandwich, and a cup of strong, hot coffee to top it off. Having appeased the beast within, I found my patch kit for the rubber dingy and restored my lifeline to the outer world of land. By now I had a need for a nap. The engine cover that ran across the stern of the boat looked inviting. It was just long enough to stretch out on and the sun provided a warm blanket. I closed my eyes and was about to doze off when I was interrupted by a knocking sound on the hull of the boat, not too far from my head.

I thought, "What on earth can that be?" I rolled up on one elbow and looked over the side of the boat into the face of a flower-child type, middle-aged woman. I'm sure 'surprise' had to be written all over my face as she laughed and said, "All is well, I just want to know if you'd like to order one or more cinnamon rolls for your breakfast?"

This question did nothing to explain what was going on. "What are you talking about?" I abruptly asked.

She laughed at my confusion, "I live on that ancient Chriscraft cruiser anchored a hundred yards off to your port side. I earn my living baking cinnamon rolls once a day for the breakfast crowd, and I deliver them at eight o'clock A.M., or there about, directly to your boat via my dingy."

I finally got the picture and asked, "How many rolls will it take to feed one average sailor?"

She quickly answered, "One or maybe two at the outside."

I ordered two and she said, "See you in the morning." She shoved off and expertly rowed her dingy to the next boat. I thought, "What an ingenious way to make a living and to do it in an environment of your choosing, like living all summer on a boat in Sucia Bay."

I then returned to my napping position, but my encounter with the floating baker so energized my brain that I shortly gave up and decided to take the dingy for a little fishing near the shore. Coming in I spotted a hole of water that looked deep, compared to the surrounding bay. This time I took the pump and repair kit with me along with my fishing tackle. As I slowly rowed along, trailing my fishing lure fifty feet behind the boat, I noticed a shiny black object barely breaking the surface of the water and following my bait. Well, so much for fishing. A harbor seal is a deterrent for any type of fishing, so I reeled in my artificial lure and returned to the boat.

The afternoon and evening were divided between reading, maintenance work, cooking and eating. I turned in early as I longed for a full night's sleep. A large sloop about a hundred feet to starboard had other plans for my night, however. The young crowd aboard filled the night air with the kind of music I hate, plus lots of whoops and hollers. I eventually became immune to them and slept the sleep of the innocent.

I awakened the next morning with the sound of someone knocking on the hull of Kitchen Pass, which brought me up with a start. Then I remembered yesterday and made my way outside, still more asleep than awake. There was the 'flower child' with two cinnamon rolls carefully wrapped in aluminum foil being carefully presented to me. Being a big time spender, I gave her a five spot and told her to keep the change. She asked if I wanted to put an order in for tomorrow, but I told her I would be pulling out after breakfast. She wished me a safe journey and paddled out of my life.

The cinnamon roles were the size of a saucer, hot, and delicious. I thought I should save one for later, but gluttony won out. I stowed my gear, raised anchor, and slowly cruised out of the harbor savoring the beauty of the water and the surroundings in general. There is something magic about a dozen boats at anchor in a remote archipelago where there isn't even a dock to say man has been here. The weather promised to be a good July day in the San Juans. This was to be my last day in my odyssey and it was important it be a good one for memory's sake.

I brought Kitchen Pass up to speed as soon as I left the harbor, which seemed to stretch for a mile. The water was sporting a small chop, which actually lifted the hull from the glue of the water. We, Kitchen Pass and I, fairly flew down Rosario Straits past Lawrence Point and Cypress Island on the way to my starting point, Skyline Marina at Anacortes, Washington. It had been a good trip; the boat had run well, the weather had been exceptional… and I was ready to go home.

Retirement Again

After working twelve years as a vocational rehabilitation counselor and reaching the age of seventy, I chose to retire again. After a year of retirement, I took a course in creative writing and memoir writing at the suggestion of my wife, Selma. Apparently she needed to get me out of the house. It was an ongoing class and four years later, because of my teaching background, I was asked by Highline Community College to teach the course to other seniors. I enjoyed this part-time employment and challenge, but after four years, I retired a third time to become a full-time author.

Since then I have published two novels: *Run Away to Tahiti,* and *Come Away With Me.* This book, *The Sixth Man,* is my third book.

Conclusion

In the beginning I was an airman in training to fight a war in the skies over Europe and Japan. It never happened... the wars ended. I, the sixth man, trained and waiting to go into battle, but like a boxer who trains for the big fight that never happened, is left with bottled up emotions. I used that energy and drive to go into the battles most of us face: choosing a career; training for that career, and working at that career. Getting married and starting a family actually took place while I was still in the service.

And now retirement... Sitting back, watching, listening, reflecting, and waiting for life's next great challenge.

THE END...or is it?

Epilogue

In the beginning, the purpose of this memoir was to explain to my three sons and eight grandchildren why I washed out of the Army Air Corp Pilot Training Program. However, some stories write themselves. This one refused to be stopped, at the end of my army career, and I will publish it in its entirety in hopes it will encourage others to do the same. "Each of us has a story to tell."

I've come to accept the fact that during wartime some things fall through the cracks. My 'wash-out' experience was one of those things. Now I can let it heal, and put it to rest.

* * *